Chicken Soup for the Soul®

The Power of Positive

Chicken Soup for the Soul: The Power of Positive
101 Inspirational Stories about Changing Your Life through Positive Thinking
Jack Canfield, Mark Victor Hansen, Amy Newmark

Published by Chicken Soup for the Soul Publishing, LLC www.chickensoup.com
Copyright © 2012 by Chicken Soup for the Soul Publishing, LLC. All Rights Reserved.

The publisher gratefully acknowledges the many publishers and individuals who granted Chicken Soup for the Soul permission to reprint the cited material.

Front cover photo courtesy of Getty Images/Richard Newstead, Lifesize. Back cover and interior photo courtesy of Photos.com/Musat (© Christian Musat), and Photos.com.

Cover and Interior Design & Layout by Pneuma Books, LLC

Distributed to the booktrade by Simon & Schuster. SAN: 200-2442

Publisher's Cataloging-in-Publication Data
(Prepared by The Donohue Group)

Chicken soup for the soul : the power of positive : 101 inspirational stories
   about changing your life through positive thinking / [compiled by] Jack
   Canfield, Mark Victor Hansen, [and] Amy Newmark.

   p. ; cm.

   ISBN: 978-1-61159-903-9

   1. Optimism--Literary collections. 2. Optimism--Anecdotes. 3. Attitude
(Psychology)--Literary collections. 4. Attitude (Psychology)--Anecdotes. 5. Conduct
of life--Literary collections. 6. Conduct of life--Anecdotes. 7. Anecdotes. I. Canfield,
Jack, 1944- II. Hansen, Mark Victor. III. Newmark, Amy. IV. Title: Power of positive

PN6071.O7 C45 2012
810.8/02/0353   2012943521

PRINTED IN THE UNITED STATES OF AMERICA
on acid∞free paper
21 20 19 18 17 16 15 14 13   04 05 06 07 08 09 10

Chicken Soup for the Soul®

The Power of Positive

101 Inspirational Stories about Changing Your Life through Positive Thinking

Jack Canfield
Mark Victor Hansen
Amy Newmark

Chicken Soup for the Soul Publishing, LLC
Cos Cob, CT

Chicken Soup for the Soul

www.chickensoup.com

Contents

❶
~The Power of Liking Yourself~

❷
~The Power of Attitude~

❸
~The Power of Persevering~

❹

~The Power of Relaxing~

❺

~The Power of Gratitude~

❻

~The Power of Giving~

❼

~The Power of Dreaming~

❽

~The Power of Challenging Yourself~

❾

~The Power of Self-Improvement~

❿

~The Power of Watching Others~

⓫
~The Power of Changing Your Thoughts~

The Power of Positive

Chapter 1

The Power of Liking Yourself

Brick by Brick

I may not have gone where I intended to go,
but I think I have ended up where I intended to be.
~Douglas Adams

I'm a bona fide late bloomer. It took thirty-eight years and a nervous breakdown for me to find my purpose.

For most people, being hospitalized with a nervous break-down might be an extreme way to figure out the Meaning of Life, but we creative types tend to write in the margins and paint outside the lines. What I tell my kids about my Mom Interrupted period is: "It was the worst time of my life but it was the best thing that ever happened to me."

How, you might ask, could you think that being placed in the lockup ward of a psychiatric institution after overdosing on prescription anxiety medication be the best thing that ever happened to you? Isn't that supposed to be the phrase reserved for more positive experiences like meeting the love of your life, becoming a parent, or winning the Nobel Prize for Literature?

All of those things are certainly among the best things that have ever happened to me (well, except for winning the Nobel Prize for Literature, because I haven't done that... yet) and I am grateful for them every day. But the nadir I experienced at the age of thirty-eight turned out to be the experience from whence so many other bless-ings have flowed.

Why? Because all of the carefully constructed walls I'd built around myself collapsed overnight, and I was left as exposed and vulnerable as a turtle without a shell. There was nowhere to left to hide, no room for Denial to make itself at home. It was just my unprotected turtle self in a place that I never want to be again as long as I live.

When you're used to putting up a brave front, to being the girl who copes and achieves and gets things done no matter what (even if "coping" involves depression, bulimia and other self-destructive behaviors) it's hard to admit to anyone that you need help—even yourself. Even in the hospital, I was desperately attempting to don the coping mask so I could get out. I was a mother and I wasn't doing my job being locked up in a hospital. Fortunately, although I didn't see it that way at the time, a doctor saw through it and kept me there.

Thus I was forced to confront the black hole I felt inside—to recognize that I was so intent on living my life to please everyone else that I didn't remember who I was. To identify the emotions I'd worked so hard and used so many desperate measures *not* to feel.

Journaling was part of the program. Writing down my thoughts and feelings was the key to more than the therapeutic progress. It opened the door to a distant memory—that once, I wanted to be a writer. I had been told that it was impractical, that I'd "never make a living as an English major," that I should major in something with a better chance of providing a lucrative job. I had ended up with an MBA in finance and fitted my round self into a square hole—good at my job, thanks to being an overachiever, but always feeling like a fraud.

I didn't believe in myself enough to fight for what I believed was right back then.

Yet where had being a "good girl" and meeting everyone else's expectations gotten me? Locked up in a psych ward, that's where.

Shortly afterwards, in an intensive outpatient program, I was in a mixed age group. For one therapeutic exercise, I had to draw a timeline of my life on a chalkboard, and explain the major events (good, bad and traumatic) to the group. It seemed to take forever because there were many events. I was worrying that the rest of the group was going to get bored before I finished. But then, even before I got to the present, one of the younger group members spoke up. "Wow," she said. "You've really been through a lot. You're so strong. I wouldn't have survived half the stuff you've been through."

I started to make the usual self-deprecating remark, but then I looked up at the timeline and I realized for the first time that I *had* been through a lot. Crazy as it sounds, until she pointed it out, I'd been so busy coping and more, striving to achieve and excel, that I'd never once stopped to acknowledge all the hurdles I'd overcome to get where I was. Okay, where I was at that point was in a psychiatric hospital, but I was still alive, and at that moment I started the process of changing my internal cue cards, replacing weak with strong, defective with creative.

Slowly, painfully, brick by brick, I had to put myself back together. In the process I examined each brick and tested it. Was it healthy for me? Was it a material I'd chosen for my own wall or did it really belong to someone else?

Doing that created a stronger foundation for the woman I am today. It gave me the courage to pursue my teenage dream of being a writer, and doing the timeline made me realize that I have a wealth of stories to tell. As I often joke, "God gave me a gift, the ability to express myself in writing. Then he gave me a lot of material."

Every time I receive a letter from a reader whose life has been touched by one of my books, I'm grateful that I was able to find purpose during the most painful time of my life.

~Sarah Darer Littman

The Little Voice

Words have the power to both destroy and heal.
When words are both true and kind, they can change our world.
~Buddha

I'm lying on the massage table when David, my massage therapist, hits a tender spot along the top of my shoulder. I groan. He digs a little deeper. I groan a little louder. When he moves higher and hits the mother lode of pain, I yelp.

"A tad tender?" he asks. "Do you want me to back off a bit?"

"Yes," I mutter through clenched teeth.

David works on the area more gently and my groans become softer. "You're really tense this week," he says, as his fingers try to unravel the knot of tight muscles that have formed from my neck to my shoulder. "I haven't seen you this bad in months. What's up?"

"April," I say. "Just April. Shakespeare was right when he said it was the cruelest month."

"How can it be cruel?" David asked. "Spring is here. Tulips are everywhere. Trees are in bud."

"Taxes," I mutter.

"Well, there's that. But you still have time to get them done."

"They're already in. I did them early this year. I'm actually getting a nice refund."

"So you should be happy and relaxed, not tied up in knots."

I grunt as another one of those knots makes its presence felt.

"And lessons. By April, I hate all my teaching material and have to spend hours developing new stuff."

David digs a little deeper into the knot and into me. "Can you reuse the new material next year?"

"Yes, and some of it is really good. I've changed my teaching style and it shows in the material. I'm building in a lot more review and the students are doing better."

David's hands continue their probing and pushing. "That's a good thing, right?"

I grunt, less from the pain and more because we're getting to the real reason I hate April. Failure. Disappointment. Regrets.

"Come on, Harriet. You're holding back and I can feel it in your body. Work with me on this."

I sigh. "Okay, since you seem as determined to massage my mind as my body today. I hate April because it's my birthday. Because I turn a year older and there's this voice that keeps telling me I haven't accomplished anything this year. That I haven't lost those twenty pounds. That I haven't finished the book I started six years ago. That I haven't sent out at least one query a week."

David's hands stop. "What voice? Who's saying that to you? I can't believe you're letting someone push you around like that."

I open my mouth to say he's right, that I wouldn't take that crap from someone. Then I realize that I've been doing just that—only the someone pushing me around is me. That voice in my head is mine. I've taken all my fears, insecurities and disappointments and literally given them a voice. And then I've used it against myself.

"It's me," I say quietly, as much to myself as to him. "It's me," I say a little louder. And then a third time even louder.

David's hands resume their kneading of knotted muscles. "So, what are you going to do about it?"

I'd lived with the voice for so long that it had never occurred to me that I could do something about it. I begin to understand that I have options. I decide to exercise one of those options. "I'm going to tell that little voice to shut up." I pause, thinking of how powerful that voice is. Maybe there's a better option. I start again. "No, I'm not going to tell it to shut up. I'm going to tell it to speak louder. Only I'm going to teach it to say positive things. To remind me of what I have done, not what I haven't."

I think about the students who like me, the other teachers who ask my advice, the writers in my online writing group who value my critiques, and the editors at magazines, newspapers and anthologies who have published my articles and stories. Suddenly I realize that my little voice will have lots of nice things to say to me—if I let it.

As for the twenty pounds and the unfinished book and all the other things that I've meant to do but somehow never did? I already know that beating myself up about my failures doesn't work. Who knows what the effect of being positive to myself will be? And what better time to test it out than in April.

For the first time this month I relax and David's fingers go from being tools of torture to being instruments of pleasure. And a little voice says, "Good for you. See what happens when you believe in yourself?"

Now that's a voice I could listen to for hours.

~Harriet Cooper

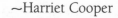

Battling
My Inner Bully

It's hard to fight an enemy who has outposts in your head.
~Sally Kempton

When I was in grade school, a boy named Scott called me Fat Lips every chance he got. He'd sit behind me on the school bus, heckling me, kicking my seat, or flicking my head with a pencil, all the time laughing in a way that made me shrink into a corner of the seat.

But much worse than Scott, and all the other childhood bullies I encountered, was the internal bully that followed me through life hissing insults in my ear. He said things like, "You should have done better," or "That was a stupid thing to say," or "Good people don't do that."

I used to believe his abuse. Because of that, I grew up lacking self-confidence, even though outwardly I was a high achiever. I excelled in school, earned a full scholarship to college, graduated magna cum laude, and became a world-traveling teacher. But I couldn't fully enjoy those accomplishments, because always, underneath, was the feeling that I wasn't good enough.

When I became a mom, my feelings of anxiety about my many failings led me to therapy. But it didn't help much. One day, after describing one of my bully's particularly cruel accusations, my therapist gave me a sorrowful look. "Oh, Sara," she said in a pained voice. "Why are you so hard on yourself?"

I could have said, "I don't know. I was hoping you could tell me that." But instead, I felt ashamed and heard another whisper from my bully: "You're so messed up, you've even got your counselor stumped!"

Around the same time, I learned that I had an autoimmune disease called Sjögren's syndrome. The diagnosis explained years of aches and pains, a troubled pregnancy, and the loss of my sense of smell. In my quest for a more holistic treatment of my symptoms, which now included dry eyes and a dry mouth, I visited a functional chiropractor. Besides recommending certain dietary changes and supplements, he suggested that I see a therapist. Surprised, I asked him why.

"Because I find that how people think greatly affects their physical health," he said.

So I went looking for a counselor again. This time I found a cozy, wise, spiritual woman named Vicki. Together we began exploring some of my mixed-up thinking. I remember our first session clearly, when I told her about the Sjögren's syndrome.

"It's an autoimmune disease," I said. "My white blood cells attack my own moisture-producing glands."

And then it struck me. "That's funny," I said.

"What?" she asked.

"I just realized, that's what I do," I said. "I attack my own self."

I doubt many doctors would agree that my thoughts had anything to do with my disease. But in my gut, I believe there's a connection. Wouldn't it make sense if, after attacking myself mentally and emotionally for so long, my physical body followed suit?

In any case, that insight made me decide to change. On my fortieth birthday, I wrote this in my journal: "This year, I want to be kind to myself."

It's been hard work. First, I learned to notice my bully's presence in my thoughts. It surprised me how often he spoke, and on how many subjects! Then, I learned to counter his cruel and faulty messages with truth. Like, "I didn't do that perfectly, but it was good enough," or "Everyone says things they wish they hadn't," or even "Good people are human and make mistakes. And that's okay." Even now, there are times when I sense my bully really wants to beat me up. That's when I have a choice—to think the old way, which leads to pain, or to be kind to myself, which leads to peace and health.

Are my efforts making a difference? I'm certain they are—at least, mentally and emotionally. As far as the effect my new thoughts have on my physical health, I'll have to wait and see. A body takes time to heal. But I can say this: when my bully tries to capitalize on the mind-body connection that I now believe in, whispering, "Look what you did to yourself!" I will stand straight and counter him with confidence:

"Yes, but look what I'm learning to do differently."

~Sara Matson

The List

He is a wise man who does not grieve for the things which he has not,
but rejoices for those which he has.
~Epictetus

I sat across from my company's director of human resources and watched his lips move as he spoke with a practiced nonchalance. "Today will be your last day with us," he said. Then he wished me well and handed me a cardboard box in which to pack up my belongings.

After twenty-two years of employment with this company, I imagined a much different parting of the ways. A recognition dinner attended by my peers would have been a more appropriate send-off, perhaps. At the very least, surely I deserved a modest cake and coffee reception in the staff lunchroom decorated with a few of those smiley-face balloons. Yet there I was, shoving a cardboard box into the back seat of my car, about to leave the place where I had spent almost half my life. I pulled out of the parking lot and glanced into the rear view mirror at the imposing brick building for one last time. My eyes looked back at me in the mirror's reflection. What now? I asked myself. What now?

I must admit that I was not generally the type of person who found it easy to take lemons and make lemonade. Yet, I had learned through my husband Bill's previous bouts with unemployment that a better opportunity quite frequently is waiting around the bend. Like the time Bill lost his job the same day we returned from our honeymoon. We were both terrified. Yet, that experience brought new employment in the South and the opportunity to experience the pleasures of southern living. After that position ended, his next job brought us back home to the North for a wonderful reunion with our friends and family. When that company went belly-up, he was hired by another organization in our area that offered him a salary large enough for us to purchase our first home. Surely some blessing would come about as a result of my unemployment.

As I sat with the newspaper want ads a few days later, however, I started to have my doubts. It seemed that in the current economy, positions for my type of work were paying exactly half of my previous salary, and benefits, if there even were any, weren't as generous either. Those facts, combined with the expense of a longer commute, made it seem that returning to work was hardly worth the effort.

Week after week I scanned each and every ad for employment carefully, never finding anything that seemed to fit my wants or my needs. One Sunday morning, frustrated, I flipped through the newspaper aimlessly. I scanned the headlines that revealed stories of natural disaster, murder, kidnapping. Sinking deeper into depression, I reached for an attempt at levity: the comics. Yet, in my current emotional state even Garfield had lost his appeal. I flipped the pages again, and there on the last page, something caught my eye: a full-color advertisement for our local college's open house to be held later that month. I ran my hand across the advertisement. How many times had I vowed to return to college to complete my degree, yet had never found the time? Well, lack of time was no longer a valid excuse. I ripped out the ad, folded it carefully, and then placed it in a kitchen drawer along with some supermarket coupons.

It took a full week before I had the courage to look at that paper again. When I did, a barrage of doubts assaulted me. How could I afford tuition? Completing my degree would require two years, at least. Was I willing to make that type of time commitment? Did I even have what it took, intellectually, to return to college after a twenty-year-plus hiatus? And then the big question: Was I just too old to embark on what seemed like such a massive undertaking?

I took my concerns to my husband. "You're worried about everything you imagine you don't have. Why don't you focus on what you know you do have?"

That night, I sat down and took a complete inventory of myself. With pen and paper in hand, I wrote down all of my assets: brains, health, drive, and desire headed the list. After fifteen minutes, I was still writing. Okay, so I had what it took, scholastically speaking, but could I afford the cost? Tuition, books, and all the other essentials were pricey, especially now that I wasn't working. Well, we had saved some money for house renovations. Maybe those repairs could wait. Then there were a few collectibles that could be sold. I did some quick calculations. The bottom line figure was barely enough to cover the first semester. I sharpened my pencil. If we cut back on dining out, rented movies instead of seeing them in a theater, steered clear of shopping malls—in other words went on a complete austerity program—we could generate some of the extra funds. The rest would have to be covered by student loans. I brought my ideas to my husband.

"No one could argue with this presentation," he said after reviewing my penciled proposal. "Go for it."

So I did. To say the following two years were easy would be a big, fat lie. There were many long afternoons spent in the library and many even longer nights spent in front of my computer. I can recall one particularly grueling wrestling match with a jammed printer as I tried to unearth a page of a report due later that afternoon, and one semester of near insanity when I decided to tackle twelve advanced credits in an abbreviated eight-week summer session. Throughout it all, I hung onto my handwritten list of assets like a lifeline. Several times, reviewing that list and switching my thinking from "have nots" to "haves" hauled me back to the shore of possibility. And, a little over two years after carrying a cardboard box of office paraphernalia home, I carried something else much better: my college diploma and the promise of a brand new career.

As I stepped down from the college's stage after commencement that drizzly June afternoon, my husband stood waiting to congratulate me. He kissed me, then squeezed my hand in his. "You're a college graduate now," he said. "I always knew you could do it."

I thought back to my penciled list, edges now worn. "So did I," I said with a wink. "So did I."

~Monica A. Andermann

Positive People Preferred, Please

Keep away from people who try to belittle your ambitions.
Small people always do that,
but the really great make you feel that you, too, can become great.
~Mark Twain

"Mommy?" A four-year-old me asked, casually scribbling some intricate free-hand composition with a purple crayon.

"Yes?" my mother replied, eyes never leaving her paperback book.

"Can I be a ballerina?"

My mother put the book in her lap. "If you want."

"Can I be an animal doctor?"

"Yes." My mother was very serious.

"Can I be a farmer like Grandpa?" He grew the best vegetables I'd ever eaten and the most beautiful and fragrant flowers I'd ever seen or smelled.

"Sure."

"Can I be an artist?" I looked down at my crayon drawing of what was supposed to be a horse.

"Why not?"

"Or a writer?" I'd just composed my first poem about ponies. I thought it was brilliant. So did my parents.

"You can be anything you want. If you want it enough, you can do it. Whatever you decide to do, Daddy and I will be behind you."

Those words reverberated through my life, leaving a deep, lasting impression. "You can be anything you want to be," is a simple yet strong message. The rest, well, it didn't really make sense until I was older, but the impact is just as powerful—and positive.

From the time I was young, my parents always told me I could do anything I wanted, I could be anyone I wanted. In no particular order (and this changed depending on day, date and age): a dancer, an artist, a jockey, a vet, a singer, a rock star, a doctor, a psychiatrist, an archaeologist, a psychic, a gem expert, a counselor, and a writer. I'm sure this is not an exhaustive list; if asked, my mother would happily add to it.

Fast-forward fifteen years, to college and the summer between sophomore and junior years. I announced to my parents at dinner, "I'm going to backpack with Veronika in Europe over the summer."

To my parents' credit, they didn't freak out. My dad replied, "Do you have enough money saved?"

I did. I'd been working two jobs. I could either put that money towards my loan or take a once-in-a-lifetime trip with my Frankfurt-based friend Veronika. The kicker was: I'd never been to Europe. Or on a plane. Or, really, done anything adventurous.

Nothing like taking a leap.

They let me go. For nearly three months, my friend and I backpacked and camped, traveled by railroad, car and on foot, and explored almost every European country. A priceless experience.

I came back a changed person. Not only did I change, but so did my (nervous) parents. But just as they'd promised since I'd been four, they supported me in whatever I wanted to do.

This included my decision to go into the music business. No, not as a singer or a rock star, but as a manager of bands. The best part of following my dream? I got to travel with bands and artists who were talented, a lot of fun, some very spiritual, and I got to travel the world. Again.

But guess what? My parents had fun, too. When one of my heavy metal bands played near my parents' house, they invited the band to sleep over. All four of them. This was during the big hair 1980s, so huge amounts of hairspray, eyeliner and make-up were used—not all by me. They took it in stride when, as everyone blow-dried their hair, the circuits in the house blew.

Did my father freak out? Did my mother melt down? Nope. They took it in stride and stayed positive, as my dad and the band changed the circuits, complete in stage dress, teased hair and make-up (the band, not my dad). Said my father, shrugging, "No big deal. These things happen."

But, even to this day, I'm fairly certain not many parents can say they hosted a rock band who blew out the power in their home.

When I went exploring my spirituality and took at least two-dozen different classes and certifications, I looked at things as a positive adventure, never knowing where it might lead. I've submitted stories and articles, some accepted, some not.

But, because I knew no matter what I did or wanted to do in life that I'd have my parents' emotional support, it gave me the courage to be bold, to try new things, to reach for my dreams, to be positive in whatever I did—no matter what.

My mantra is repeated within a portion of a quote attributed to the German philosopher Goethe. "Whatever you can do or dream you can, begin it. Boldness has genius, power and magic in it." I've never wavered from that, staying positive, knowing that the Universe is this wonderfully vast and magical place.

Courage is key to positivity, along with an open mind and a sense of wonder, fueled by a loving support system. It unlocks opportunities I could have never envisioned.

Throughout every bump, every situation, I've stayed positive. For me, positivity is the charge that magnetizes your aura, drawing great things to you. Is it like *The Secret*? I don't know. I've never read *The Secret*. What I do know is this: if negative thoughts invade your mind, they also invade your heart, your soul and your body, until eventually you begin to rot from the inside out.

I often tell my friends how much my parents pumped me up

with positive thinking, how they stood by me no matter what. Most of them tell me that was not their experience. I want to cry for them. I cannot imagine how different I'd be if it were not for all that parental positivity.

I prefer positive people. Negative people with dark personalities are dream killers, sucking joy from the marrow of the soul.

Last year, I decided to make a leap of faith again. Stepping off into the yawning abyss of unemployment, I declined an offer to move cross-country for a job I'd had (and liked) for eighteen years. Instead, I rationalized in my brain, I'd start my own business… and I'd write.

No matter what.

Just the other day, I said to my mother, "I know that these little writing jobs that pay nothing will lead to something. I just have to finish my book, and I know my agent will be able to sell this one. I feel it." At that moment, I did. I still do. I believe it to the core of my soul. I have no doubts whatsoever, but the key is courage, to move forward, to finish it.

Instantly, Mom replied, just like she had forty-five years earlier, "I know you'll do it. I believe in you."

And somehow, just knowing that, makes me believe it even more.

~Syndee A. Barwick

Feeling Lucky

Those who wish to sing, always find a song.
~Swedish Proverb

"Oh, honey, come here," a friend of mine said, pulling me into a hug. "Last night, when I went to pick up my daughter from softball practice, I drove right by your husband's office. His truck was still there and it was almost 8:30. You poor thing," she added, patting my shoulder.

I nodded. "He finally rolled in a few minutes after nine."

"I feel so bad for you," she said. "Being home by yourself with all of those kids. It must be so hard on you."

I nodded again. Poor me.

It was the same story the next time I ran into this woman. And the time after that too. Every time I saw her, she was quick to offer her sympathy for my terrible circumstances.

My friend's heart was in the right place. Her own husband traveled frequently for his job, so she knew what it was like to miss her man, as well as carry most of the childcare and household responsibilities by herself.

We were in the same boat, so why shouldn't we play the woe-is-me game together?

One reason: I hated the way it made me feel.

I'd head into my local Walmart with a shopping list and a spring in my step, but after bumping into my misery-loves-company friend,

I'd leave the store with a heavy heart and resentment simmering toward my husband. (As well as an ample supply of chocolate and Cheez-It crackers—comfort food at its best.)

These little pity parties were not good for my marriage. Or the size of my backside.

So I decided to change the way I thought about my situation.

The next time I bumped into my friend and she launched into poor-baby mode, I tried to look on the bright side. I shrugged and said, "Yes, Eric got home late last night, but he was working on a new project. If this deal comes through, his company may be able to hire someone else and then Eric's job will be easier." I shrugged and added, "So a year from now, he might be able to be home a lot more."

She nodded. "That's nice, but what about right now?"

"Right now, I'll admit that things are tough, but they're not nearly as bad as they could be," I said. "Our husbands both have jobs, and in this economy, that's a blessing."

"But they're both gone all the time," she said, scowling.

She was right, but I wasn't ready to start the pity party. "Yes, but our husbands' jobs allow us to stay at home with our children and still manage to pay our bills," I reasoned.

She nodded. "I never thought about it that way. I do like being at home with my kids."

"Our husbands love us enough to work hard so that we don't have to work," I shrugged and added, "well, at least not outside of our homes."

She nodded again, more thoughtfully this time. "I used to work at a bank. The job was all right, but I missed my kids and I hated being away from them."

"I know what you mean," I said. "I was a teacher, and I loved my summers home with them. Now I get to enjoy being with them year-round."

"Yeah," she said, "but now, instead of missing my kids, I miss my husband."

I shrugged. "Didn't you miss him when you worked at the bank too?"

She chuckled. "Good point."

Score one for me, but I wasn't done yet. "And think about this. At least our husbands are at work. A lot of men are gone at least as long as our guys are, but they aren't working. They're in bars and bowling alleys."

"And the really bad ones are at other women's houses," she added with raised eyebrows.

I smiled. "So I guess that makes us some of the lucky ones."

"Hmm, I'm one of the lucky ones," she murmured and then she grinned at me. "I'm really glad I bumped into you this morning. I feel better than I have in months."

I felt pretty good too. And why shouldn't I feel good? I have a husband who works too much.

But he does it because he loves me. He does it so I can be a stay-at-home mom, which for me is a dream come true. He does it so I can live in a comfortable home and drive a reliable car. He does it to provide for our family and even take me on the occasional vacation.

I won't be attending any more pity parties because as it turns out, my hard-working husband has given me plenty of reasons to feel really, really lucky.

~Diane Stark

No More Excuses

The person who really wants to do something finds a way;
the other person finds an excuse.
~Author Unknown

It took over my body. It hurt to walk and sometimes even to talk. The joints in my jaws dislocated. TMJ surgery resulted in eight weeks of sucking mashed potatoes through a straw. Over time, my fingers cramped and pulled as they became weak and disfigured. The pain was unbearable.

After seeing numerous specialists, I was diagnosed with rheumatoid arthritis, the kind that attacks the joints and cripples people. Surgeries to correct deformities on my inflamed hands and wrists were undone when the disease raged out of control. Reluctantly, I put my pride aside and quit my job as a law school secretary. I had no choice.

My doctor was baffled. For me, even the most up-to-date medications weren't effective for long. After months of treatment, most of his patients would have found a drug that worked for them. He kept searching for answers, trying new drugs as they were FDA-approved. At that point, the best I could hope for were brief reprieves.

Thankfully, he didn't give up. Instead, he resorted to less conventional methods. "From one to ten, write your pain level down every day," he suggested. By documenting my progress, we could see if a combination of medications would be more effective and, at the same time, find out if stress or my diet played a role.

So, I wrote in my journal every day, careful to include anything I thought might be significant. The past few years had been rough. I had been through a stressful divorce and was trying to rebuild my life. Now with a destructive disease added on, how could it get any worse? On paper, the message came through loud and clear—negative thoughts were controlling my life.

For my health, I had to turn my thinking around. Dwelling on my problems would only make me worse. So, as difficult as it seemed, I started by taking a good look around me. When I took my mind off myself, I realized I was lucky in many ways. I had two wonderful children, a family who loved me, and I wasn't dying from cancer or heart disease. It could be much worse. With that in mind, I resolved to find a way to make the disease I hated so badly work for me instead of against me.

I dug down deep and surprised even myself. Just under the surface, I found courage and determination I never knew I had. In my Bible studies, I was influenced by the wisdom of King Solomon. He said we had two choices: Live a cheerful life and enjoy good health, or allow a broken spirit to dry up our bones. I decided to go with his first suggestion. I began that day to accept my disability and vowed to get on with my life. In order to make it work, I had to do away with negative thinking.

My decision to think positive led to positive actions. First of all, at forty years old, I went back to college. It was there that I found out what I already knew—I loved to write. How would I write with crippled fingers? My past jobs involved a lot of typing. At one time, I could navigate the keyboard with my eyes closed. Those days were gone.

A friend suggested voice recognition software. It would recognize my voice and, like magic, it would type what I said. I liked the idea, but I was limited to where I would work. My house was a busy one and I really enjoyed the camaraderie of family and friends.

Then, one day, quite by accident, I picked up a fat pencil laying on my desk, like the one I had used in first grade. With the eraser end down, I held it in my right hand and pecked out letters on the keyboard with relative ease. Then, with my left thumb, I pressed the left shift key for capitalizations. It wasn't easy, but my brain adapted quickly. I couldn't use my handicap as an excuse anymore.

Like anything worth having, my plan involved work and commitment. I got busy reading everything I could from experienced writers, learning how they got started. I checked out books at the library and I read every magazine I could get my hands on about the subject. The stories where courageous people overcame insurmountable obstacles were my favorites. I was convinced that the way I handled my illness could inspire others with debilitating diseases. As I read my Bible and self-help books, I gained the inspiration and encouragement to write my own stories.

I made some difficult, albeit, necessary changes. Although I had lots of friends, I made a conscience effort to surround myself only with the ones with positive upbeat attitudes. Uplifting friends lifted my spirits.

Also, I stayed as active as possible and lost myself in worthwhile projects, especially those that would help somebody else. I noticed I was smiling more, even when I didn't always feel like it. I formed friendships with people who had their own challenges to overcome. No matter how bad I felt at times, there was always someone worse off than me. We inspired each other to keep on keeping on.

It was one of the best decisions I had ever made. Instead of dwelling on what I couldn't do, I woke up each morning with a welcome wave of optimism. Despite my handicap, I was seeing each day as an opportunity to move forward.

As I continued to write, the more consumed I was by it. And, the more I concentrated on my stories, the less pain I felt. Now, instead of sitting idle with a heating pad on my shoulders and tears in my eyes, I had a notebook in my hand, writing down new ideas for my next story. When I woke up in the night hurting, I thought of things to add to my writing.

The more stories I wrote, the more stories formed in my head. I wrote many articles about coping with my disease, but other stories involving my dogs, my childhood, wildlife on our farm and a local murder mystery rounded out my hobby. I rallied my courage and began submitting them to magazines. My confidence grew as I started hearing from editors. Many said "no," but a few said "yes." My life began to change, one story at a time.

Today, I feel good about my life. The negative thoughts have disappeared and positive ones have taken their place. Now, I realize what a significant role worry and fear played in the onset of my disease. Still, I smile, knowing that when I thought it couldn't get any worse, I made the effort to change my thought pattern and that made all the difference. Negative thoughts cannot thrive unless they are nurtured. Get rid of them and positive thoughts will take over. Take Solomon's advice and chose a cheerful heart. It works.

~Linda C. Defew

The Honors Class

Don't live down to expectations. Go out there and do something remarkable.
~Wendy Wasserstein

The motley looking group of eleventh graders didn't look like any "honors" U.S. History class I'd ever imagined. They shuffled into my classroom, which I'd painstakingly decorated with Presidential portraits and colorful maps and framed copies of the Declaration of Independence and the Constitution, with an "attitude" that was apparent even to a rookie teacher.

Which is exactly what I was. Fresh out of college with a degree in history, a teaching certificate, and not a lick of experience. I was grateful to have a job, even if it was in one of the rougher high schools in the city where I lived.

"Good morning," I said brightly. I was greeted with vacant stares. "I'm so excited to have been selected to teach this honors class," I continued. "They usually don't let first-year teachers do that."

Several of the students sat up straighter and cut their eyes at each other. Too late, I wondered if I should have tried to hide the fact that I had zero teaching experience. Oh, well. "We're going to do things a little differently in this class because I know that all of you want a challenge."

By now, every student was staring at me with a puzzled expression.

"First off, let's rearrange these desks," I said. "I like lots of class discussion, so let's put them in a big circle so we can all see each other's faces." Several of the kids rolled their eyes, but they all got up and began scooting the desks out of the traditional straight rows. "Perfect! Thanks. Now, everybody choose a seat and let's play a game. When I point to you, tell me your name. Then tell me what you hate most about history."

Finally, some smiles. And lots more as our game progressed.

Amanda hated how history seemed to be all about war. Jose didn't like memorizing names and dates. Gerald was convinced that nothing that had happened in the past was relevant to his life. "Why should I care about a bunch of dead white guys?" was how he put it. Caitlyn hated tricky true-false questions. Miranda despised fill-in-the-blank tests.

We had just made our way around the circle when the bell rang. Who knew fifty minutes could pass so quickly?

Armed with the feedback my students had given me, I began formulating a plan. No teaching straight from the textbook for this group. No "read the chapter and answer the questions at the end" homework. These kids were bright. They were motivated. My honors class deserved to be taught in a way that would speak to them.

We'd study social and economic history, not just battles and generals. We'd tie current events into events from the past. We'd read novels to bring home the humanity of history. *Across Five Aprils* when studying the Civil War. *The Grapes of Wrath* to learn about the Great Depression. *The Things They Carried* when talking about Vietnam.

Tests would cover the facts, but also require higher level thinking skills. No tricky true-false questions. No fill-in-the-blank.

At first, I was surprised by how many of my students used poor grammar and lacked writing skills. And some seemed to falter when reading out loud. But we worked on those skills while we were learning history. I found that many of the kids were not only willing, but eager to attend the after-school study sessions I offered and to accept the help of peer tutors.

Four of my students came to love the subject matter so much that they formed their own "History Bowl" team and entered a countywide contest. Though they didn't take first place, they were ecstatic over the Honorable Mention trophy they brought home to our classroom.

The school year came to an end more quickly than I could have imagined. Though I had grown fond of many of my students, the ones in the honors class held a special place in my heart. Most had earned A's and B's. No one had averaged lower than a C.

During our final teacher workday before summer break, the principal called me into her office for my end-of-the-year evaluation.

"I want to congratulate you on a great rookie season," she said with a smile. "Especially on how well you did with your remedial kids."

"Remedial kids? I don't understand. I didn't have any remedial classes."

Mrs. Anderson looked at me in a strange way. "Your first period class was remedial. Surely you saw that indicated at the top of the roll." She pulled a file folder from a drawer and handed it to me. "And you must have suspected the students in that class were below average by the way they dressed and the way they carried themselves. Not to mention their terrible grammar and poor reading and writing skills."

I opened the file folder and removed a copy of the roll from my first period class. There at the top, plain as day, was the word HONORS. I showed it to Mrs. Anderson.

"Oh, dear," she said. "What a huge mistake! How did you ever manage, treating slow students as though they were…"

I couldn't help but finish the sentence for her. "As though they were bright?"

She nodded, looking more than a little sheepish.

"You know what, Mrs. Anderson? I think we've both learned a lesson from this. One they didn't teach in any of the education courses I took. But one I'll never forget."

"Nor will I," she said, circling the word HONORS with a red marker before placing the paper back in the folder. "Next year, I may just have this printed at the top of all the class rolls."

~Jennie Ivey

The Power of Positive

Chapter
2

The Power of Attitude

Making Chicken Soup in Prison!

What doesn't kill you makes you stronger.
~Kelly Clarkson

"Take off all your clothes and wait in there." I walked into the small cell and waited twenty minutes as a corrections officer took my clothes and put them in a box to be mailed to wherever I asked. A large man then examined me from head to toe and then some.

I signed some form confirming where my clothes would be sent together with a half dozen other forms, one of which was my designation as to where they should send my body if I died in the federal prison into which I was now being processed.

After the mug shot, fingerprinting and DNA swab, I was given a handful of green prison shirts and pants, together with some underclothes, and directed to walk a half-mile up the road from the "medium" prison where I had "self-surrendered" to the "camp" where I would spend the next year and a day. I had pled guilty to two tax misdemeanors wherein I declared all my income, filed accurately and on time but didn't enclose a check. I had always managed to pay my taxes somehow, if not perfectly on time. I always seemed to be able to pull a rabbit out of a hat around tax time but this time I had run out of rabbits. Then I ran out of hats.

I followed the driveway to the camp and was greeted by the

unofficial "mayor" of the camp who showed me around and finally helped me set up my bunk. I had the top bunk in a room with seventeen others who nodded hello to me. This was not The Pierre hotel on Fifth Avenue where I often stayed as a guest of a major network for whom I worked as an on-air legal analyst for several years. There was no mini-bar and I had no cell phone which would ring often as some cable news producer would call me for a "pre-interview" before I would appear on CNN or MSNBC or FOX to opine about the interesting case of the day.

In some manner of ironic injustice or perhaps, justice, I had become the interesting case of the day. As I told a reporter on the courthouse steps at my sentencing, "I screwed up and the judge was very fair. My life is not over and I hope to learn from this experience." Many people watched my mini-speech on YouTube and told me how impressed they were that I was so upbeat. Only I knew that I was lying to myself. I was convinced my life *was* basically over.

As I lay in my upper bunk I kept trying to reassure myself that this time would pass quickly and maybe I would have a decent life to go back to. Again, although I was considered an effective advocate in the courtroom and on television, I consistently failed to convince myself that there would be a life after this prison camp.

After essentially hiding under the covers for three days in my bunk, I came to the conclusion that Ashton Kutcher was not going to run up to me to tell me I was being "punked" and this was an elaborate prank. I really needed to meet all these guys and get to know them. They would be my family for a long time. All they knew about me was I was some moderately famous lawyer in 56 upper. I later learned that the PNN (Prisoner News Network) had me tagged as a lawyer who bribed a juror. I hesitated to correct them when I heard that—it was a more interesting crime than the tax misdemeanors. When I did finally dispel that rumor, I substituted it with a story that I beat up some bikers in a brawl on the Jersey Shore. Absolutely nobody believed that but the story got a lot of laughs.

I spent a lot of time listening at first. I wanted to learn the language. By the time I had been "down" for a week, I had picked up so many new words and phrases that I kept a journal of them for a book I began writing. Oddly enough, the prison library had a copy of my first book, *How Can You Defend Those People?* Like I said, irony ruled here.

It was my fifth or sixth night in 56 upper when I began to think about the scene in the great Bill Murray movie *Stripes* where all the newly inducted soldiers introduce themselves. Each one is wackier than the next. The best is a character named Francis who insists that everyone call him "Psycho." In a loud and appropriately maniacal tone, I found myself belting out his lines from that scene to the general population of my seventeen bunkmates.

"IF ANYBODY TOUCHES MY STUFF... I'LL KILL YA."

Dead silence in the bunk room as the other inmates tried to assess whether I was having a nervous breakdown.

"IF ANYBODY TOUCHES ME... I'LL KILL YA."

Now a few were laughing—they had seen the movie or it was just so damn funny coming from this sixty-four-year-old Jewish lawyer who has been under the covers since he got there.

"IF ANYBODY CALLS ME FRANCIS... I'LL KILL YA."

Everyone was laughing and from that moment on, until the day I left the camp, my fellow inmates would come up to me with some variation of the "I'll Kill Ya" line.

A few days later there was a "roast" in the dining hall celebrating the discharge of one of the guys who had been there for a few years. I had only met him briefly but the class clown in me asked to be one of the speakers. I opened with "I never gave a speech to a *captured audience* before but..." I then crammed all my new prison words into a speech about nothing, making sure I used all the prison terms in the absolute wrong context. I got a lot of laughs and again it broke down so many barriers between myself and the very diverse collection of inmates. We all had our own mug for coffee or juice or whatever. To mock my lack of "prison creds" I drew a big skull and bones on my mug with a black magic marker. A few months later I learned that the skull and bones were the "colors" of a major nationwide prison gang!

For the rest of my time at the camp, I did my best to meet and really get to know as many of my fellow inmates as possible. They were fascinating and I really made good friends with so many. Oddly enough, once one is discharged from a federal correctional facility, it is against the rules to continue any such friendship. Go figure.

I felt very fortunate to have had the means to allow other inmates to feel comfortable with me through my offbeat humor. I met and became very friendly with a variety of people with whom I shared only some measure of criminal conduct. Yet, I learned to like and trust so many of them. The level of civility and simple courtesy that existed in the camp was greater than one could possibly imagine.

When I left there, I promised to stay in touch with everyone but, as mentioned earlier, it is not allowed. I wish it were.

My life was not over. As was mentioned in a news article about my return to the practice of law, I never thought I would need to hit the "restart" button. I recently heard from some of the inmates who read that article about me. They were happy for me but more importantly, very happy to see that there can be life after a prison camp! My experience gave them hope. That almost makes it all worth it.

~Mickey Sherman

10

Feeling Like a Superhero

The human spirit is stronger than anything that can happen to it.
~C.C. Scott

It was a normal day. I came home from work, had a few casual words with my roommate, got the dog into her harness and leash, and headed out for a walk. I had moved to downtown San Diego just seven days ago, so Chibby, my four-pound Chihuahua, hadn't been on a good long walk for a few weeks. I'd been focused on moving and therefore had been ignoring her a bit. Tonight was the night we were going to get her some exercise and explore the new neighborhood.

I headed towards the marina and cruise port simply because I hadn't walked in that direction before. I made a left down Ash Street and was delighted to see the ocean and some cruise ships lined up at the pier in front of me, many adorned with lights and glimmer. Then I noticed the Star of India parked there, a historical ship and tourist attraction. I was excited to be living near such a fun place with so much going on. I mumbled half to myself and half to Chibby that we should walk over there and take a look. Then it was dark.

When I emerged from that darkness, I realized that I was looking at the inside of an ambulance. I began to scream, "What am I doing in here? What happened? Where's my dog?" A paramedic replied, but I don't remember what his answers were. The scissors were cold as they ran up my leg, my abdomen, my stomach, my chest, and to my neck. He was cutting my clothes off to examine the extent of my injuries. Then it went dark again.

Apparently I had been hit by a city trolley. The local news said I was chasing my dog, who had gotten loose and run across the tracks, and that I ran after her. The reporter said the trolley hurled me thirty feet, and they showed pictures of my shoes lying about fifteen feet apart from each other. I'd been knocked out of them when I was hit and thrown.

A few weeks later I obtained the police report. The picture the policeman painted still haunts me. "As I walked up," he wrote, "she was sitting cross-legged with her dog in her lap. She was missing her front teeth and covered in blood. She was crying, and she asked me if I could help her find her teeth. I took her dog from her, and she just kept asking, 'Where are my teeth? Can you help me find them?'" I must have been in shock.

When I got to the hospital I received emergency surgery on both wrists. Both bones in my right wrist were pulverized, and my left wrist was also broken. The surgeon and his team wrapped wire around the bones to hold the pieces together, and screwed in metal plates to hold it all in place while the bones healed.

After surgery I was wheeled into what was to be my home for the next nine days, Room 522 in the trauma unit. I was placed on a liquid diet and I was unable to move. A close friend tells me that for about four days I was a vegetable, clearly feeling defeated by my circumstances. On the fifth day however, according to him, it was apparent I had made the decision to fight for my health. My personality returned and I even got out of bed to hobble down the hallway.

Now that I had come out of shock and was able to comprehend my situation, the doctors explained to me why my teeth were jutting out and some were missing. My left eye socket, both my cheeks, my nose and my jaw were all shattered into pieces; my jaw also cracked in half. On day seven I had facial reconstruction surgery. They inserted wire mesh, eighteen metal plates, and over sixty screws to hold my face together.

Once I was released from the hospital, I went home to my new apartment, where my mother lived with my roommate and me for the next six weeks so she could take care of me. I could barely walk, and both wrists were in casts so I couldn't do much for myself. My mother did an amazing job taking care of me, and several friends stopped in to visit or sent flowers and cards to wish me well.

I don't know how I ended up in front of a trolley that day. Perhaps I never will. While I don't remember anything, I can guess I simply wasn't paying attention to my environment. I caused this accident to happen, and I will have to live with that for the rest of my life. But despite all of the unknowns, I do know this about resilience and the physical and emotional healing that comes after trauma: your attitude matters.

Less than a month after the accident I was back to work teaching at a college. It was hard and I was in pain, but I was also much farther along in the healing process than the doctors expected. In fact, after surgery the doctors told my mother that it was absolutely not possible that I would be ready to work so soon. But there I was—ready, willing and able. I hadn't even had dental work done yet, so I taught my courses with missing teeth for several weeks, until they could get a flipper for me. I wasn't going to let the accident get in my way.

Whenever I see my wrist surgeon for checkups he tells me I am his poster child for attitude and how it affects the healing process. He says he gets so many patients with a broken pinky finger who hate life and complain that they can't do anything, yet here I am with two pulverized wrists and a face made of metal—happy as can be. He is absolutely convinced I have healed so miraculously because of my positive attitude.

But I don't think positivity comes on its own; the biggest life lesson I learned in all this was gratitude. I am lucky to have a family that dropped everything to come to my rescue. I also have a lot of friends who supported me then, and persist in their support now as I continue to heal. I imagine it would have been hard to remain positive if I had felt alone.

I also kept the little things from getting the best of me. I couldn't pour milk into my cereal bowl, I couldn't close my bras, and I couldn't blow dry my own hair, for example. Instead of feeling sorry for myself I found ways to get around these daily obstacles. My mom poured the milk into little containers so I could pick it up, I purchased bras that close in the front, and I bought a lightweight hair dryer. Being as normal as possible kept me from feeling defeated, and helped me remain positive.

Ultimately I realized that I am not a victim of circumstance. I see myself as a survivor rather than a victim. A 150-ton trolley going twenty miles per hour hit me and I lived. I think that makes me a superhero.

~Catherine Mattice

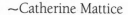

11

Bloom Where You Are Planted

*Things turn out best for the people who
make the best out of the way things turn out.*
~Art Linkletter

I was smitten from the moment I laid eyes on that adorable condo, with its sunken living room and the gorgeous French doors that opened onto the flagstone patio. I convinced my husband Joe that "happily ever after" awaited us on the other side of that threshold. The threshold with the elegant front door flanked by full-length beveled glass windows. The one located at 6823 Crooked Lane.

Right away we put our house up for sale and in less than a week someone made us an offer. I took it as a sign from Heaven and mentally started feathering our Crooked Lane nest. The same day we accepted the buyer's offer we put a deposit down on our dream house. Let the packing begin!

As I filled each box I pictured myself cooking sumptuous suppers in that beautiful wide-open kitchen, or soaking in the luxury of the Jacuzzi after a long day at work. Yep, living was going to start just as soon as we were settled into our new home, and I could hardly wait. Joe, on the other hand, had his own fantasy list of activities (or lack of them) that he mused over. The thought of being relieved of his responsibility to mow the grass and shovel snow made him practically giddy.

As we packed, the usual paperwork and appointments ran their course. We were approved for our new mortgage without a hitch and our house on Spring Mill Avenue passed all routine inspections. Not a snag in sight. Settlement day approached and with it our excitement about moving to Utopia grew steadily. We counted down the days and never counted on trouble, but trouble was waiting right around the corner.

I stared across the table at the empty chair just as the grandfather clock in the corner of the real estate office struck three o'clock. The buyer of our home was now officially thirty minutes late. This seemed unusual since he was a real estate agent himself.

Our own real estate agent frantically called the buyer's office and cell phone. When we had waited a full hour my husband stood up and said, "We've had enough. We're leaving, and unless you can prove that the buyer has come to some physical harm that prevented him from contacting this office, the sale is off." Then we walked out.

We drove home in shock. Well, I was in shock. Joe barreled past shock and didn't put the brakes on until he got to rage. The whole time we ate dinner I'm certain there was smoke coming out of his ears. Neither of us could accept that the sale of our house progressed to the point of settlement without our own real estate office following up on the legitimacy of the buyer. We never asked questions because, well, because we had no experience selling a home and when our agent said everything was fine, we believed that everything was, in fact, fine. Silly us.

At about seven o'clock in the evening our real estate agent called to say that he finally spoke with the buyer, who confessed he had too many irons in the fire at the moment and was having a little difficulty securing a mortgage. Of course our agent George assured us that if we would just grant the buyer an extension of a few weeks all would work out.

Joe put the phone on mute and said, "What do you think, Annie?"

There I stood among stacks of packed boxes, having hitched my wagon to the house on Crooked Lane with "Let's give him another chance" right on the tip of my tongue. The look on my financially prudent husband's face spoke volumes. I drew in a deep breath, and then said, "No way, Joe. He had his chance and I don't think we should bank any longer on his empty promises. There's something crooked going on here and I don't trust this guy."

Joe gave a sigh of relief, delivered the news to George, and then hung up the phone.

"It's official, Annie. The sale of this house is off."

"What do we do now?" I asked, hoping Joe had an ace up his sleeve, but in my heart I knew better.

"This," he said, as he dialed the number for the real estate agent of our condo on Crooked Lane.

I had to leave the room. Just thinking about having to swing two mortgage payments until our house sold was making me sweat in places where I didn't even know I had glands. I knew for sure Joe would never agree to a swing loan or any other high interest quick fix, and I shared the same mindset. At this point the odds were no longer in our favor. Even without being in the room, I knew Joe was going to explain our situation and ask if we could be released from the agreement to purchase the condo on Crooked Lane.

When Joe hung up the phone he came into the living room and flopped down on the couch next to me.

"What a mess, Annie. What a big, fat, exhausting mess."

The owner of Crooked Lane agreed to let us out of the contract as long as our real estate agent's office sent a letter explaining what had happened. They were disgruntled but cooperative. Though our agent would much rather have talked us into giving the buyer another chance, he agreed to send the letter all the same.

When the dust settled, Joe and I decided to pretend that our little house on Spring Mill Avenue was Crooked Lane. And that's just what we did — mortgage-wise, that is. The mortgage payment on the new house figured to be almost twice what we were paying on Spring

Mill Avenue. So every month we wrote a check that was almost twice the amount of our scheduled payment.

We've made some cosmetic changes over the years, like tearing down the old wood paneling and installing hardwood floors, but we certainly have no Jacuzzi. And all these years later my husband still grumbles when the grass needs cutting. The amazing news is that last December we made our final mortgage payment on this little house of ours, fifteen years ahead of schedule. That's quite a positive outcome in a world where top-heavy mortgages abound. We don't have a mortgage. We have a deed and equity. We have pride and peace of mind, in a cozy and comfortable home that we have grown to love. But mostly we have firsthand knowledge that sometimes you just have to look on the bright side and bloom where you are planted.

~Annmarie B. Tait

12

Easy as A, B, C

Being in a good frame of mind helps keep one in the picture of health.
~Author Unknown

I felt way more tired than a twenty-eight-year-old should so I went for a checkup. The blood tests came back. I had Hepatitis C.

I had no idea what it was but I figured having a virus wasn't a big deal. So, when the doctor looked worried, sad even, I fought the urge to put my arm around his shoulders to console him. I asked a few questions, but the walls in the rooms began to move in on me and his voice became white noise and I couldn't understand anything. He pulled out a prescription pad and wrote "Liver Biopsy." I didn't know what that was either. He gave me a number to call and I left.

The breeze felt good as I walked past Columbus Circle and back to my office. From a private conference room I called Susan, my M.D. friend who worked for Doctors Without Borders.

"Do you know what Hepatitis C is?"

"Yes, it's a horrible disease, usually chronic. The liver erodes. It causes cirrhosis."

"But it can be cured, right?"

"Sometimes. Or people can get a liver transplant. But the body can reject the new liver and then the patient dies. Why are you asking me?"

"I just came from the doctor. He said I have Hepatitis C and…"

"What?" Susan gasped.

"The doctor said to see a gastroenterologist, whatever the heck that is. And I need a biopsy."

"Oh my God," she said, panicky, like I'd be dead in ten minutes.

I looked up "Best Doctors" in the latest issue of *New York* magazine and made an appointment. Dr. Gastroenterologist was out-of-network so my insurance said no to his three-hundred-dollar fee but I went anyway.

I told friends about my diagnosis but each one shot me a look of pity that said, "You're a goner," so I quit talking about it.

Once in Dr. Gastro's office I asked questions. He had olive skin, an aquiline nose and stood six feet tall. I imagined him naked until he opened his mouth. He sounded cranky and superior, which made me want to kick him. His dour expression and blank stare reminded me of actors playing sociopaths on Lifetime. So much for bedside manner.

He explained the virus in minute detail, which I appreciated, then showed me a poster with illustrations of a healthy liver versus an inflamed, swollen, undesirable one. I began to sweat and sat down. He told me to schedule a biopsy with the "girl" at the desk, who was old enough to be my mother. The address for the test was a hospital. That made me want my mommy, though I hadn't called her that since grade school. I hadn't even told my parents yet—I was loath to worry them—but my attempt at maturity gave way to fear. I called them for support. As always, they were willing to drop everything and come to the appointment with me. Relief loosened the tension in my neck—a smidgeon.

When it was time, we three went to the hospital. My father's brow was furrowed, but it usually was anyway. Mom was grinding her teeth, jaw muscles twitching as she stared at the drab, gray carpet. Their nervousness was infectious but I was grateful they were there.

Finally, a woman in white shoes and whiter smock led me to a room, handed me a cotton shmata and instructed me to put it on, opening to the front. After twenty minutes, and with goose bumps on my legs, I was led to a bed on wheels. A nurse gave me a round blue pill that looked like a Valium and told me it would make me sleepy.

Next thing I remember: Dr. Gas-Man stuck a biopsy needle in and yanked out a piece of me. I hadn't felt the slice of the blade thanks to local anesthesia but when he snatched that piece of liver it felt like I'd been sucker punched and I couldn't catch my breath. He rolled me onto my right side—right where it hurt. I was in agony as a nurse wheeled me into post-op.

In a follow-up visit with Gastro-Guy he said the biopsy showed my liver was normal size and that was very good. Then he prescribed a regimen of interferon alpha-2b. He showed me a sample kit with syringes and told me I'd have to inject it. Just seeing the needles filled me with terror. He recited side effects in a disconnected monotone. "Many patients experience flu-like symptoms, suicidal depression, and…"

Wait a minute, I thought. That sounded worse than what I had. He handed me a prescription that I knew I was never going to fill. When I got home, I called friends to ask if they knew any good doctors.

My friend from Woodstock sent me to a nutritionist whose specialty was "holistically healing chronic diseases." Her hair was wavy and long, her blouse loose, her skirt flowery—she looked like she'd just come from a Grateful Dead concert. With a warm smile she asked many questions. I watched as she wrote a customized chart in curlicue script. I was to eat millet with carrots on Mondays, brown rice with celery on Tuesdays, barley soup on Wednesdays and so on. At the top of the chart she wrote, "No sugar. No soda. No processed foods of any kind." The thought of life without Diet Coke or Ben & Jerry's made me want to die. Thankfully she wasn't expensive. I shoved her handwritten chart in my pocket and left, thinking, "Next."

Doctor number five was an organ specialist. "I treat everything from the mouth to the anus," he said. How lovely for him. Like Gastro-Man, he suggested interferon. When I asked about the success rate, he said, "50-50."

"So, half are cured?" I said.

"Not exactly. Of the half that respond well to interferon alpha-2b, half of those see the virus return after six months and need to repeat the treatment." I thanked him, left, and thought, "Next."

Help came when I met doctor number ten. I'd heard of him through a family friend who'd been diagnosed with stomach cancer and given two months to live. After she put herself in the care of this man, she lived another ten years. Dr. Gerald Epstein was smiley and chubby like Santa. He welcomed me by cupping my hand in both of his. It felt gentle and caring and I liked it. He showed me his book, *Healing Visualizations: Creating Health Through Imagery*, then asked me what I liked to do. I told him I liked working as a commercial artist but really loved to paint. That's when he said, "I want you to paint a perfectly healthy liver, hang it next to your bed, and stare at it every morning when you wake and again when you go to sleep. Imagine that your liver is as perfect as that painting."

Skeptical, I expressed doubts and confessed my fears of slowly dying with chronic pain from cirrhosis.

"Forty percent of people with chronic Hepatitis C live out their entire life with no symptoms and die of old age. Just be in that forty percent."

He said it so matter-of-factly it sounded as easy as Abraham Lincoln saying, "People are as happy as they make their minds up to be."

I borrowed an illustrated medical encyclopedia and studied the healthy liver as I rendered it with acrylic paint on watercolor paper. It took two hours and looked perfect. I bought a frame, hung it on my bedroom wall, then meditated on it as if it were an exact replication of my own liver.

Dr. Epstein also told me to get annual blood tests to keep an eye on my liver enzymes, eat healthy, and stay away from toxins — drugs, alcohol, cigarettes and processed foods. That was twenty-five years ago. I've followed all of his advice and now I'm fifty. My liver enzymes are as low as they were when I was first diagnosed. They are only slightly elevated, just enough to show that the virus is still in my system but it is dormant. I just got a liver ultrasound that showed my organ is the perfect size and color. Just like the one in my painting. That's what positive thinking did for me.

~Dorri Olds

Re-Attaching

When I came to, both eyes were bandaged shut. I could open my right eye inside the bandage, but everything was still black. My head throbbed as if it had been tumbled in a cement mixer, and the pain was beginning to claw through the numbness on the left side of my face and forehead. The surgeon had fitted a silicone buckle around my left eye to hold the retina to the back wall—his second attempt to re-attach it. The first operation had held the retina for only a month. This one had been far more invasive—"the whole nine yards," as he put it. And he warned there might be additional laser procedures to make it adhere cleanly. Then, if all went well, two more operations would repair some of the damage caused by the reattachment surgeries. My life had been forever altered.

"Are you awake?" a woman's voice asked. "How do you feel?"

I did not answer. I was angry, so nail-spitting, window-smashing angry I did not dare to speak. I wanted to stay shut in this dark cave. Even if the buckle held the retina in place this time, my vision was already permanently impaired—double vision, lack of peripheral sight, poor depth perception, and all-around fuzzy and crooked pictures of the world, none of it correctable by glasses. I had a great surgeon, but it was impossible to line up the retina exactly to where it had been and the retinal tear and the laser stitching would distort how I saw. Without surgery, of course, I would have soon lost all vision and the eye would have to be removed.

"How do you feel?" the nurse said louder.

I did not want her to rip off the bandage over my good eye yet—I didn't want to face the world as a handicapped man. I didn't want to start a life in which I could never again do anything that might jar loose the retinas of either eye, for the good eye was now at high risk as well. No jumping, running, softball, tennis or heavy exertion. No stomping on the plastic rocket toy with the grandkids.

After the first operation, I had trouble judging depths and often took awkward stutter steps at stairs and curbs. With diminished peripheral vision, I had collided with people in supermarkets. Once I'd walked through a screen door, which was both comical and unsettling. These embarrassments forced me to walk in slow motion. My whole life had become about holding back and being careful. With double vision, I often reached for the ghostly doorknob instead of the real one or stabbed the plate instead of the bean with a fork. After this second operation, I'd have even less vision. The miracles of modern technology would not magically transport me back to my previous self. I did not know who I was and did not want to leave the darkness and expose this strange person to the world. I didn't want people thinking this person was me. I didn't want this to be me.

"How do you feel?"

How did I feel? Here's what I wanted to tell the nurse:

A. This was not supposed to happen to me. Most retinal detachments are either genetic flaws that run in families or are caused by impact injuries from things like boxing gloves, car crashes or explosions. My family had no history of retinal problems and there were no bar fights on my résumé. This problem belonged to someone else. The FedEx guy ought to reclaim it and deliver it to the right address.

B. I have things to do—an agenda to finish before I grow feeble or handicapped. Just let me finish a few things in the next five or six years before springing this on me. One day during a leisurely walk, poof! My retina detaches. The next day, people are slicing into my eye, vacuuming out its natural gel, strapping a buckle around it and filling my eye with oil. There should have been warning signs.

C. My life is over. Oh, I'll go on breathing. But what's the point of living a maimed life? I'm not tough or noble enough to be a brave handicapped person.

I spoke none of this aloud, but that's how I felt. I lay in the hospital bed like stone. Then my wife's hand touched the back of mine. Her fingers ran around the IV tube and up and down my fingers. Her touch softened me. In my mind I told her, "I want to live again. I don't want to be like this for you." Carol said nothing aloud, but as she stroked my hand, I heard her speaking to me.

A. There does not have to be a reason for this to happen. It did happen. It's a fact. Something happens to everybody. We don't get to choose what or when. You've been lucky, husband, very lucky, that something big did not happen before this. Maybe now you can appreciate better what you had. This is your life — none of it belongs to anyone else.

B. You have an agenda? Nature does too. And guess whose agenda wins? So you need to revise yours. This might be an opportunity to try new things, take new paths you never saw before. Maybe your goals were too limited. As for warnings, life isn't the Weather Channel.

C. Your life is over only if you believe that. We cannot control what happens to us, only how we react to what happens. Joys and sufferings are both written into our contract for life. If you react with anger and despair to the suffering, that's what you'll have left. If you react with courage, energy and humor, that will be you. Your life will be worth living if you want it to be. You can't control your eye being detached, but you can decide if you want to be detached or not. And, pal, no matter what condition you are in, you and I are attached.

My wife shuffled aside as the nurse — now a bit peeved — leaned closer over me and repeated, "Are you awake, Mr. Bauman?"

I whispered hoarsely. "I'm getting there."

~Garrett Bauman

The Adventure of Change

Change always comes bearing gifts.
~Price Pritchett

I'm a military brat. When my father was a marine officer, we moved twelve times in fourteen years. When people hear this, they say, "That must have been hard on you."

I disagree. Each move was an adventure, an opportunity that contributed to who I am as an adult.

At family meetings, my parents would announce, "We're being transferred." Then the map would come out and we'd go into a huddle.

"This is where we are. This is where we are going." My father's fingers landed on our current home state and with the other hand, he pinpointed our next home.

I might have been sad to leave behind a favorite hiding place but I looked forward to finding a new one at the next place. I was exposed to the different seasons when we moved from the East to the West Coast. In school I learned the history of more than one state, something I wouldn't have been exposed to if we hadn't moved. My brothers and I got to visit many amusement parks and museums across the country as we traveled. These experiences were only some of the common threads among military families.

As my family ticked off the trip miles, my mother engaged us in a plethora of games, including my favorite — listing state license plates we saw. I was fascinated to see the variety. I'd wonder where the other families were headed. Were they moving too? Were they headed to Grandma's house or were they out for a local trip?

If we hadn't moved across this great country, I wouldn't have spotted a Kaibab squirrel, admired the petroglyphs of Zion National Park, or wondered at the hoodoos of Bryce Canyon. I wouldn't have giggled as we dipped deep in the water on a river float, screeched as I reeled in a trout from a babbling creek, or gazed in wonder at the Atlantic and Pacific Oceans. Although I love my Tex-Mex, the taste of true Cajun food and fresh seafood gave me a desire for a variety of cuisines. I doubt I would have tried chicken shawarma if I hadn't tried an assortment of dishes as a child.

Although the distances seemed vast when my dad would show us the map, some of my fondest memories involved the miles we covered. Our longest trek? From North Carolina to California in the summer of 1970. My parents broke each trip into segments. As an adult, I surmised it was easier on them to shoo four kids out of the car to run off energy at frequent stops. But as children, we delighted in the adventure of each break.

My parents scoped out the national and state parks along the route, and researched the hotel and camping options. Camping usually won out. With six of us, I suspect it was the cheaper solution. This led to memories such as crawling into a tent on a clear evening in the Rocky Mountains and waking up to more than eight inches of pristine snow blanketing our tents, the ground and picnic tables. When we opened the flaps of our tents, we stared in wonder at the crystal white of the landscape and then huddled back into cozy, flannel sleeping bags for a late start that morning.

Breakfast over a Coleman gas grill always tasted better than a meal cooked on a kitchen stove. Camping meant more effort for my parents than for my brothers and me. We'd clamor out of the car, help unload a few things, and leave our parents to do the real camp setup. For my brothers and me there were critters to chase and a half-hearted attempt to gather kindling for a fire. With the smell of pine needles in the Rockies, or the squish of sand between our toes on a beach, we'd be off and return as mealtime approached.

As Dad announced, "Just a little farther," we always became antsy. Would it be a big house? Would it have a bedroom for each of us? Would the back yard have enough room to toss a ball? When we pulled into our new home's driveway, I remember the excitement of solving those mysteries. My brothers and I ran from one bedroom to the next, discussing which room belonged to whom. I don't remember any arguments. It seemed as if each house was made just for our family and specific bedrooms fit our needs and personalities. Once we'd staked our claims, we'd run out the back door to see what was there. Each varied environment influenced me.

One of my favorite homes in Camp Lejeune, North Carolina, gave me a tremendous love of nature. I remember gasping when I went out the back door. Woods! Not twenty feet from the back porch, a forest of pine, beech and ash served as the property line. It didn't take the four of us long to disappear into the trees with the promise to stick together and not go too far. We spent many afternoons discovering birds, lizards and other critters among the leaves of that forest floor. By the time we'd moved away a year later, we could each explore without getting lost.

From the stops along the route to the mysteries awaiting us at the end of our journey, our military life provided opportunities that serve me well as an adult. I'm never bored, always curious to learn, and usually look at any change as an opportunity to grow. Military brats can't say, "I've lived in this house for twenty years," but we can brag about the different states we've explored and the friends and adventures we've experienced.

~Gail Molsbee Morris

15

Perspective

No life is so hard that you can't make it easier by the way you take it.
~Ellen Glasgow

Dyan is one of those down-and-out people wandering the street with her stolen shopping cart from Safeway stuffed with everything she owns. I've always steered clear of the homeless—I never could understand why they chose to walk the streets day and night instead of living in a nice warm home.

I used to sniff haughtily, "I have a home, I am in school, and I have a marvelous family. Really, why should I care about these people?"

My husband would correct me. "Some of those people have lost their own homes and their own livelihood, sometimes even their own families, and they have nowhere to go." I'm ashamed to admit that after listening to him I felt only a little less disgusted.

Then my husband lost his job. One day we had a good income and I was getting my B.A. in psychology and the next we had absolutely nothing. He had been laid off four years before and we used up all our savings and then had to resort to bankruptcy. So this time when he lost his job we had nothing to fall back on, and in this financial climate he couldn't get anywhere near the paycheck he had been earning. He was able to do consulting work but we still had to pinch pennies and juggle the monthly bills. Thankfully our house and two cars were free and clear. We weren't through paying off the bankruptcy, though, so my lawyer suggested selling our house and one of the two cars. I was terribly depressed and thought how much easier it would be if I just ended it, or like Dyan, became a homeless person everybody steered clear of, with a stolen shopping cart that contained every possession I owned.

In mid-December of that year my newly married daughter gave me $100 as an early Christmas present. It took all my fortitude to keep from crying in front of her. Once she left, I decided to drive down to our local Walgreens where I might be able to afford a few things that would make our house Christmassy, as well as some stocking stuffers. So I got in my car and turned the ignition. Nothing. My head fell between my hands that had been white-knuckling the steering wheel. "Oh God, please, no! We can't afford to fix this car! What's next?"

I was only thirty feet away from the bus stop when the 58 zoomed past. "That's what's next," I sniveled. I sat down on the wooden bench to wait the twenty minutes for the next bus. I put my heavy purse that contained the $100 down on the bench beside me.

The air was fragrant, for behind me was a group of mugo pines huddled together in the front yard of the house unlucky to be just behind an ugly bus stop. Suddenly, a shadow blocked the weak sun, while dirty clothes and stale body odor assailed my nose.

"Anybody sitting here?"

I looked up. Oh gosh, it was the stolen cart lady. In answer, I picked up my purse and held it tightly against my stomach.

She pushed her shopping cart to the side of the bench and sat with a sigh. "My, it feels so good to sit."

I leaned as far away from her as I could.

She rested her head against the back of the bench. "Feel that sun?"

My forehead wrinkled. "What sun?"

"Even the warmth of this pretty feeble sun feels so welcome when the temperature's fallen to just above freezing every night since October."

I was dumbfounded. She sounded so well educated. A nod was my own educated reply.

I finally looked at her and she at me.

"Why are you so dejected?"

I broke eye contact and pulled myself up. "Why would you think that?"

"I've never seen such a hangdog expression, complete with red nose, pale face, taut lips and bloodshot eyes." She leaned forward. "I'm right, aren't I?"

Now a homeless lady was concerned about me. In minutes I had sunk below this woman. How embarrassed I was! Nevertheless, I lost my self-possession. My shoulders slumped and I covered my face. Though I didn't intend to, I began to weep, "What's happening to me?"

"Money troubles?"

I nodded unwillingly. "Our bankruptcy lawyer recommended that we sell our house."

I looked down at her reddened, rough hand as it cupped mine.

"There are worse things than losing a house."

"Worse things? How could things be worse?"

"You could lose your husband."

I swiped at my face. "Lose what?"

She gazed across the street. "In 2005 my husband and I had just gotten excellent jobs. Together our salaries came close to $200,000 a year. We lived in Chico and moved into a gigantic house that we could just barely afford. That same year, he lost his job and a short time later, so did I. So of course we lost our house and we had to move into a cramped rental. We argued every day. Our marriage dissolved when he got another job and took up with his secretary." She glanced down at her hands. "One day, after doing my grocery shopping, I couldn't get into my own house. I went from window to window looking for a way in. When I got back to the front porch, two bags stuffed with my giveaway clothes were waiting for me. I never saw the inside of my house again.

"I stayed with my girlfriend who was separated from her husband but when he moved back in I was asked to leave. Where could I go? I had $200 in my purse and no access to our credit cards or our joint bank account. My parents live in the East and they would have helped me, but I was so embarrassed I couldn't tell them that I had lost everything. So I begged a ride from two drivers and found myself here." She sighed. "That was almost seven years ago." She suddenly smiled. "But I don't have any bills to pay and no responsibilities. I'm free as a bird. Just haven't any wings."

I was embarrassed that I had been blubbering and complaining to a homeless person. Her story made mine pale in comparison.

"Why don't you look for a job?"

She gestured down her body. "Would you hire someone like this?"

I didn't know how to answer that so I remained mum.

The bus came and as I stood I said to her, "You can stay with us. We have room. That is, until we sell the house." I couldn't believe how dispassionate about selling the house I was. "We're at 5600 Coleman."

"Thanks. But I like being free. It's just the cold that I don't like." And with that she also stood and reached for her shopping cart. "See you around, Mrs...?"

"Buckman."

"I'm Dyan, just Dyan."

On the bus, as Dyan receded into the background, I turned back around and smiled—a house is just a house after all. I felt happier than I had in days.

~L.R. Buckman

16

Strong Enough to Ask for Help

Don't be shy about asking for help. It doesn't mean you're weak,
it only means you're wise.
~Author Unknown

Last week at the supermarket a young gal named Tara who was bagging my groceries said, "Can I help take these to your car?"

As always, for the eight years since my spinal cord injury I said, "No thanks." But that particular day, I was in trouble. I had overdone my exercising the day before. Hence, I couldn't lift my feet to walk and had to shuffle instead. Tara could tell I was hurting. "Let me just help," she said sweetly.

When I finally said, "I'd love your help," I should have felt a great sense of liberation because it was the very first time I had agreed to someone helping me in all of these years. Instead, I felt like a failure.

On our way to my truck, Tara and I became friends. But at my truck, nineteen-year-old Tara became my teacher.

When I eventually agreed to her suggestion to sit in the front seat while she loaded the groceries, I put my head in my hands and cried. "I feel like a two-hundred-year-old helpless wreck. I hate that someone's putting my groceries in the truck."

She stood by the open door where I was sitting. "I know you could have done this yourself," she said. "But it was so much easier to let me do it." And then she said a life-altering sentence, "Getting help should never make you feel bad. It should always make you feel good."

I will never forget her words. Talk about an attitude adjustment.

She tentatively raised her arms to hug me. When we hugged, it was one of the most meaningful hugs of my life.

At home, I plunked myself down on my favorite "plunking" spot. It's in front of the fireplace where I hang out on large pillows. My husband, Bob, came in and plunked next to me. When I told him about the groceries, he tenderly brushed away my tears with his fingers.

"Sweetheart," he said. "Why is it so hard for you to ask for help?"

"Probably denial about my physical state."

"I think it's two other things," he said. "One—asking for help makes you feel inferior and two—you think you're bothering somebody. And three..."

"You said 'two.'"

"I just thought of a third."

"I'd so love to hear it." I covered his face with a pillow.

He took the pillow away and said, "If you do that again, I'll..."

So I did it again.

He managed to say, "Is this subject a tiny bit touchy?"

"I can handle it," I lied.

"The third is that asking for help reminds you of all the things you have a hard time doing or can no longer do at all."

This time I covered my own face with the pillow and said, "I hate this!"

"I know." And with that, he helped me to a standing position. That's something he's done hundreds of times. Yet I have felt guilty every single one of those times... until now.

It was because of Tara that I changed my way of thinking. I told Bob my new conclusions: "By asking for help, does that make me inferior? Of course not. Am I bothering someone? Who knows? But if I am, whose problem is that? Will asking for help remind me of the things I can't do? Heck, yes."

Bob knew my crusade was successful because of a pizza.

When he opened the pizza box I brought home the next day, he was astonished and said, "It's round! You asked for help!"

You see, before I met Tara, I'd never let anyone carry a take-out pizza to my truck. Instead, using my cane with my right arm, I'd awkwardly carry the pizza box with my left, resulting in the box constantly tilting one way and then the other. By the time I'd get home, that round pizza would be a smushed pile of cheesy red gunk in the corner of the box.

Bob and I plunked down in front of the fireplace and ate.

"How did it feel to accept help?" he said.

"Well, my new way of thinking helped. But the part about reminding me of things I can't do? Like carry my own pizza? That didn't feel good."

He took cheese off my chin and ate it. (We eat like monkeys.) "Sweetheart, you may never get used to the things you can't do. But it's better to be aware of that than to hide under the pretense of 'I don't need help.'"

And so, I have learned the following:

1. It does not diminish me to ask for help.

2. A nineteen-year-old gal was more influential than a shrink I saw for two years.

3. A round pizza doesn't taste nearly as good as a pizza all smushed up into a luscious gooey pile of cheesy doughy gunk in the corner of the box.

~Saralee Perel

Nurse and Patient

Life shrinks or expands in proportion to one's courage.
~Anaïs Nin

All I could hear was the sound of my feet hitting the pavement for those last few steps of my daily five-mile run. Those last few steps always hit the pavement the hardest but were the most melodic to my ears. As much as I loved my run, I loved it most the second it was over. I think I liked the idea of training for the New York City Marathon. That's just who I am (or who I was). I did things big—for the challenge. Some might have called it arrogance. My friend Sue called it "the power." She said I had it over every aspect of my life—work, men, marathons—whatever I wanted.

I remember an underlying feeling that I was invincible. I felt comfortable in my life and in my own skin. At twenty-two, I became a nurse, immediately went back to school in pursuit of my master's degree, bought my first home at twenty-five and felt like I was completely untouchable.

I went home, showered and went to work. I worked in a Pediatric Intensive Care Unit where the parents were just as much the patients as the children—sometimes more so. I never minded. I loved my patients and their families. Coming from a crazy family myself, I guess I understood. At that point in my life I didn't even know any children. That is probably what made me effective at my job. I was caring and sensitive but when I looked at a sick child I didn't see my own baby the way some nurses did.

I had a gift for dealing with "difficult" parents too. I guess I saw it as yet another challenge. If I could get those parents to trust me to take care of their sick child long enough for them to go take a shower or eat a meal, I knew I was a success. That was all the validation I needed. Many people say the PICU is one of the most challenging areas in nursing. In retrospect, that is probably why I chose it initially. That job was stressful, sad, heart wrenching, rewarding—and it made me feel like a superhero.

I had lost a patient at work the night before and, when I came home, I wanted to blow off some steam with my usual routine. The difference was, I was angry on this run. I wasn't really paying attention and was just sort of going through the motions waiting for some endorphins to kick in and make me feel better. Tears were still streaming down my face—a side of myself I never let anyone see. In fact, I was the type of person who denied her feelings so much that, if I had to cry, I usually did it in the shower. The theory being—if your face is already wet, it doesn't count. But, on that particular day, I couldn't hold back. I was so upset, in fact, that I didn't pay much attention to the tingling in my legs that morning.

The next day, I was able to turn off some of the emotions that had made me weep so uncharacteristically the day before. I guess I was less distracted because the tingling had become very apparent now. It didn't keep me from running, but it was noticeable. After all, I was training for a marathon. I didn't have time to worry about a little tingling. Several days later, I was out at dinner with a handsome lawyer whose name I don't even remember now. Over our Greek salads I said, "Shin splints!" Clearly all of this training was giving me shin splints. That was it! It was the obvious explanation and I couldn't understand how I didn't realize it sooner.

The funny thing about denial is that it usually has an expiration date. About two weeks later, I found myself in my doctor's office asking for an MRI. I suspected I had multiple sclerosis and wanted to go through the formality of ruling it out. He laughed at me and said,

"You nurses are the worst — you think you have everything." We had known each other a long time and were friends, so even though he thought I was a total hypochondriac at that point, he appeased me for the sake of our friendship.

It was a Tuesday. I don't know why I always remember that but I do. I guess the day your life changes forever you remember the details. My friend the doctor called. His voice was different. He started to cry and said he was so sorry he had laughed at me. I knew what that meant because my legs gave out and I sat down on the bed but, at the same time, I was confused. It was surreal. I couldn't speak. It wasn't until he actually said, "You have multiple sclerosis" that I simply said, "Okay" and hung up the phone. I hadn't even told anyone that I was having the testing done because I never really thought this would be the outcome. Now I had to tell people. Once you start telling people it becomes real and it is so much harder to live in denial once it's real.

I was so angry. I was angry that I might not be able to do all the things I wanted to down the line. I was angry that my family and friends might look at me differently. I was angry that I had to consider changing my career path. Most of all, I was angry that I couldn't run that stupid marathon!

Then I started analyzing why I got MS. Maybe this was all pay-back for the way I treated the men I dated. I was a terrible daughter growing up — a real delinquent. My mother always said I put every gray hair on her head. I used to beat up my sister. Maybe if I had been nicer all those years, this wouldn't have happened to me. What if I promised to be a better person? Maybe all of this would go away. I could be good. I could be a good girlfriend — even settle down. That would kill two birds with one stone. That would make my Italian mother the happiest woman in the world and I would be better in the relationship department.

It started me thinking very philosophically about why bad things happen to good people — or do they? It kept coming back to me that maybe bad things just happen to bad people and I clearly fell into that category. I became a saint overnight because, if the same principles applied, then good things were going to happen to me because I was going to be the next Mother Teresa if it killed me.

Needless to say, this did not work. The plan was doomed from the start. The last thing I am is a saint. The truth is, sometimes things just happen. There is no rhyme or reason to it. It just happens. Some people believe everything happens for a reason. I happen to be one of them… but I'll get to that later. In the end, it was not worth the energy to try to figure it out why this happened to me and, the truth is, none of us will ever truly know anyway. I just found that it served me better in the long run to focus my energy on getting better.

At some point you realize that this thing that has invaded your existence is simply not going to go away. Despite all of your yelling and screaming, crying and begging, this is it. For me, surprisingly, that point was not until much later when I had my second episode.

It sort of hit me the first time I had to give myself an injection. I sat with the needle in my hand staring at my leg for over an hour. I was a nurse for crying out loud! What was wrong with me? I had given more injections throughout my career than I could count but, for some reason, putting that pointy metal object into my own body felt completely unnatural.

I went from being "me"—larger than life—to someone I didn't recognize. Someone I didn't like or even understand. I felt lost. I had no idea that so much of my self-esteem was tied to my work. I was used to being the caregiver, not the receiver. I was humbled. This was something I couldn't control and I hated that. People told me just to let go, relax and let someone else take care of me for a change but there was nothing relaxing about letting go for me. All I wanted was to cling to my former self, my former life and everything I once was.

When I was first diagnosed, I decided I was going to control this disease—it was not going to control me. Well, I have since amended that notion. I can't control this disease or the randomness of it but I can manage it to the best of my ability and embrace the unexpected. The only control I have is to control my response to some of the bizarre things my body has done over the last decade since I was diagnosed with MS.

I started to understand the unpredictability of this illness. I came to realize that one day I may be sick and the next I may be fine. It took me months (even years) to really understand. Years can go by and nothing but minor inconveniences that everyone suffers will come up and then something can come along and knock me on my ass... but that's life, isn't it? There's nothing so unique about me.

In some ways, I really feel like I've been given a huge gift. I have learned to go with the flow in ways I never knew I could. I have since been thrown more curve balls than I can count but they don't knock me off my game because I've learned to trust that I can handle whatever gets thrown at me. I have since survived breast cancer and a bilateral mastectomy too. I'm not saying it was easy but I think positively, surround myself with positive people and I believe in myself and in the power of positive thinking.

While I tend to be a little more cautious than some people when it comes to my health, I take a lot more risks when it comes to my life. I try to live and enjoy every moment that I can and do all the things I want to do. I've scaled the Great Wall of China, climbed the Eiffel Tower, seen Big Ben, partied at Mardi Gras, been on a shark expedition, landed by helicopter on top of a glacier, walked among the redwoods, stared at the ceiling in the Sistine Chapel and I live in the greatest city in the world... New York! (This is probably my greatest adventure of all.)

I'm still a nurse and I'm still a patient. I'm not defined by either one. My identity is not wrapped up in what I do or what I have. They are both contributing factors in my life but they are not who I am.

My life is not over because I hit a bump. It has just shifted routes, but that's okay because my next stop is the Galapagos Islands. I'm still thinking big.

~Sidney Anne Stone

The Power of Positive

The Power of Persevering

The Strength

A wise man will make more opportunities than he finds.
~Francis Bacon

I waited half an hour, set the board, and sat in the studio reviewing my questions another five minutes until the telephone lines flashed. I always got butterflies before every interview.

"Hello?"

"I'm so sorry I'm late. This doesn't usually happen." I could hear the woman on the line was a little out of breath. The line went silent.

"This is Connie Chung. How are you?" My heart sank.

Connie Chung was an icon, one of only four women anchors to make it into the elite club of major evening network television news. For almost an hour we talked about the industry. When I asked if she ever had a mentor throughout her trials she turned around and offered to mentor me. When I asked why she wanted to do it she simply replied, "Because you're good."

That afternoon I rushed home and told my mother what had happened. Deep down I felt a sense of competition with my mother, and her response always made me feel under-appreciated. "Good for you."

I had been the president of a prestigious high school, argued with trustees, the school administration and chairs of departments over what the right direction to take the school was, and after a friend of mine passed in my senior year from cancer, I assisted in raising tens of thousands of dollars for charities that would aid others in their battle for survival. I worked for her front-row seat at my graduation. Instead of enjoying those moments as a family, negativity brought us down.

Until then I had been searching for something that I would never get — that sense of love and acceptance in a house full of negativity. A risk would allow me to open myself to the world again and receive all the positive energy that I needed. I knew that I could do whatever I was called to do, but first I needed to get rid of all the negativity in my life. I packed my bags, and without looking back, I walked out of that house.

Radio became therapeutic for me. It became my way of connecting with others, and telling their story. My ability to book high-level guests and celebrities led to my own talk show, The Gary Duff Show. It would air to a Malibu, California audience, while I continued to host a live morning talk show in New York.

Eventually all the words of encouragement from past guests and colleagues helped me to re-build my confidence levels. "I can do this," I kept telling myself, and pushed even harder to find my next niche.

One of my chief mentors, John Mullen, known for his no-nonsense attitude as New York's WBLS FM Program Director, helped me to partially develop this faster decision making process. Where can I go now? What can I do next? Who can I grab for my show? "You're incredible at booking." He told me. "I've never seen anything like it."

Another friend, Joseph DeRosa, who once served as Charlie Rose's Chief Engineer at Bloomberg, put the idea of possibly working there in my head. "Really?" I thought. "They're always looking for people like you," he'd say.

People had faith in me and so I developed faith in myself. Their positive attitudes towards themselves and towards me helped me develop my own positive attitude, leading to productive interactions with celebrities and adding to my list of mentors.

I may not have started life surrounded by positivity but I sure feel that I am surrounded by it now. It's amazing how positivity builds on itself.

~Gary Duff

Chicken Soup for the Soul

Blind Faith

Leadership is action, not position.
~Donald H. McGannon

"Why?" I pleaded for an answer. "Oh, God, why is this happening to me?" I moaned as I buried my head in my pillow.

I was in my prime. I had just turned nineteen. I was a sophomore at a prestigious Ivy League women's college and I had a plan. I was going to study abroad, graduate, go to law school, get a good job at a top law firm, find a man, get married, start a family—have it all. I wasn't supposed to go blind. That wasn't part of the plan. Yet, there I was, blind, lying helpless on my childhood bed in my parents' house, tears streaming down my face as I gasped for air between heaving sobs.

God will never give you more than you can bear, I thought, in a futile attempt to calm down. For a split second, my nerves settled. Then, the thoughts of what was to come flooded back into my head. I shuddered and cried out, "Oh God, I just can't bear it."

I was used to going to doctors. I had endured hundreds of examinations and had undergone dozens of operations ever since I was four years old and diagnosed with juvenile rheumatoid arthritis, cataracts, glaucoma and uveitis. I was a seasoned patient, not afraid of any doctor, needle or procedure. Operation? No problem. Only one day after laser surgery to reduce the pressure in my eye, I was outside swinging on the swing set simply because it was a beautiful day and I loved the sense of freedom that swinging on a swing gave me. Even when I was ten years old, sitting in the examination chair for a post-operative checkup in Boston and the doctor told me and my parents that the retina in my left eye had detached during surgery, I didn't flinch. I simply accepted the news and happily walked the several blocks to the ocularist's office where I was promptly fitted with a starter prosthesis for my left eye. I still had the sight in my right eye. It wasn't great vision—I was legally blind—but I could see. That is how I always was—at least with those sorts of things—resilient, optimistic.

But, that day, in that examination chair, I was shaken to the core by my greatest fear—being blind, being disabled. My fear of blindness and being seen as disabled is what took me to the brink when I was fifteen. Not only the thought of being different, but actually being ostracized by my peers, sent me spiraling into a deep depression. I cursed God and asked Him why back then. Now, here I was all over again, no longer visually impaired, but completely blind—after a sudden flare-up of my condition.

"Will I get my sight back?" I had asked my doctor tentatively. I feared the answer, but had to ask.

He paused. "I don't know. Hopefully," he said in a low, sincere voice.

Hopefully. I repeated the word in my mind and remembered the serenity prayer. I couldn't change this. I would have to go on. So, that is what I did. I continued with the plan I had originally charted. Little did I know, this was part of a bigger plan.

Only a few weeks before I had my flare-up, in a city three hundred miles away, a man lost his sight as well. He had been diagnosed with glaucoma as an infant. After going totally blind as a toddler, doctors restored the sight in one of his eyes. He had lived with that sight for over twenty-five years until in a freak accident with a pair of pliers, his sight was gone in a second.

His name was Lance and our paths did not cross until nearly two years later when he and I were in Morristown, New Jersey training with our first seeing-eye dogs. It wasn't love at first sight, and not just because neither one of us could see. He was brash, cynical, and arrogant, but he was also kind, intelligent, and funny. We began a six-year courtship. We traveled together with our seeing-eye dogs, walking, taking planes, trains, buses and taxis blindly and boldly going wherever we wanted. We shared our hopes, dreams and fears with one another.

One day, Lance took me in his arms and said, "You're my inspiration."

I smiled. "You should know sappy lines from eighties rock songs don't work on me," I said jokingly. He knew they did.

"No. I mean it. You're the reason I want to be better. You inspire me. I didn't know what was possible until you showed me."

"Well, that's the way it's supposed to be. I'm your girlfriend. You should think that about me. If you didn't, we'd have a problem." We laughed.

I wasn't ready to accept what Lance was trying to tell me. He saw something in me that I could not see and that led to a stunning moment in my life, when I realized one of my childhood dreams, and when I also started to see the bigger picture about my blindness.

I was adorned in my cap and gown and doctoral hood, about to graduate from Cornell Law School. I picked up my seeing-eye dog's harness handle and ascended the steps to the stage. The dean called my name. I took one last deep breath, rolled back my shoulders, lifted my head and commanded my dog "forward."

A sudden thunderous tidal wave of applause carried me across the stage. Screaming, cheering, clapping from every direction. I was dumbfounded, moved and enlightened. This really was it. This was the answer to the question I had asked years before. Why? This was why. I was so focused on my blindness being only about me. Yes, I was the one who overcame it in order to graduate, but by overcoming it and accomplishing my goals, I unknowingly was inspiring those around me.

This is what Lance was talking about. My journey could help others and now that I knew, I was compelled to share my experience and everything I had learned. Together, Lance and I formed

Blind Faith Enterprises LLC to motivate, educate and inspire others to reach their highest potential. I truly believe that there is a reason for everything and we all do have a purpose. It might not be easy to see exactly what the reason or purpose is, but that's because we are looking for it with our eyes instead of feeling it with our hearts. I am so thankful for being able to inspire Lance and that he in turn helped me realize my purpose in life.

~Angela C. Winfield, Esq.

Rolling Uphill

*Obstacles are those frightful things you see
when you take your eyes off your goal.*
~Henry Ford

"I can tell you right now, you're not going to pass this class." My physics instructor paused, rubbed wearily at his pale, cold eyes, and elaborated. "First, you're a woman. Second, you're too old to be a student."

I couldn't believe my ears. As he droned on, offering special help if I wasn't willing to play it smart and drop the course, my heart sank and my mind raced. It was 1985. Hadn't Geraldine Ferraro run for the vice presidency? Helen Reddy had been singing "I am woman, hear me roar" for nearly fifteen years. I couldn't believe this Neanderthal. Could I really be too old? I was twenty-six. As a young divorced mom, I faced struggles in college, but I hadn't considered my age to be a barrier. Tucking my notebook into my green backpack, I rose, thanked the professor for his time and dragged myself from his office, my shoulders sagging in dismay.

I'd walked about ten feet when indignation straightened my posture and lightened my step. I was a straight A student. I was determined. I had a big sister with a master's degree in engineering. Physics—or rather, this antique of a physics professor—would not defeat me. If he thought I'd withdraw from his class, he was mistaken. He'd waved a red cape before me, and I would charge.

Charge I did. I ran headlong into a big, tall, wide brick wall. My dad the engineer tried to help me over the phone. My sister the engineer gave me her *Schaum's Outline of College Physics*. My brother the whiz kid tried to tutor me. My daughter Elaine encouraged me with hugs. She also invited me to take frequent breaks from my studies to read stories or play blocks with her.

Without her interruptions my brain would have exploded. The first week's homework assignment took me ten hours to complete. It was a set of ten problems. At one problem per hour, it would be a long semester.

One day the professor lectured on friction. He drew a simple diagram of a car parked on a hill on the chalkboard. Then he began spouting gobbledygook about mass and gravity and friction and scrawling on the board, spittle flying as he warmed to his topic. Finally he turned to the class and asked, triumphantly, "What happens when the friction is adequate?"

Involuntarily, I made an upward motion with my hand, at an angle.

He snickered. "When the friction is adequate," he intoned, "the brakes work. Cars seldom roll uphill," he added, sneering.

I wanted to hide.

This misogynistic, supercilious physics teacher was likely to kill me, I thought. I had a full-time job, a full load at school, and a young daughter. I hadn't budgeted ten hours a week for physics homework. I also had an acceptance letter to the University of California, San Diego, my dream school. My admission was contingent upon satisfactory completion of this physics course.

One evening I poured out my heart, and my frustration, to my mom. "It makes me crazy, Mom! I know I'm not too old to learn this. And I know I'm smart enough. But my brain just isn't wired that way. It takes me an hour to do a single homework problem."

"How are your grades?"

"Funny you should ask that. I'm getting As on all the tests. He lets us use a single page of formulas and notes. And the problems are very similar to our homework problems, so I study my homework and memorize everything. I can work the problems, but I don't understand why the right answers are right."

"Well," my wise mother said, "if you're making the grade you need, just keep at it."

"But I want to understand!"

"Of course you do," she soothed over the phone. "And maybe by semester's end it will make sense. But don't you need this course to transfer? You can't quit. You're so close to your goal. And nobody's brilliant in everything. I know it's hard, honey, but just hang in there."

She was right. This course was the toughest one I'd faced, and it was crucial to my educational goal. No rheumy-eyed, obnoxious professor would stand between me and my dreams.

Nobody's brilliant in everything. My mom offered me a tremendous gift with those words. She gave me permission to be mediocre, to do my very best and yet receive just-okay results. In this case, just-okay would advance my education. Failure, or quitting, would not.

I quit grumbling. Physics might become clearer, as Mom had suggested, or it might not: my task was to pass the class. I resolved to ignore the instructor's arrogance and focus on cranking out that homework and memorizing the problems so I could pass this miserable course and move on with my life.

I pictured myself as that improbable car I'd suggested during the friction lecture, rolling uphill. The image made me laugh. It felt good to laugh about physics. I hadn't tried that before.

The weeks wore on. I still spent ten hours a week on my physics homework. I continued to memorize problems in order to pass the exams. But now I laughed as I studied. I just needed to roll uphill and get through the course. Then it was on to university, where no further study in physics would threaten my future.

In November, twelve weeks into the sixteen-week course, I pulled my notebook from my green backpack and settled into my seat. The instructor arrived, took out his notes, wiped his pasty forehead and commenced a lecture on fluid dynamics.

I sat and listened, trying to identify the strange sensation floating about in my head. Suddenly I recognized the feeling. I understood! I wondered if a giant light bulb blazed over my head. I could hardly contain my excitement, squirming in my seat like a second grader before recess.

When class ended I raced to a pay phone. "Mom! I get it!" I shrieked into the phone.

"What did you get? Are you all right? Is Elaine okay?"

I calmed myself with a deep breath. "In physics class today, Mom—it all made sense! Not just the stuff he taught us today, but all of it! Just like you said it would!"

"I said it might," she reminded me gently. "I'm glad. I'm so proud of your hard work."

"Mom, I don't think I would have made it if you hadn't encouraged me the way you did. You offered me a different perspective. You gave me room to be average at something. You reminded me what I had to gain."

"Well, I'm your mom. That's my job." I could hear her smile right through the telephone line.

At semester's end I stood outside the instructor's office, examining the list of final grades. His door flew open. "Miss Seiler?"

"Yes?"

"You passed this class with the highest point total ever. Congratulations."

He extended his hand. I hesitated for an instant, and then I shook it.

"Please excuse me," I said, withdrawing my hand from his clammy paw. "I have to go pack. I'm moving to the university this weekend."

~Sheila Seiler Lagrand

Chutes and Ladders

You can never quit. Winners never quit, and quitters never win.
~Ted Turner

The late afternoon sun streamed through our living room windows, my four-year-old son Evan's sticky handprints smudged across the glass. He and I sat on the carpet, his *Chutes and Ladders* game sprawled out before us.

"It's your move, Mommy," he said.

I was preoccupied. I'd just gotten a rejection letter on my book, and as much as I love playing with my kid, a grown person can only take so much *Candy Land* and *Hungry Hungry Hippos*. My mind swirled with self-pitying thoughts: Was this where all my years of writing had led? Was this my destiny? I could almost feel my brain withering.

I shook off the melodrama and refocused on the game. I already had two fully-grown children and I knew all too well how fast this precious time would pass. Moments playing with my kid were what really mattered—and who cared what that stuffy agent thought, anyway?

Evan spun the dial. "Woo Hoo! I'm gonna win!" he shouted as he moved his playing piece up the ladder.

The object of *Chutes and Ladders* is to move 100 spaces to the winner's spot at the top. Along the way, you are provided "Ladders" that allow you to skip spaces and move to the top, and then there are "Chutes," long slides that send you reeling back to the bottom.

Lately, Evan had been obsessed with the idea of winning. In fact, he saw everything as an opportunity to win. When we got out of the car, he'd race me to the front door. He'd finish a glass of milk, slam it down empty on the table and exclaim, "I win!" But he, like every four-year-old, was having a hard time with the concept of "losing."

So when we'd play games like *Candy Land* or *Don't Break the Ice*, I tried to teach him good sportsmanship. When he'd win, he'd shout, "I win and you lose, Mommy!" He didn't say it with any malice, and technically he was right, but I explained to him that even in winning we must be gracious, and encourage the other person for playing a good game. After that, whenever I lost, he'd gently pat me on the back and say, with a sweet expression and sing-songy voice, "Congratulations, loser."

Once again, Evan roused me from my daydreaming. "Your turn, Mommy."

I spun the dial, and just happened to get the ladder to the winner's circle. I won. He looked crestfallen. He dropped his playing piece and started to pack up the game.

"Aren't you going to say 'Congratulations, loser' to me, Mommy?" he asked.

And suddenly, the importance of this moment sunk in. My son wasn't a loser because his roll of the dice was different than mine. He wasn't a lesser person because his journey set him back on the game board. My head was spinning as I related this preschool game to my whole life. I could see our family's history on the multi-colored spaces....

The Dexters' Real-Life Chutes and Ladders:

1993 — My struggling business turns a profit after four years of loss: Ladder

1994 — It burns down: Chute

2003 — We take out a loan and build my husband's recording studio: Ladder

2004 — It floods: Chute

2009 — We finally pay off our debt: Ladder

2010 — We're sued: Chute

But did we ever pack up the game and walk away? No! We kept rebuilding, kept going after our dreams. We knew that other "chutes" could be in our future, but the winner's circle was still up there.

So I told my son, "Wait a minute, why don't you finish the game?"

He looked at me confused. "But I lost, Mommy."

I answered, "Just because one person makes it to the top first, doesn't mean the rest of us lose. You keep going."

So he did, and bless his little heart, every time he got close to the top, he'd land on this one terrible chute that would take him right back to the beginning. And I'll be darned if that didn't happen four times in a row. At first it upset him. A lot. But after the fifth time, it became ridiculously funny to both of us. Evan was laughing so hard he fell over in his chair. It took him another half hour to finally make it to the winner's circle, but boy-oh-boy was that a sweet moment. We jumped up and cheered—the victory all the sweeter for having been so hard earned. Isn't that just like life?

And of course I caught my own reflection in this lesson. I thought I was teaching my son something that day, but I'm the one who really needed to learn the value of persistence, and hope, and what's more—a sense of humor. When I think of all the times I've been discouraged—the times I just knew that someone else had already done it better, faster, slicker than me, whatever it was. All the times I packed up the game and quit, because someone else had made it to the top first—they had written the better essay, the more brilliant book. All those times, I walked away from my own chance to win.

I certainly wasn't going to teach my son that there is only one winner, or that every situation is either win or lose.

I believe the winner's circle still looms up there for every one of us. Some of us may take a long time to get there. We may be four years old, or forty, or twice that (Betty White's resurgence at 88? Helloooo!). The journey will look different for all of us. Some of us might get knocked down that chute five times or more, while others take the ladder straight up. It doesn't matter.

What matters is that we find our own way, and persevere.

It's like I told Evan that day. "Don't pack up the game. Keep going."

We started a new way of "playing the game" that day, and you know what? It's much more gratifying for all of us.

By the way, my book eventually sold.

Ladder!

~Hollye Dexter

My Husband the Winner

Let perseverance be your engine and hope your fuel.
~H. Jackson Brown, Jr.

My husband Steve has always been a positive guy. I'm more the "prove it to me" type. Back in 1999, we ran an in-home day care and I was diagnosed with rheumatoid arthritis. There was a game show on called *Greed*. After he watched it a couple of times, my husband decided that he could do way better than any other contestant/group he had seen and it became his mission to get on this show.

He searched both the Internet and the newspaper ads to find out how to get on. It didn't take long before he got himself an audition. This meant taking off an entire day of work. Our son Adam stayed home from high school to help me.

My ever-lovin' got through the first round and was asked to stay for a possible taping that day. He didn't make it, but was told he'd be called soon for another "possible" taping.

Given my health and the fact that our son took off from school, we discussed the matter, and while my husband didn't like the idea of giving up on his dream, he agreed that if he didn't get to do a taping the second time, there'd have to be a "promise" instead of a "maybe" to go a third time.

He was called and off he went—this time our daughter Sarah arranged her work schedule to be my designated helper for the day. Again, he left at 6:30 a.m. (something I couldn't even get him to do during the normal workweek) and he returned well after dark.

The outcome—he was in the group that was supposed to be up next when they stopped taping for the night! They asked who'd be able to come back for a "possible" taping. Steve was so intent on proving he could win that he said he'd absolutely be there. After hearing this, I was a tad angry. We had agreed, but his positive feelings about winning had somehow dimmed his memory!

A few weeks later, the producers called and gave him a choice of taping days. He explained the situation and they said they'd do their best, given this was the third time he was making the drive and taking time off from work. Our kids split the difference on helping me for the day.

It was "college week" on the show, and fortunately for my husband, the last group of college kids crashed and burned early. The outcome—he was made team captain. Three men, two women. The other two men were "taken out" by the two women, so the women were slated to receive the share that the men they booted off would have received.

Neither woman wanted to boot my husband because he had "cleaned up" their mistakes and got them to the $500,000 level! So the three of them went on to compete.

Then came the category—JAMES BOND MOVIES.

Did I mention Steve is a movie fanatic? The women gave wrong answers, which my husband corrected. Then he answered his own question and then the spare one.

Yes, he swept the $500,000 category. The women wound up getting $200,000 each while the man who made sure they won went home with $100,000!

He called me on his way home. I asked if he had a good time and how he did. "Did you at least get $10,000?" He said no. I told him I was glad he had fun anyway. He asked me to add a "0" to the number. "Why? Adding a '0' won't change anything. One '0' or two still comes to the same nothing."

"No, I mean add a '0' to the $10 grand."

"You're kidding." He assured me he wasn't! We were sworn to secrecy until the air date. We didn't even tell our kids.

It couldn't have come at a better time. My health was fading fast. Steve got the first payment several months later and then we had six years of annuity payments. That money saw us through closing our business and re-inventing ourselves in new careers.

We were still treading financial waters when our daughter announced her engagement. The last installment was what we used to host her wedding and reception.

If it hadn't been for his positive mindset and perseverance, I honestly have no idea how we would have made it through those years. Thank goodness he's the man he is and that his love of movies is as strong as his love for our family.

~Carine Inez Nadel

Just Reward

He conquers who endures.
~Persius

"I am not going to the award ceremony this year! Please don't make me go." I sat with my daughter at breakfast the morning of the high school senior award ceremony. We'd had this battle every time there was an award ceremony, ever since she'd come to the conclusion that no matter how hard she worked, she wasn't going to win an award.

But this year, I knew something she didn't.

"Oh Tori, it's your last year of school. I... saw a letter at a PTO meeting. Your friend Jesse is going to get an award. You should be there to cheer her on."

I got one of those looks teenagers are so good at, but as she walked out the door that morning she reluctantly agreed to attend the ceremony.

My wonderful, sweet daughter is incredibly bright but so profoundly dyslexic that she really didn't learn to read fluently until she was about twelve, and she still struggles to express herself coherently in writing. Every mother, of course, thinks her child deserves an award, but I knew that if one was given out for hard work and a "never say die" attitude, Tori would have no competition. She never gave up, even during the dark days when we were desperately searching for help for her, terrified she might never graduate from high school, much less go to college.

When other kids were singing or acting or doing sports after school, Tori doggedly worked at special programs, spending hours every week trying to get her tangled brain to decode the written word. She sacrificed summer vacation time and Christmas break in her endless push through the many programs available for dyslexics. Each one helped a bit and enabled her to finish high school and get accepted into college.

But unfortunately the one thing she'd never been able to achieve were school awards, and we'd endured many teary afternoons after award ceremonies.

After she left the house, I quickly got dressed and took one last look at the letter the school had sent me. It was an invitation to the award ceremony, sent only to parents of students who would be receiving awards. Her positive attitude and determination, which often bolstered my husband and me when the battle had worn us down, was finally paying off, and I would be there to see it.

As I walked to the school in the sweltering early June morning, I contemplated how I was going to get in without her seeing me. I didn't want to spoil the surprise! When I approached the high school parking lot, I could hear the buzz of teenage excitement. I scanned the sea of blue graduation gowns, which the kids were required to wear to the ceremony, but fortunately didn't see her. I scooted into the blissfully cooler auditorium and grabbed a seat in the first row behind where the students would be seated.

They all marched in a few minutes later, and, of course, in that 800-seat auditorium, she was seated right in front of me! She spotted me about a second after I spotted her. But just when I thought all was lost, she said, "Oh, you're here for Jesse. That's nice of you." This being our first senior award ceremony, she didn't know about the parents being invited to come.

The awards droned on for a while until we got to the Eleanor Shipler Award, given to a student who had improved and put forth exceptional effort in English. And the winner was Tori! When she turned around to look at me, the shock and joy on her face made every hour of struggle we'd all put in worth it. She walked up and got her award, beaming. When she got back with her envelope, she asked me if I'd known. I told her I knew she was getting something—but not an English award! The ceremony continued and, in the end, she also won a second award for her work with the backstage technical theater crew.

It turns out, as I discovered later from the Shipler family, the award was meant by Eleanor, a former English teacher, for exactly the kind of kid Tori was—not the student with the highest average, but one who tries hard and puts her best effort forth to improve her English skills. I couldn't have been prouder.

I snapped lots of pictures outside and then, trying not to embarrass Tori too much, snuck away from the crowd of seniors eagerly anticipating the annual pool party that followed. As I walked I heard "Mother!" Not being the only mother in the crowd, I ignored the voice, until I heard a very insistent, "Karen, wait up!" It was Tori. Surprised and pleased that my eighteen-year-old didn't mind being seen with me, I waited until she caught up. I don't think her feet touched the steaming sidewalk as we walked home.

She shook the envelope, rattling the contents.

"What do you think it is?"

"Probably a letter and a check," I answered.

"Can we frame the check?"

I laughed. "No, Tori. We'll cash the check and use it for your education. We'll frame the letter."

And so we did, along with her high school diploma. I can't say which she treasures more.

~Karen Lewis Jackson

I Named Her Lily

Every child begins the world again.
~Henry David Thoreau

"You will never, ever be able to adopt this child." I read the words again. "Don't even think about it." The e-mail went on to explain all the reasons why it would be impossible for me to adopt the girl I had left behind in China.

I thought back to that day. She was on the other side of a room filled with kids, mostly girls, at the orphanage in Nanjing. She was already grown, a teenager, not a child. She glanced at me and smiled. I fell in love. "Don't be crazy," I told myself. "You have four kids already. You do not need another child." But I made sure to get her photo and her name before she walked out of the room. Just as she disappeared from view, she looked back at me and smiled shyly. It was all I could do not to run after her. I didn't know if I would ever see her again.

Once I was back home, I found a way to sponsor her in school and correspond with her. Her delicate Chinese characters were a magical secret code. Whenever I got a card or letter from her, I would race to one of my friends who spoke and read Chinese to translate. I scribbled down every word so I could read them again later.

Meanwhile, I started making inquiries about adopting her. I sought advice from adoption agencies, from friends at the State

Department, from former law students of mine now practicing in China. Surely someone could give me some encouragement.

But no one did. No matter where I turned, the answer was the same. She was not on the list of children available to adopt, and there was no way to get her on the list. She would soon be over the age limit. The Chinese government frowned on people selecting their own child, especially before being approved. And no, there were no exceptions. Not ever.

Why, then, was I so sure that she was meant to be my child?

I didn't give up. I kept asking. And then, in the midst of all the discouraging responses, I got an e-mail. "I have spoken with someone who thinks that she can help you." The first glimmer of hope. Oh, but so many things had to fall in place in my country and hers, through the bureaucratic red tape of two governments. I didn't hesitate. "Let's get started."

It was only then, when I thought that it was possible, that I sent a letter to the person who mattered most. I wrote to this girl I had only seen for twenty minutes and asked her if she would like to be part of my family. I described our life and sent pictures. I tried to be as honest as I could. I told her I couldn't make any guarantees, but if she wanted me to be her mother, I would do everything in my power to make that a reality. She was about to make the most important decision of her young life.

The days stretched into weeks as I waited for her response. When it came, I stared at the one English word in the midst of all the indecipherable characters—mother. My ever-patient friend soon translated the rest. Yes, she would like to be my daughter.

Now we were in a race against the clock. Everything had to be completed before her next birthday. Like Cinderella when the clock struck midnight, she would then be over the age limit. There was no room for errors or delays.

If I wrote about all the people who made heroic efforts on both sides of the ocean to make miracles happen, it would take up this entire volume. Many of them I never knew and couldn't even thank.

But step by step we got closer to the time when I would get on the plane and go to China to bring her home.

With the adoption plans moving forward, I wrote to ask her if she wanted an English name, and if so, what name appealed to her. She replied that in China, parents give their child a name that represents a wish or hope for the child. She wanted me to choose her name, to state my wish for her.

I thought about all that had transpired since I met her. I thought about her courage to leave behind everything that was familiar to her. It was like being born again.

So I named her Lily, the flower of Easter, the flower of life resurrected, with the hope that her new life would bring her joy and fulfillment.

A year and a half after that fateful day when I watched her walk out of that room, I sat in another room in Nanjing, waiting for her to arrive. When she walked through the door, I saw that same shy smile. I said hello to her in Chinese and held out my hand. With the pure trust of a child, she put her soft hand in mine, and we began our new life together.

I recently ran across that e-mail from the expert telling me that I would never, ever be able to adopt that girl. I just smiled. Never, ever underestimate the power of a mother's love.

~Galen Pearl

Just Finish

Runners just do it — they run for the finish line
even if someone else has reached it first.
~Author Unknown

Jeff Ortega lost the eighteen-year-old son who shared his name two weeks before I met him on a roadway in Tulsa, Oklahoma. But I didn't know that when he caught up with me about fifteen minutes into my run of the final leg of the 2011 Tulsa Route 66 Marathon Relay. Four of my other co-workers had just run their five-mile sections, and they counted on me to finish strong on that cold November morning.

I didn't know if I would. Truth was, I'd started off the run with a bad attitude, a negative one for sure. The wind whipped my face too hard, chapping my lips before I'd even started. All around the race the November chill set in and promised to stay, never allowing temperatures to get out of the forties. As I waited at the University of Tulsa for my section to begin, I watched rain misting outside from thick clouds.

Race day had proven miserable and left me questioning why I always signed up for races like this one. It was my first time in Tulsa; I'd never been more ready to hop in my Honda and head back to Oklahoma City.

When Jeff caught up with me on the race trail, I could see immediately that something had gone wrong. His stride looked painful; I saw him wince more than once. I wondered for a split second if he'd fall out like some of the other marathon runners I'd seen on past runs.

"You can do this," I told him encouragingly, breaking the ice between cold breaths. I realized I'd hit a pace where talking didn't feel painful.

"I don't know if I can," Jeff admitted. Then he told me how on mile six, sixteen miles back, he'd felt a sharp pain rip through one of his legs, an injury that screamed with every step. He told me he'd wondered for the last few miles if he should quit the race all together. This seasoned marathon runner wrestled with a body that had broken down.

"You can't quit now," I chided as our feet fell into place. "We're almost done. You're almost done."

Jeff nodded. "I want to keep going, but I'm afraid," he said. "I don't know if I can make it, if I even want to any more."

I guess that's when I knew that I had to run with him. I guess that's when I knew I needed to force him to think positively.

For the next few minutes, we got the formalities out of the way. He told me about his home in St. Louis, how he worked for a company there. I mentioned I had just moved to Oklahoma City to anchor the 9 p.m. news. He explained how he had come to Tulsa as part of a running group of about seventy people. I told him I'd spent the last few years in Cincinnati.

"Cincinnati?" Jeff said, and then his face changed. "My son, he lived around there with his mother."

Right then and there, between huffs and painful steps, Jeff told me the real reason he'd come to Tulsa.

Just two weeks before, his son had fallen off a balcony at a home in Lawrenceburg, Indiana. Just eighteen, Jeff Jr., was gone in an instant in an accident no one could explain, a life moment that made sense to no one on earth.

Father and son had loved running and bonded over the physicality and the body stress that came with a race. Now this grieving man had just two and a half more miles to finish a race he and his running group had dedicated to his son's memory.

"We're all wearing black," Jeff told me. "But I think I'm the last one to finish, you know, since I got hurt."

I looked down at my own black North Face jacket, at the fleece that wrapped me against the cold and the black pants that matched. "Well, I've got black on too," I replied. "So I guess now I'm running in memory of your son as well. I'd be honored if you'd let me."

Jeff smiled.

Over the next two miles, he shared with me some of his memories. We laughed; we cried. We kept pace. Jeff told me about how much his son impacted the world around him, how the boy he loved had an infectious spirit unmatched by anyone he'd ever met. I told Jeff about my own loss, how I'd buried my father when I was ten and run down my own road of grief.

And then, we saw the sign for 25.9 miles. We only had .3 miles until the finish.

"Do you have something left?" I asked Jeff. "Can you finish strong?"

"Yeah," said Jeff resoundingly. "I do."

We picked up the pace, pushed harder, and watched the runner's chute come into our sights. The finish was there; it was happening. For me, it had been a run of just over five miles, for Jeff it had been a journey of 26.2.

Somehow, we both were about to leave that race as different people.

The rest of my relay team fell in step with me, but I could hardly hear their cries of "We did it," and "Woohoo" as I crossed the line with Jeff. I only thought about him, about what those seconds said about life, about struggle and journey. Then we crossed the line. I saw his family cheering for him, the runners waiting to pull him in their arms.

Before I knew it, I hugged him too. And sobbed.

So did he.

"I want you to meet my son's mother and my family," he said, and pulled me over to the tent where they all waited. Someone showed me a huge poster of Jeff's son, all the family photos they'd brought. We all hugged again, and cried some more.

Somewhere among all the 2011 Tulsa Route 66 Marathon photos is one of Jeff and me. We've got medals around our necks, big smiles on our faces.

You wouldn't know by just looking at the photo what had happened along the race route. But we know, and we always will.

The best races in life aren't the ones you win. The best races in life are the ones where it takes everything you have just to finish.

~Sara Celi

26

Gardening with My Son

You can bury a lot of troubles digging in the dirt.
~Author Unknown

In the weeks following my divorce, my once neatly tended garden turned into a near jungle. The grass stood at least a foot high, the flowerbeds were overgrown with weeds, and the whole place had a dry, deserted look to it. Looking out the window one morning, I saw two of my neighbors huddled together, looking at my garden, talking, and shaking their heads with disapproval. I knew my garden was a mess, but then, so was I.

Even though the marriage hadn't been the happiest one, and I should have been relieved that the fighting was finally over, I felt sad and desolate. When we married we had loved each other so much. We had been together for nearly twenty years. What had happened to us?

Five years into the marriage we had bought a house in a newly developed area. The house itself was beautiful, but the garden was atrocious. By any stretch of the imagination it couldn't even be called a garden. Over the years we had planted and sowed, weeded and watered, until at last our garden was the envy of the neighborhood. And now it was a shadow of its former glorious self.

"Mom, we have to do something," my fifteen-year-old son Dieter said halfway through May. "We can't have the place looking like this.

Let's clean up the garden and plant some things. Everyone has tulips and narcissus and those purple flowers—what are they called again?"

"Irises?"

"Right, irises, and we have nothing."

"The garden is a mess, honey," I said. "Nothing will grow in there now."

"Then let's clean it up," he said. "We'll do it together."

I wanted to, but it seemed like an enormous job and I didn't feel up to it. I didn't feel up to anything. Some days it was an effort just getting showered and dressed.

Seeing his anxious face, I agreed to the job, but I wondered how the two of us were going to manage turning that wilderness into anything halfway decent looking. The grass was so tall and there were so many weeds. It was going to take weeks to get everything done.

"Don't look at the whole thing," Dieter said when we were outside. "Pick a flowerbed and concentrate on that. I'll get started on the grass. Whatever we don't finish today, we'll finish tomorrow."

So I did. I got a bucket and a trowel from the garage and got started with a flowerbed nearest to the house. As I dug, Dieter mowed.

It was hard dealing with just that one flowerbed, but seeing Dieter so hard at work I knew I had to keep going. We were going to do this together, so I had to do my share. After a while I found that I started to enjoy myself. Smelling the scent of fresh cut grass and feeling the warmth of the sun on my skin was a welcome change to watching TV all day.

At noon the lawnmower fell silent. When I looked up I noticed that a good portion of the grass had been cut.

"Done for the day?" I asked Dieter.

"Time for lunch," he said. "Aren't you hungry? I am."

As a matter of fact, I was hungry, which was also a change. More often than not I skipped lunch because I didn't feel like eating.

"You got a lot done," I said over cheese and tomato sandwiches.

"So did you," Dieter said. "That flowerbed is starting to look good."

"It's just soil," I shrugged. "Without flowers it's not even a flowerbed."

"For now, yes," he said, "but we could go to the garden center and get some flowers."

I nodded. "We could."

"Do you want to take a nap or shall we carry on?" he asked, putting our plates into the sink.

"Let's carry on," I said, and found that I was actually looking forward to going outside again. "I want to finish that patch today."

Every day we did a little, and once all the grass was cut, Dieter joined me in the flowerbeds. Some days we only worked an hour, some days we worked the morning, and some days—when Dieter was back at school—I found myself working alone.

I can't say that I went through the days singing, but I did get up in the morning with more enthusiasm. I ate breakfast, lunch and dinner because I had an appetite again, and at night I slept like a log.

At the garden center I bought roses and dahlias, asters and daisies, freesias and gladiolus, and my all-time favourites, pansies.

There had been a time when I couldn't stand the sight of pansies, when their cheerful faces mocked me and I much preferred the company of a weeping willow. Not anymore—now I was attracted to pansies again, and I was going to plant them on either side of the driveway. They were my "Welcome Home" flowers.

Sometime in June I was outside watering the roses when one of my neighbors came outside and smiled. "Looking good, my dear," she said. "You and Dieter have performed a near miracle. You really brought that garden back to life."

As I glanced over the trees, shrubs, and flowers I noticed the pansies bobbing their yellow and purple faces in unison.

I felt good, for the first time in a long time. I actually felt like my old self again. I wondered, had Dieter and I brought this garden back to life, or had it brought me back?

~Conny Manero

27

Taking Time to Listen

The most precious gift we can offer anyone is our attention.
~Thich Nhat Hanh

Leah was an eight-year-old patient suffering from fiber-type II disproportion. She was completely paralyzed and had been on a ventilator since she was three weeks old and hadn't gained the strength to open her eyes until she was six years old.

I was sent to her home as her home health nurse. It took several weeks to learn to communicate with her. She would blink for yes, but would not blink for no. It was probably a year before I actually believed she understood what I was saying and could respond appropriately.

At age nine, Leah received a computer from the state as part of her home schooling program. I would put in computerized books and she learned how to hit a button with her chin when it was time to turn the page.

Leah loved to hum. I would sing children's songs like "Row, Row, Row Your Boat" and "Itsy Bitsy Spider" and she would hum along.

By the time Leah was ten, we would have complete conversations with her using her eyes to communicate.

When Leah was eleven, I started taking care of her a few evenings a week and started work as a school nurse.

Ironically, I ended up working with Leah's speech therapist. When I mentioned this to Leah's mom, she told me that the speech therapist thought Leah had brain damage and would therefore not try to challenge Leah.

I asked the speech therapist, Paula, what she thought of Leah. Paula said that Leah was cute but had no real speech abilities and couldn't communicate. She made some "baby talk" but it was just nonsense. When I tried to explain differently, Paula told me I suffered from wishful thinking.

The next evening that I took care of Leah, I brought a tape recorder. After getting permission from her mom and explaining to Leah what I planned to do, I started recording. I would ask her what song she wanted to sing and she would hum a bar to let me know. Then I would sing a bar and she would hum the next. We went through several songs this way, trading off bars. At one point, I lost my place and forgot my line. Sensing my hesitation, Leah hummed the line for me. We recorded this exchange for a half hour.

The next day I handed the tape to Paula and asked that she please listen to it. She took it into her office to listen. A half hour later she came out with a shocked look on her face.

She told me she had to completely redo Leah's curriculum.

Five years later, at the age of sixteen, Leah now integrates with regular students at a nearby high school. She has a communication board to help her speak and an electric wheelchair to help her get around. Since she's still on a ventilator, a nurse accompanies her to school. But Leah is popular and her classmates love to help her out when needed.

In the eight years since I first started caring for Leah, I have learned a lot. Never assume that because a patient can't talk or move that she's not a bright child who has a lot to say if someone takes the time to listen.

~B. Lee White

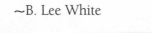

The Power of Positive

Chapter 4

The Power of Relaxing

Don't Sweat the Small Stuff

There are always flowers for those who want to see them.
~Henri Matisse

While I was living in the south of France, I drove all the way to Barcelona to purchase a very special guitar. Once I was back in the States with my treasured, finely finished wooden instrument, my father asked if he could play it. He loved flamenco guitar music and decided to show off his skills. Before I knew it, between strums, he was tapping on the smooth cedar top of my classical guitar with his fingernails! This technique, called "golpe," is commonly used while playing the colorful rhythmic flamenco music of Spain.

Guitars meant for playing such music had tap plates on their soundboards to protect the finish from fingernail damage. My father did not realize that my classical guitar did not have a tap plate. I was horrified, but I politely said, "Here, let me show you what I can play" as I took back my guitar.

I hate to admit this, but for years, whenever I played my guitar, I couldn't help noticing the marks in its fine cedar finish. I felt bad about feeling annoyed because my father was so nice to me and I really loved everything about him.

After having my third child, I didn't have as much time to practice, so the guitar stayed safely in its case for years. During that time, my father passed away tragically. Although I was very much at peace with our relationship, which helped me during the grieving process, I was of course extremely sad for a long time. Then one day, I was in the mood to start playing my guitar again and I opened the case for the first time in a long while. I gathered up my favorite pieces of music, set up my music stand, and got out my tuning fork. As I started to tighten the strings, I noticed the fingernail marks on my guitar.

It was a moment that took my breath away. Those marks—my father had made them—yes, my father had made them. He was there—a part of him was there on the polished cedar top of my guitar. How wonderful! I was so happy to see those little scratches made by the tapping of his fingers and all of a sudden my guitar was even more special than ever before. My father was a very wise man and I learned so much from him when he was alive—and now he was still teaching me. My perspective on what was important changed. What had once seemed like defects on my guitar were beautiful little souvenirs of time spent with my father.

I vowed from that day on to always appreciate life's little moments with the people I loved. And whenever I find myself about to "sweat the small stuff," I think of my father. And I think about my beautiful guitar with its lovely tap marks.

~Pamela Rose Hawken

29

The Healing Power of Toilet Paper

With the fearful strain that is on me night and day,
if I did not laugh I should die.
~Abraham Lincoln

A letter to the editor in our local newspaper complained about nocturnal pranksters stringing toilet paper on residents' trees. That letter brought a flurry of responses defending this act as being a harmless tribute to friends: "It's an honor to get toilet papered," admonished one writer, "and good clean fun for teenagers!"

Reading these letters brought me chuckles and then tears as they stirred up old memories of my mother's ninety-second year—a year Charles Dickens would describe as "the best of times, the worst of times." She was terminally ill that autumn. And I watched, powerless, as my mother's vigor and grit gave way to frailty and despair.

Mom's ninety-second year was also my tenth one as her caregiver. A decade before, I helped her, as she liked to call it, "break out" of the nursing home where she resided. It was a fine facility with a caring staff. But Mom didn't want or need skilled care; she wanted to live on her own and just needed some assistance to do so. Being in a more restrictive environment than was necessary had plunged her into a clinical depression; she got out of bed only at mealtimes and spent the rest of each day staring at the ceiling, disconnected.

And so I made a leap of faith. With her doctor's blessing and my determination to help Mom live independently, I found her an apartment, furnished it, and hired a few part-time caregivers to assist us.

The risk paid off, and I was abundantly rewarded by seeing my mother once again enjoying her life. Icing on the cake was Mom's eagerness to resume our fun-filled weekly outings—"adventures," we called them—exploring country roads to discover what lay around each bend: a field of flowers, an old barn or maybe a country café to stop at for pie and coffee.

It was during these years of Mom's need and my help that we became closer than we had ever been.

Though I still look back and wonder how I found the time and energy to manage Mom's home and helpers, along with my own home, family responsibilities and job, I did handle it—one day at a time. Mom was happy and thriving; that kept me strong and resolute.

Then, ten years later, Mom was diagnosed with cancer. Following on the heels of her chemotherapy, she suffered a series of strokes that made walking difficult.

As Mom's health declined, my caregiving duties increased, leaving little time for things like adventures. Those days the only unfamiliar roads we traveled were the ones leading to Mom's new symptoms and my corresponding duties. Who had time to even think about fun or outings?

Then, one balmy September evening, for some inexplicable reason, I invited my mother to do a thing neither of us had ever done: "Let's go toilet papering!"

I picked her up around twilight that evening and headed to a store to buy our double-ply ammunition. We devised a plan to paper the yards of her two other children, my brother and sister, and to hit a few of her grandchildren's homes, time and energy permitting.

This outing would push my mother to her physical limits. Was I making a mistake? Her usual bedtime was 9:00 p.m. and it was already 8:30; we always used the handicap spaces, but this night, to avoid notice, I parked a full block from our first stop.

At that distance, we snuck arm-in-arm down the dark walk

leading to my brother's home. Mom's steps were labored, but her attention was focused on the clear, star-studded sky and gentle autumn breezes.

Once in his back yard, I guided Mom to a small tree and handed her a roll of toilet paper from our canvas bag. Without hesitation, she shot it skyward. We watched the white ribbon sail over the crown and glide down the other side, leaving a streamer of well-placed Charmin.

I retrieved the roll and handed it back to Mom; she had both hands clasped over her mouth to keep from laughing out loud. Hugging each other, we glanced toward the patio doors and spotted my brother relaxing in his recliner. The sight of him so oblivious to our presence emboldened us to continue our shenanigans.

Bent over and leaning on me, Mom shuffled from tree to tree, gleefully pitching rolls like an ace. We were in a timeless cocoon where pain and burdens didn't exist. Finishing the last tree, we stood a while to survey our handiwork; the moonlit yard looked like a surreal wonderland of shimmering white streamers. Mission accomplished, we headed back to my car, giggling all the way like two schoolgirls. Mom was to paper a dozen trees in four family yards that unforgettable evening.

We both knew this would be one of our last outings, but the lesson we took from it would ultimately help carry us through the rough days that lay ahead. Mom and I resolved that night to make some play time every day, in whatever way we would be able; I added crayons and coloring books to our shopping list.

The day after our big adventure, Mom and I sent an anonymous card to each of our victims, signed, "From your EXTERIOR decorators." We laughed all the way home from the post office. In the coming weeks, Mom and I shared many more laughs after each of us received calls from puzzled family members wondering who had done those strange things.

Our family Thanksgiving gathering was at my home that November. To accommodate the thirty-some guests, I set dinner tables in my basement recreation room. My brother, sister and their families made many trips up and down the stairs that day to help carry food and dishes, and to use my first and second floor bathrooms.

That evening, my sister was the last to leave. At the door, she pulled an envelope from her purse, handed it to Mom and then kissed us goodbye. Baffled, Mom read the note: "From your INTERIOR decorators."

For the first time that day, I had a chance to go upstairs; the entire second floor was strewn, top to bottom, with toilet paper!

My mother's last year was marked by physical decline. Nevertheless, we kept our resolve to share some simple fun each day. Those lighthearted moments were like a salve on our stress, and they are the ones I'll always remember. Toilet papering had taught us that play is, indeed, powerful medicine!

~Toni Becker

Try a Smile

The world always looks brighter from behind a smile.
~Author Unknown

I was at the post office early that morning, hoping to be in and out and on my way at the start of a busy day. Instead, I found myself standing on a line that zigzagged through rope-defined lanes and oozed out into the hallway. I had never seen so many people there and it wasn't even a holiday. Someone must have made an announcement that I obviously missed, welcoming patrons with as many packages as they could possibly carry to bring them in at the exact time I needed to have my own parcel weighed. The line moved excruciatingly slowly. My mood turned edgy, then annoyed. The longer it took, the angrier I became. When I got to the counter—finally!—I concluded my business quickly and curtly and strode past the line that was now extending past the front door.

"Excuse me," I said, trying not to be too pushy. Several people had to shift to make room for me to get to the exit.

I strode out grumbling under my breath about inefficiency and how I was going to be late getting to my dentist appointment. I was scowling as I headed into the parking lot.

A woman was coming across the lot in my direction. She was walking with determination, each step pounding the ground like a mini-jackhammer. I noticed that her brow was tightly furrowed and she looked as if she could breathe fire. It stopped me in my tracks. I recognized myself and it wasn't pretty. Had I looked like that? Her body language said that she was having a really rough day. My anger melted away. I wished I could wrap her in a hug but I was a stranger. So I did what I could in the brief minute before she barreled past me—I smiled. In the space of a second everything changed. I could tell that she was startled, then somewhat confused. Then her face softened and her shoulders relaxed. I saw her take a deep breath. Her pace slowed and she smiled back at me as we passed each other.

I continued to smile all the way to my car. Wow, I thought. Look what a simple smile can do.

The rest of the day felt like a meditation on smiling. I became aware of people's expressions and my own, of the way we show our emotions so plainly. Now I use that awareness on an everyday basis, letting it remind me that when I am fighting the world, or see someone else in that position, I can try a smile. More often than not, the energy of the moment shifts with that one little gesture. The smile on the outside turns inward and the day becomes new again, turning a bright face toward the activities that are yet to come.

~Ferida Wolff

Eighty-Five Percent

Let us be of good cheer, remembering that the misfortunes hardest to bear are those which will never happen.
~James Russell Lowell

I n my earliest years my older sister and I bounced from place to place. Our parents separated when we were toddlers, so we made the rounds, staying with Grandma, with our dad, with his friends, and then back again to Grandma's.

As if these uncertain circuits weren't enough to disquiet even a tranquil tyke, one time I even lost the company of my sister, the closest thing I had to a security blanket. At age four I became hospitalized for several weeks with double pneumonia.

Then when we were five and six, an aunt and uncle adopted us. But my childhood continued to be peppered with predicaments. In addition to the normal childhood diseases of those pre-vaccination days—measles, mumps, whooping cough, and chickenpox—I also contracted scarlet fever, which kept me bedridden for weeks. I'd barely recovered when I had to be hospitalized again, this time for a tonsillectomy.

I became a nervous wreck. I realize now how frustrating it must have been for my adoptive parents, watching while I ran through the gamut of self-soothing behaviors. I covered all the bases. I chewed off the entire left collar of my red boucle coat. I sucked my thumb, even licking off the acrid iodine Mama painted it with. I rocked myself to sleep, banging the bed against the wall so violently that my entire family complained of lack of sleep. And, most embarrassingly for Mama, I'd huddle under my bed, shivering in fear, if visitors showed up.

Nowadays, the average parent may be better educated about the impact of childhood trauma and might seek out professional advice. Back then, though, my family hadn't a clue. Dr. Benjamin Spock's book on baby and childcare wouldn't even be published until I was nine. So bless their hearts… my adoptive parents tried every ploy they could dream up to deal with me, an abnormally anxious child, as I struggled to get through the days and the nights.

"What's the matter with you?" Mama would demand, as I sobbed uncontrollably when she turned off the light at bedtime.

I was scared to death all the time. I didn't know why. Nothing seemed to calm me down. Not promises of ice cream or bluffs to drop me off at a nearby police station if I didn't like it where I was. No treat or threat succeeded in seducing or scaring me into tranquility.

In those days in our suburban Southern California neighborhood, people didn't chauffeur children to school. We simply walked. We'd been warned to look both ways before crossing streets, and not to jaywalk. Nevertheless my heart began to pound every time I came to an intersection. What if I stepped off the curb and a car came around a corner hit me and I died? Thank heavens I only had to cross three streets to reach Bryson Avenue Elementary. If there'd been a fourth I might have made "Ripley's Believe It or Not!" column as the youngest heart attack victim ever.

By the time I turned eight and my family moved to Oregon, I'd settled into a daily routine of waking up early to enumerate the dozens of imaginary landmines I'd be called upon to sidestep if I were to live until nightfall. "What if" became my dismaying morning mantra.

Then things changed. Miss Magee, my new teacher, decided I should skip third grade because of my high reading scores. She worked with me after school to catch up on long division and multiplication. She stared down the boys who called me "Terri Termite" because I chewed my pencils. She suggested to my parents that I be given a baton for Christmas because I'd had my heart set on one for years. She let me read every book in the little three-room-schoolhouse library. She praised my book reports, gently reminding me to write on, and not between, the lines.

Most of all, she helped me to distinguish between my negative and positive thoughts. She told me that as a child she'd been afraid, too, but at her Friends Church she'd learned to believe she had an Inner Light. This Inner Light would always lead her to find positive ways of viewing the world. So she suggested that when I awoke in the morning I ask myself what wonderful things I'd be doing that day, rather than wondering "what if."

It was hard at first to change my thinking pattern. I'd grown used to viewing each new day as yet another struggle to avoid trouble. But Miss Magee would check with me at recess, and I had to be ready with an answer when she'd ask what positive thought I'd selected for that day.

"Picking crab apples in the orchard," I'd say. Or "Reading *Dandelion Cottage*." Or "Helping Grandma shell peas."

If I fell back on my old habit of looking for the worst possibilities, Miss Magee would remind me that when I learned my multiplication tables I'd had to practice them a lot to get them right. Now I had to practice looking for positive possibilities, over and over, until it became automatic.

Gradually, I grew more comfortable around other children and even trusted a few enough to make friends. Of course I still encountered woes. Once I caught poison oak, and once I cut my foot stepping on a piece of broken glass while wading in a creek. Though these were uncomfortable experiences, somehow I'd grown mature enough to realize that minor rashes and gashes were only that... minor.

Now I realize that I had an undiagnosed anxiety disorder as a child. Its repercussions have remained with me for life. Now, though, whenever I lapse into dread, I force myself to think of what positive activity I'll soon engage in: an hour with a Dickens novel, a walk with my dog, a dish of frozen yogurt... something wonderful.

When I married my late husband in 2000, he told me he could

never understand worry. A man who spent his career in the gaming industry, Ken appreciated statistics and odds. Somewhere he'd read that eighty-five percent of the things that people worry about never come to be. And worrying can't alter the final outcome of the remaining fifteen percent, he'd remind me. If I voiced what he determined to be unreasonable concern, he'd just cast me a baleful glance and murmur, "Eighty-five." Gradually, I picked up his phrase.

Oh, I still have some telltale anxiety traits. I'm not a hoarder, but I like a well-stocked pantry, and probably have a dozen more cans of soup than I really need. I've never lost my keys in over fifty years, but I still check several times to make certain they're in my purse before I leave the house. I still have that recurrent dream of not being able to locate the classroom where I'm scheduled to sit for a final exam.

Worry? Yes, but not excessively. Eighty-five percent of the time I'm thinking positive!

~Terri Elders

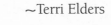

Uncovered

While we try to teach our children all about life,
Our children teach us what life is all about.
~Angela Schwindt

I consider myself to be a fairly positive person now. I wasn't always that way. Living in the attic of your sister-in-law's home in the middle of July without air conditioning and only a twin-sized mattress for a family of four can bring out the worst in you.

I remember the night very specifically; it was July 12. The clock read 2 a.m. and the temperature gauge 105. The sweat was pouring down my forehead—and not just because it was hotter than a sauna in the attic—but because I was dejected. Earlier in the day I had received news that I didn't get the job. That made it three jobs in a row where I had been one of the final two candidates—only to lose out in the end.

Friends and family kept telling me that they "understood" because they had "been there." Did they really understand and had they really been there? Had they really had the carpet suddenly pulled out from under them? Everything that is comfortable: job, health, house, car, freedom, future security—GONE!

Despite the heat, I pulled the covers over my head and curled up in a little ball. The tears started streaming down my face, dampening my already dampened pillow. I felt so alone, even though I was sharing a twin-sized mattress with my wife, three-year-old daughter, and one-year-old son. I started punching my pillow and obsessing over what I was going to do.

I can't remember how long I lay in that position trying to hide my tears from my family, but I remember it seemed like an eternity. I stayed there as long as possible because it was the only place that felt safe and secure from the world around me. Those were the darkest moments of my life. As a man I can't think of anything worse than feeling like you aren't measuring up, that you can't even take care of yourself, much less your family!

I grabbed another pillow to throw on top of my head to hide further and further from the "real world" out there. I must have fallen asleep because I woke up to a little bit of light creeping under one of the pillows. I heard a bird chirping outside the only attic window. I rolled over because I still didn't have the energy or the emotional stamina to pull the covers down.

But then I heard laughing. My two kids were having a tickle fight on the other side of the tiny mattress. They stood up and started jumping up and down and smiling and laughing and carrying on as only kids can do. Or, can adults do that too? The kids grabbed two pillows and started relentlessly clobbering me and wouldn't give up until I picked up a pillow and fought back. I couldn't. I couldn't face another day "out there" so I pretended to be sleeping. Another strong blow to my lower back. "Daddy!" "Daddy!" "Wake up!"

After a few minutes of trying so hard to hide my feelings of shame, disappointment, and discouragement, my kids started pulling down the covers and wouldn't stop until they could see my face. They pulled harder and harder. I pulled harder and harder to stay in my little cocoon of safety and security. I heard more laughing. My kids thought this was one big game of tug of war. Didn't they know that Daddy was a loser?

More pulling of the covers until finally more light appeared. More laughing. I finally gave up. My kids had won, but not just at our tug of war game. They had won because they had reminded me that they didn't care whether or not I had a job, they didn't care how much money I made, and they didn't care where we slept. They only knew there was joy in the moment.

If you want to learn how to stay positive, spend a day admiring your children or grandchildren. Watch how their joy isn't dependent upon their circumstances. Watch how they love without strings attached. Watch how carefree they are and how even the simplest, most insignificant experience can make them so happy. Thanks to my children, I have learned how to stay positive even when life has taken its toll.

~Tom Kaden

The Onion Room

Instead of complaining that the rosebush is full of thorns,
be happy that the thorn bush has roses.
~Proverb

I would have quit if I weren't the boss. It started when my first patient arrived thirty minutes late but demanded she still be seen. "It wasn't my fault—traffic was terrible."

The next patient screamed at my secretary for trying to collect a co-pay. After smoothing my receptionist's ruffled feathers, I entered the next exam room only to be handed a massive pile of forms needing completion—by tomorrow. Stir in the twenty minutes on hold with an insurance company, a patient hostile about her forty-minute wait, and a man who fainted when his blood was drawn, and my day became as enjoyable as a balloon ride in a tornado.

The final straw? Mrs. Smith informed me she had stopped her blood pressure medication a month ago and had replaced it with an herbal remedy she learned about online. The website claimed the 100 percent all-natural herb had "miraculous powers" to lower blood pressure.

"I'm just more comfortable going organic," she insisted. "According to the Internet, the blood pressure pills you prescribed are a synthetic poison." She glared at me as though I'd prescribed arsenic.

By stopping her "synthetic poison," her blood pressure registered a dangerous 220/110. In short, her all-natural, organic herb was nothing more than an expensive placebo—she might as well have swallowed a fistful of crabgrass. But try telling her that!

I exited her exam room a full hour behind schedule. My head pounded like a kettledrum and my neck muscles felt tighter than a banjo string. I rolled my neck, relaxed my jaw, and inhaled several deep breaths. The charts on my desk resembled the Leaning Tower of Pisa. I flopped into my chair for a two-minute respite and tackled the medication refills.

What had possessed me to hang a medical shingle? My mental image of *Marcus Welby, M.D.* shared little in common with the modern internist's life—insurance hassles, paperwork, and patients who believe the Internet over their physician.

I scribbled my signature on the last chart, lugged the unwieldy heap to my medical assistant's desk, and braced myself for the next disaster. Malpractice lawsuit? Cardiac arrest? Power outage? Employee catfight? Today, they all seemed possible.

I bustled into the next exam room and greeted Marge Moreland, a pleasant forty-year-old, who gazed up at me with red, puffy eyes. She looked as though she'd cried non-stop for a month.

Not surprisingly, she'd made the appointment to investigate what could be done for her irritated eyes. One by one I eliminated all the usual culprits: crying jags due to stress or depression, new mascara, pink eye, allergens such as ragweed, mold, dust, or animal dander. I scratched my head, perplexed. She then commented, "I think it's my workplace."

I nodded. "I get it. You work in one of those 'sick buildings' we hear about and now you and your co-workers all walk around with red, swollen eyes."

"No, none of the others are affected, just me."

I glanced up from writing in her chart. "So why do you think it's your job if none of your co-workers are affected?"

"Cause they aren't in the onion room."

"The onion room?"

"They have me peeling and slicing onions eight hours a day."

"You slice onions eight hours a day?" I couldn't imagine! No wonder her eyes were red.

"Yes, and the room is small and unventilated."

Surely torturing an employee in a non-ventilated onion room for eight hours a day must violate OSHA safety laws. Rage welled up in me like a geyser.

I exited the exam room, stomped to my office, and rang up the local OSHA officer, ready to demand he investigate and improve her work conditions. Imagine my amazement when he informed me he had already investigated the room and no laws were violated. There was nothing legally he could do. "Since onions are just a type of food and are not a toxin or poison, my hands are tied."

"But her work environment is intolerable. How would you like to chop onions all day?"

"I can hardly stand to walk into the room, let alone inspect it—the odor is overwhelming. Trust me, I get a call at least monthly on that position. The turnover is unreal."

I returned to her exam room and broke the bad news. I shook my head in disgust. "How long have you been stuck in the onion room?"

"Three months. My boss says I've lasted longer than any previous employee," she boasted.

I crossed my arms. "Why do you stay?"

"I'm hoping to be promoted to cabbages."

"Cabbages?" I bit the inside of my cheek to keep from laughing.

"The slaw room. It's the next step up in the company and it comes with a fifty cents an hour raise."

I stared at her in awe, chagrined at my own bad attitude and petty complaints. Here I'd sputtered all morning about a few insurance hassles, an overzealous Internet reader, and a heap of paperwork, while this poor woman endured the noxious odor and irritation of chopping onions for eight long hours a day—all for minimum wage. Yet somehow, she looked forward to a promotion to cabbages?

Now, whenever I'm having one of those days and I'm tempted

to whine, I remind myself it could be worse. Much worse. I could be chopping onions.

~Sally Willard Burbank

Becoming
the Sunflower

Keep a green tree in your heart and perhaps a singing bird will come.
~Chinese Proverb

I was wandering in the floral section of the supermarket in the middle of a Tuesday afternoon. I felt oddly out of place, like I was cutting school or doing something I shouldn't be. Normally, I would be at my desk at work at this time on a weekday, but it had been months since I was laid off from my job. Normally, the heady fragrance and profusion of color would have made me happy. But this was not a normal day. I was upset and depressed that a pink slip was the thanks I got for my knowledge, loyalty, and dedication as an architectural computer draftsperson for the county school board for eight out of thirty years of my career. I felt like I had no purpose. No one needed my talents or me any longer.

Every day, I made a list of things I wanted to get done. I wanted to clean the house, organize my mountains of art supplies, and run all those errands I didn't have time to do when I was working. I'd start those tasks, but before I could finish anything, I would either run around the living room crying loudly or curl up in a ball on the sofa in a gray mental haze and do nothing. I was so miserable that I totally ignored my husband, yelled at my kids, and pushed them all away. Months of wasted time went by in which I could have been doing something… anything.

Applying for jobs was frustrating. There were no openings for what I had been doing. I didn't know what else I even wanted to do. I felt too tired to be interested in doing anything. I wished for something new to just plop into my lap and say, "Here you go; this is right for you." But nothing did.

So there I was, in the floral aisle, fingering the velvety petals of an insanely bright yellow sunflower when these words suddenly popped into my mind. "Be a sunflower in the garden where you're planted." What did that mean? On the one hand, the sunflower was like that smiling yellow happy face logo you see everywhere… that have-a-nice-day cliché. I certainly wasn't in the mood for that. I was too busy wallowing in my unemployment depression. But on the other, it was as though the blossom spoke to me and planted that message in my brain. Maybe I desperately needed it to.

I had been spinning my wheels agonizing about my income, but I think my pride was hurt worse than my pocketbook. I did get meager unemployment checks. And, thank goodness, I had a husband to keep a roof over my head. I was really grateful for that. Instead of wasting time and mental energy worrying about the bills, I realized I needed to just face the reality of it, cut non-critical expenses, and plan out the rest. When I visited my twenty-eight-year-old son at his home, I had watched him spend money on extravagances like vacations and new cars. It made me feel jealous and angry that he was so wasteful. But on reflection, I realize that we were in different circumstances and at different stages in life. He had a good, high-paying job. I had what he had when I was his age. There was no reason why he shouldn't be enjoying his life since he could afford it. I had to learn to accept my new circumstances. There would be no more new clothes and dinners out for quite some time.

The thought about blooming where I was planted meant to me that I should make the most of what I had. It made me realize that while I did not have much money, I did have time. There were so many things I once enjoyed that I had put off or quit doing when

I was working an eight-to-five job. I loved to draw and paint, but it had been years since I had time for them. I had a passion for writing, but I hadn't had time for that in years either. I had taught myself to play the flute years ago too, but it had been gathering dust. I didn't know if I even remembered how to play a tune anymore. I had teenage kids and housework that need my attention.

It was time to become a sunflower and flourish where I was planted, in my forced retirement with the luxury of free time. I found a part-time job teaching reading, math, and art in a literacy program for low-income elementary school children at my county library. My new job is wonderfully fulfilling. It doesn't pay all my bills, but it does bring me joy. My career is not back on track yet, but at least I feel needed again. I work four afternoons a week. Now I have time to be that sunflower.

I am writing again now and have even published a few things. That's extremely satisfying. I put art lessons together for my students. I am on speaking terms with my husband again. And now, I feel good about helping my own kids with their schoolwork and interests. I even manage to squeak out a few tunes on my flute when the mood strikes me. Until a full-time job comes along, I love my spare time!

~Lisa Wojcik

Being a Positive Expert

The cyclone derives its powers from a calm center. So does a person.
~Norman Vincent Peale

It was a routine colonoscopy. Although groggy from drugs, I was awake enough to see the concern on Dr. Gottleib's face. "You need surgery."

After the surgeon told me that I'd lose forty percent of my colon, he listed the possible complications: infection, heart attack, stroke, pulmonary embolism, and death. My knees were shaking as I left his office, and my husband Jim and I sat on a bench outside his door. I called on Pollyanna's spirit.

Pollyanna, the young fictional character, had been my best friend growing up. She, like me, had a bushel of trouble, but she practiced the glad game. Each morning I bowed to her, and started looking for reasons to be happy. She inspired me to a lifelong commitment of finding positive choices. Therapy had helped me balance Pollyanna, who often bypassed her true feelings to jump into glad. I'd learned to acknowledge and accept all of my feelings, and still choose a positive way to live my life.

"I've got ten days to get ready," I said through tears.

Although a part of me was in shock, I knew that I had some big questions to answer. Was my spirit sending me a message? What did it need? Was it my time to die? How could I best support my immune system? What ways were the most helpful to honor my fears, yet contain them. How was I going to tell my body and colon about the trauma it was to endure?

I began to make lists, one to satisfy my left brain and one to engage my right. Left: cancel everything, update and revise will and living will, get acupuncture, book energy session with healer, write love letters to my children, plan music to listen to during surgery, organize post-op healing sessions, ask a friend to be with my husband on day of surgery, etc. Right brain: meditate, create healing collage, do dominant/non-dominant handwriting, daily self-healing using Reiki, create prayer-mantra to engage immune system, etc. I would practice what I preached and taught regularly as a nurse consultant. Richard Bach's quote came to mind: "You teach best what you most need to learn." Well, here I was, determined to be the best student to get ready for the trip of my life.

For many years I'd used Lucia Capacchione's book, *The Power of Your Other Hand: A Course in Channeling the Inner Wisdom of the Right Brain*. I didn't understand how the process worked, but I'd had tremendous success in accessing information from within that helped me take better care of myself. I took my journal and with my dominant hand (right) I wrote a love letter to my body, telling it the news. I thanked it for its wisdom and told it I needed its help to get ready.

Pausing, shifting to a spacious meditative mindset, I picked up the pen with my non-dominant hand (left), and in big scrawly letters printed the first response that popped into my mind. One word, "DIE." I was not surprised. I shifted the pen to my right hand, and in words that you'd use for a young child, I wrote that dying was a possibility, but the bigger possibility was that we would live to a ripe old age. I asked what was needed.

Back and forth went the pen with tears flowing. To my surprise an image of a Civil War surgery table kept recurring in my mind. Although I didn't understand it, I trusted the process and continued. Some part of me believed that I was going to have surgery without anesthetic. My right hand wrote about twenty-first century medicine, explaining how surgery would be done with me in a drugged "sleep."

I detailed the sophisticated medical advancements that made surgery a very common and successful thing.

Somewhere within me, the fear began to melt, and my solar plexus and belly relaxed. There was almost an internal click, after having addressed something that was beyond my rational mind.

During the ten days, however, I had times of anxiety, each issue needing specific attention. With each upset, I balanced Pollyanna's perseverance with concrete action steps. I tapped my body using EFT (emotional freedom technique). I rolled my eyes using EMDR (eye movement desensitization and reprocessing technique) to help keep me in the present. I made up wellness songs and sang them as I took my daily walk. I made a healing mandala with crayons. I wrote positive affirmations, taping them up around my home so that they caught my eye and strengthened my mind. I snuggled with Jim, and watched some romantic comedies. I indulged in ice cream, mashed potatoes, and macaroni and cheese. I stayed in the present as much as I was able to, intuiting what action (if any) was needed.

At five in the morning on the day of my surgery we pulled into the hospital parking lot. My friend Jan, who was going to stay at the hospital with my husband, pulled in behind us. I ran towards her, arms outstretched, shouting, "I am ready." Carrying my suitcase and three boxes of chocolates for the surgery staff, the three of us walked to the surgical department.

It was not easy being the patient, instead of the nurse. And the surgery was painful. But years of positive-mind-practice, along with painkillers and great post-op care came together effortlessly.

On the fourth day post-op I plastered my belly with gold star stickers, surprising the surgeon. He surprised me too. The polyp he removed had ten percent cancer cells (in situ), but he was discharging me four days early because I was doing so well. I would not need radiation or chemotherapy because all the cancer cells had been contained in the polyp.

Pollyanna rushed to my side. I needed her. I was in disbelief and knew that it would take time for the news to sink in. I also knew that I would work with my body-mind-spirit to maintain my wellness.

Family and friends would support me. I'd handle each step as it came along, consciously and with as much grace and positivity as possible. My training as a positive expert came in handy.

~Shirley Dunn Perry

The Gift Horse's Mouth

Don't look a gift horse in the mouth.
~Proverb

My most prized possession is nothing special to look at. It's not flashy or expensive, or the latest model. Though it's over twenty years old and has managed to survive a lot of wear and tear, it's not an antique. There are black scuffmarks on its sides, some unidentifiable stains on the threadbare gray carpet, and the seats are frayed and ripped, held together with duct tape. Last year the engine gave out and we had to spend our first summer landlocked. We'll never do that again; we all agreed it was too depressing.

Can you picture it? Have you guessed what it is yet?

The Bayliner appeared in our lives through an odd series of coincidences. Out of the blue my father—who rarely gives gifts, and almost never gives useful ones—mailed us some shares of tobacco company stock. Though the stock was doing extremely well financially, I didn't want it because of the moral dilemma it represented. For years I breathed my dad's secondhand smoke, watched my friends try unsuccessfully to give up cigarettes, and was disgusted by people who used our favorite parks and beaches as their personal ashtrays. I disliked tobacco companies on principle. My father knew this and was purposefully setting up a situation where my ethics would be forced to clash with our growing family's chronic need for money.

This realization got under my skin and I found myself stewing about what to do for several days. Turning the various possibilities over in my mind like the pieces of a Rubik's Cube, I kept hoping that eventually I'd come up with an answer that would allow me to accept the gift while still being able to look at myself in the mirror every morning.

There really is such a thing as serendipity. One day, my husband's co-worker happened to mention that he had just bought a new camper. His wife wanted him to sell their boat because she hated the water and was afraid to take their four-year-old daughter boating. In his usual impulsive way, Neil arranged for us to all meet him at the boat launch and take his boat for a test drive.

It was a hazy, hot, and humid summer evening when Neil and I drove our three toddlers to the lake, zipped the boys into their life jackets, and cruised slowly out of the marina. Drifting at a leisurely pace along the shoreline, I gazed at the setting sun, a red fireball over the horizon, and inhaled the smells of barbecues and campfires at the summer cottages. I heard the ducks calling to each other as they skimmed over the water and felt the throb of the engine as it cut through the wakes of passing boats.

I felt at peace, as if I had come home. I had forgotten how passionately I'd always loved everything associated with the water and how much I'd always wanted a boat of my own. We had never had one growing up. My parents shared an equal dislike of recreational water sports and doing things as a family, so my sister and I were forced to rely on the generosity of friends and neighbors to access the seafaring life we craved.

As the warm wind lifted the hair off the back of my neck, I felt like that fourteen-year-old girl again. I had to have this boat or I would sink into a deep depression. In a sudden flash of insight, I understood that if this boat were ours we would never, ever be like my family was; the boat wouldn't let us be. I motioned to my husband to cut the engine and we drifted to a stop. Amidst the kids complaining and begging us to go faster, I shouted, "I want this boat!"

His eyes widened and he stared at me, speechless. For years I had been the one who put the brakes on our expenditures, the practical mother who monitored all purchases and finances with an iron fist. He wasn't sure how to respond, and for once I didn't push him for a quick answer. We sat in a silence fraught with unspoken meaning.

Finally he asked, "How would we pay for it?"

"We'll sell the stock!" I declared joyfully, realizing as I said it out loud that the perfect solution I'd been searching for all week had just been revealed. Finally my dad, unbeknownst to him, would be giving me something that our family really wanted, a gift that could be the vehicle for creating many fond memories over the coming years, a rare commodity in my own childhood. The emotional weight that I'd been carrying around since receiving the stock magically lifted and my mind began to soar with the endless stream of possibilities that owning a boat would give us.

Looking at my three little boys, their eyes filled with excitement and longing, my heart overflowed. "Do you really want to buy this boat?" I asked, and their gleeful cheers made us laugh out loud.

The next morning we sold the tobacco stock and bought the boat. Psychologists call this a "corrective experience," which means taking a difficult, painful memory and recreating it, this time with a positive outcome. Every time we go waterskiing or tubing with our friends, each weekend that we trailer our boat to explore a new lake or waterway, or whenever we take the boat out at night to watch colorful 4th of July fireworks explode over the water, our family constructs a happy memory to replace one of my sorrowful or depressing ones. Our boat has been the source of many unusual adventures including a brand new remote-controlled airplane, our yearly trek to Frontenac Island, a family we saved from drowning, and a gold Italian bracelet that was almost lost forever.

Whenever times are tough, money is tight, or cold winds howl outside, all I have to do is close my eyes and imagine driving our boat to the middle of the lake on a hot summer day and jumping into the cool clear water. I instantly feel better.

The night before my oldest son moved to Michigan, I asked him what he would miss the most when he was gone. Not even hesitating, he replied, "The boat." And that's why this boat, my first but hopefully not my last, will always be my most prized possession. It allowed me to transform the cigarette money, profits earned at the expense of people's health and the environment, into the rock solid foundation on which I built the home I'd always wanted, proving once again that you should never, ever look a gift horse in the mouth.

~Sue Henninger

The Power of Positive

Chapter 5

The Power of Gratitude

The Thank You Note

Kindness, like a boomerang, always returns.
~Author Unknown

Many times we do something positive or say something kind, but we don't see the impact it has on other people. We may practice these "random acts of kindness," but we never know what happens next. One time, I was lucky enough to find out.

I was returning from a business trip to northwest Wisconsin when I stopped to refuel and get a snack at one of those travel plaza/gas station combos on the expressway. It was late, I was tired, it was starting to rain, and all I wanted to do was get home, but home was still more than two hours away. I was feeling slightly crabby, and my back hurt from all the driving.

I went inside to buy some veggie chips and a sparkling water. The checker smiled at me, and we chatted for a moment. I don't remember exactly what she said, but I do remember the kindness she showed me. Our brief interaction brightened my spirits, and when I got back in my car, I had a smile on my face. My car and my stomach were both refueled, but more importantly, I was refreshed. Her small act of kindness kept me going on the last leg of my journey home.

The next week, I was cleaning my purse, and I came across the receipt. The receipt reminded me of the clerk's warmth, and it had the address of the store. On impulse, I decided to write a quick thank you note to her manager. I normally don't write thank you notes—in fact, except for my wedding, I've never written many notes of thanksgiving or gratitude—but I've learned to heed such promptings.

Initially, I felt a little awkward, embarrassed even, to be writing a thank you note to a gas station manager, but I set aside my "feelings" to listen to my gut. I told the woman's manager exactly what I've just shared with you—that his employee's kind words and caring attitude stood out to me, brightening my trip home. It took all of five minutes to write the note and affix a stamp to the envelope. I dropped the missive in the mail, and that was that.

That is, until a week later, when I received a thank you note for my thank you note. That clerk—Robin is her name—wrote me back. As a result of my note, she received a commendation from her manager, a company award pin, and then, to top it off, a merit raise. I was stunned, and the note brought tears to my eyes. Robin's kindness inspired me to return her positivity, and there it was—a small, mini chain reaction of goodness.

In these challenging times, it's especially important to spread joy and gladness whenever and wherever we can. Whether it's a note or a kind word or even just a smile, a little gratitude goes a long way. More people complain than give thanks, and I've heard it said that it takes ten kind words to overcome a single harsh one. It sometimes takes a conscious effort on our part to say more positive words than negative ones, and to do more positive things than negative ones, but the ripple effect of that goodness is powerful.

Mother Teresa advised us to "do small things with great love." Oftentimes, when we do such small things, we don't get to see the effects of our kind words or deeds, but every so often, we're blessed to discover the positive outcome. If there's one thing I've learned from writing that short note it's to give in to the impulse of kindness when it strikes.

You never know what good may come of it or where it might lead you.

~Jeanette Hurt

The Book of Good Things

*Enjoy the little things, for one day you may look back
and realize they were the big things.*
~Robert Brault

College: the best of times, the worst of times. That's how it was for me at least. In the best of times I was able to embrace new experiences, dig into new subjects, and enjoy making new friends. In the worst of times I was confused about what I wanted to study and where I was headed in life. I changed my major once and considered changing it again.

Then came the second semester of my sophomore year. I decided to take the semester off since I would be studying abroad all summer and earn a semester full of credits then.

So I headed to Washington, D.C. to live with two friends who were spending the semester doing internships. The experience of living on my own, earning money for rent and food and fun, was an eye-opening but positive experience. I discovered I loved living in the city—the surprises of urban existence.

The joy of it all made me want to capture the experience on paper. I began to keep a "Book of Good Things." I bought a small notebook and kept a running, numbered list of everything that delighted me. Anything could make the list: the guy who sang at my metro stop, Dorothy's ruby slippers at the Smithsonian, the funny things I overheard on the bus, the salad I ate for lunch. It was all in there.

Months later, when I was back at college after my summer abroad, I ran into the worst of times: a full-blown depression, except I didn't know that's what it was called. I cried all the time, and I felt utterly lost. I didn't belong at this school in the Chicago suburbs anymore, but I couldn't admit that to myself or anyone else.

It was my Book of Good Things that gave me one of the many nudges I needed to make some changes. Flipping through the pages and pages of things that brought me joy, I realized that much of what I loved was in D.C. and I began to see that something I loved to do was express myself on paper.

I wonder now what would have happened without my Book of Good Things, which still resides in my garage in a box labeled "College." Keeping track of the delightful random moments—those urban snapshots that made my heart so happy—helped me to see who I was and where I belonged. I moved to Washington, D.C. to attend American University and I changed my major to communications. From that point forward, the confusion and depression were gone and I knew I was on the right track. It is amazing where gratitude for the small things can lead you.

~Nina Taylor

Thanks to CF

Attitude is a little thing that makes a big difference.
~Winston Churchill

One of my first despairing cries when the kind young doctor told us our nine-month-old son certainly had cystic fibrosis was, "Oh dear God, my baby's going to die." Indeed, it was all I could think of those first foggy days and weeks (probably even months). My baby's going to die. My baby's going to die. My baby...

And then he wasn't a baby anymore. He grew into a toddler like any other toddler. He yelled "No, no, no" with all his might. He swallowed his medicine-laden applesauce. He watched *Little Bear* DVDs during his thrice-daily pulmonary therapy sessions (patting all over his chest and back to loosen thick mucus for coughing up). He ran from me naked and peed on the floor. He occasionally was hospitalized with IVs. He learned colors, letters, Mama, Daddy. He was cute. He was naughty. He did need extra care to be healthy, but he definitely was not dead.

Numerous hospitalizations throughout the years do stymie some developments that experts like to point out on those charts that petrify new parents; they also boast some developments—ones that are more complex to quantify but are the stuff of a real, good life. He did figure out how to walk—who cares when? He fought on and was strong. He did achieve a black belt—who cares that kids he'd begun with made it a year earlier? His triumph took longer than the others but he prevailed. He played well the cards dealt him, as we all must. I admit that parents of chronically ill children feel a strange mix of swagger and humility at their victories. They're sweeter. More costly. Accomplishments, I propose, should be measured by depth as well as height. Thanks to CF.

Slowly, over the years, our perspective shifted.

The pulmonary therapy sessions, once such an imposition, have forged a close relationship that remains to this day. The high nutritional standards, once such a stressor, have forced me to research and refine my culinary skills. The logistical logjam of hospitalizations, once so confusing, has created a certain comfort level in that setting. The existential anxieties, once such a depression, have demanded discussion of the tough topics. Appreciating these silver linings has enlivened our family, from good cooking and stronger bodies to spirited conversations and an easygoing lifestyle. We had more babies and had more fun with them. We saved less money and went out for more ice cream. We dug deeper into our faith, looking for a fix, and discovered profound purpose and consolation. Are we sadder? Sure. But we are wiser and more understanding. Thanks to CF.

Does this mean we take our wisdom and float along with folded hands? Absolutely not! We write letters requesting research monies; we volunteer at fundraising events; we sign up for walks and drug studies and surveys; and we talk. Some things we now know more about, some things less. In some ways our world has shrunk to just our family; in some ways our world has expanded to include people, organizations, and ideals. Thanks to CF.

Now seventeen and the eldest of seven, he is the family favorite. The kids all think he is so cool. They pine for his super bedtime snacks: a shake, a pile of cookies, and yogurt are a regular tray full. When IV necessities require a two-week hospitalization, they are green with envy: He gets a television in his room! He gets whatever food he desires delivered right to him! He gets to handle his own needles! We construct a chart to organize who spends what time there, ensuring no one loses out on visits with the biggest brother. He is the king. Thanks to CF.

So we hope and donate for a cure, and in the meantime, we live a good, new, normal life. Every single person, CF or not, must march on with our own unique set of talents and troubles. Sometimes the march is more of a tiptoe. Or a bayonet charge. Or a shouldering by friends. We push ourselves this way now; we encourage all our children this way now; we see other people this way now. Thanks to CF.

~Allison Howell

40

The Journal

For each new morning with its light,
For rest and shelter of the night,
For health and food, for love and friends,
For everything Thy goodness sends.
~Ralph Waldo Emerson

I t was almost Christmas in 1997. After going through a sad divorce I was happily remarried and enjoying life once again. My wonderful husband Joe and I went to work each morning to jobs we loved. On the weekends we went dancing at the local country western roadhouse. All of our children were doing well and were happy for our happiness. We were in a very good place and grateful for all that we had found in each other's love.

While I was Christmas shopping for my sisters at the local bookstore, I saw a display of gratitude journals. I decided to buy four of them, one for me and three for my sisters. My plan was that beginning on January 1st, we would write five things every day that we were grateful for in our lives. I looked forward to sharing my good life with my journal.

Starting the journal was fun, and I found five things to be grateful for every day without any problem at all. With my life sailing along so joyfully, it was easy to be grateful. I enjoyed the simple pleasure of sitting at my vanity every evening and writing my five entries. I entered the names of new friends we met and the musicals we saw together, the new restaurants we tried, the touching things my husband said to me, the exciting things my sons were doing, and the encouraging comments from the parents at work. On and on the words spilled from my pen.

But my life changed quickly and unexpectedly. On a Wednesday afternoon in early February there was a knock on my door that changed my life forever. When I opened the door, two men who worked with Joe stood in front of me with distraught expressions on their faces. They told me that Joe had been found on the floor in his office and taken to the hospital. They came to take me to see him. I climbed into the company car with shock. It was an icy day and the ride to the hospital was painfully slow. With the pinging sound of ice hitting the roof, I prayed to and bargained with God for Joe's life during the entire ride. But, it was too late. My husband had already died.

Keeping my gratitude journal wasn't so easy after that. Through February and March the pages of my journal stayed empty. I was too filled with fear and sorrow to make room for gratitude and optimism. But as the weeks went by, I began to realize that it is during the hard times that we most need to find and acknowledge the good things in our lives. I remembered learning at church that we are to be thankful in all circumstances. We're not expected to be thankful for all circumstances, but we are to be thankful in all circumstances.

I didn't want to be the kind of person who gave up on life. I decided to take on the challenge of being thankful and positive in the midst of my grief. Once again I sat down at the end of the day and tried to find five things that I was grateful for and write them in my journal. What had been so easy before my husband's death became a nightly struggle.

My first new entries into my journal were like those beginning steps that a little one takes on her first birthday. They were wobbly but determined, and often ended with a fall. One evening I remember crying and writing "I'm glad that this day is over" five times. But I stuck with it and slowly my gratefulness for life returned. By making myself write something every day, I forced my soul to see and feel the good mixed within my pain. The sun still rose, the flowering dogwood tree bloomed, the toddlers at the center still reached their arms out to me, the robins came back, and I could laugh at a corny joke once again!

Instead of trying to figure out the answers to all of my problems by myself, I asked God to send the right people into my life to help me. Again and again He did. A real estate friend found the perfect small house for me, and my family and friends helped me move into it on a warm day in May. Some family members and close friends donated money to help me out, and co-workers covered for me on days when I was clearly struggling. My sons knew when to comfort me and when to make me laugh. My best friend and her husband met me every Friday night for dinner and never once made me feel like the proverbial third wheel. Blessings just gushed into my life, and every night I listed them in my journal.

I still cried into my pillow some nights, but I began to understand that I was lucky to have memories so good they were worth crying about. It wasn't easy, but I began to feel powerful and strong enough to handle my life with grace and a sense of humor. I became the person I was meant to be.

I remarried three years ago, and despite many bumps along the way, my positive outlook continues to bring joy and contentment into my life. Even though my pessimistic husband Tom teases me about being a Pollyanna, I know that life looks better through the lenses of gratitude and positivity. Life is going well for me now, but I am wise enough to realize that I will face more difficult times. I know that I will be sad again, but I also know that with time a thankful optimism will replace my tears and carry me through. The twelve-dollar cost of that journal I bought so many years ago was such a small price for the lesson of a lifetime!

~Audrey Smith McLaughlin

41

Celebrate the Small Stuff

Why not learn to enjoy the little things—there are so many of them.
~Author Unknown

I t was the first Tuesday in November. Election Day. And my kids were out of school. So I was all set for a relaxing day of enjoying the nothingness of having a day off. Until Amazon. com came along and spoiled it.

"As someone who has ordered *Chicken Soup for the Soul* books in the past," the e-mail read, "we thought you might like…"

"No, Amazon.com, you are wrong. I would not like that book," I wanted to say. "Because I submitted a story to that book. And if you have it for sale and I never heard back from Chicken Soup for the Soul, then that means my story wasn't picked."

So I sulked for a moment, then got over it and went to the gym.

While at the gym walking on the treadmill, I thought about a blog post I had read the previous day. The author frankly stated that if you don't learn to be happy along every step on your writing jour- ney, you will never be happy. The author basically outlined a writer's journey from finishing that first manuscript all the way to making it to the top of the bestseller list. And how, at each step, we soon forget how happy we were at that previous step and quickly begin looking forward to the next step. But we never take enough time to celebrate the "now."

After thinking about that blog post, and in light of the fact that Amazon.com had just burst my bubble, I made up my mind to celebrate everything I had accomplished so far in my writing career. And the first thing I needed to celebrate was the fact that I had already been published in Chicken Soup for the Soul, even if I didn't get into that particular upcoming title.

But I didn't stop there. I also called my husband and told him we were going out to celebrate that night. I said, "I know we haven't accomplished anything big. But we've accomplished a lot of small things this year, so we need to celebrate." I even listed the things our kids had accomplished thus far in the school year, so we were taking them out too.

His response: "Cool."

When I got home and told the kids, my middle school daughter wanted to know why we were going out on a Tuesday night. I told her, "Just to celebrate our small successes."

"Like what?" she wanted to know.

So I listed some of them for her, such as her older sister (a senior) scoring high enough on her ACT to qualify for scholarships; for herself having her first basketball game that week; and for her little brother (a kindergartener) miraculously surviving school.

She replied, "Shouldn't we at least wait until Thursday to see how I do in my first game?"

I said, "Nope. We're celebrating the fact that you made the team."

She shrugged. "That's no big deal."

"Did everybody who tried out make the team?" I asked her.

"Of course not," she said.

"Then you have something to celebrate," I said.

But some amazing things happened that day after we made the decision to go out and count our blessings—more blessings came our way. That very day, I received an e-mail from Chicken Soup for the Soul notifying me that another story I had submitted made it to the final round of selections for one of their other books (my second that year!). That evening, during our celebration dinner, my husband placed an envelope on the table and told me to open it. Inside was a bonus check from his job! After dinner, I checked my e-mail, and, believe it or not, got notification that I had received money in my PayPal account from a writing contest that I had won a couple of months before. All these things in one day — the same day we, as a family, decided to celebrate the small stuff!

But the blessings didn't stop there. I had been praying for new living room furniture for a very long time. Over a year, actually. It might have been two. But I refused to get new furniture using credit or any type of payment plan. I just continued to pray and hope. Well, wouldn't you know it? In one single day, with the bonus check and the money from the contest, I had enough to buy new furniture — without credit!

And, I believe with all my heart that those blessings were a direct result of our decision to count our blessings and be happy right now rather than waiting for our big payday to come and make us happy.

I have heard that Oprah once said, "The single greatest thing you can do to change your life today would be to start being grateful for what you have right now. And the more grateful you are, the more you get." And that, my friends, I can testify, is the honest-to-goodness truth.

~Linda Jackson

From Misery to Meaning

Could we change our attitude, we should not only see life differently, but life itself would come to be different.
~Katherine Mansfield

When I first arrived in Guangzhou, China for my two-year assignment, the contrast to the life I had led in the U.S. was overwhelming. I knew I had agreed to live in a "hardship location," but despite all the books I had read, I was unprepared for the culture shock I experienced in China's third largest city. Suddenly I belonged to a minority of two thousand expats among ten million Chinese.

I could not understand a word around me and never recognized where I was because I could not read the signs. I had to constantly clear my throat because of the pollution from the factories and thousands of motorbikes. Combined with the high temperatures and the humidity, it resulted in a permanent gray haze over the city. I felt suffocated by the crowds I encountered wherever I went. From my taxicab sitting in the jammed traffic, I saw ailing beggars in the streets and old women carrying heavy loads on their bent backs. It made me feel guilty for being a rich white woman and helpless because I was lost in a world I could not relate to. Everything I saw seemed so dismal, so depressing. It didn't take me long to despair and I yearned to be anywhere else but there.

One miserable day, I was complaining to a European colleague. When she told me she had been in Guangzhou for eight years and loved it, I was stunned. How could we experience the same place in such contrasting ways? It was as if we were living in two different universes. She was happy and upbeat. I was depressed and homesick. Where I saw smog, traffic jams, and language barriers, she saw adventure, opportunity, and culture.

I wanted to look at my surroundings the way she did but I did not know how to do it. During the following sleepless night, I challenged myself to identify three things in my environment each day that I would classify as "positive." It could be anything, as long as it was somehow good or encouraging. In the gloomy world I lived in, this was a difficult exercise. I really had to force myself to be open-minded and creative.

I had a hard time finding the first positive thing around me. But I was determined, and later that afternoon, walking through the crowded streets I started to see things. A smiling child on his mother's arm. Yes, that counted! A man in a business suit buying a piece of melon from a street vendor and giving it to a beggar. I would not have noticed this scene if I had not forced myself to look. Two women joking as they chose a (live) chicken in the meat market. That was three for Day One. I had made it. I could do it again.

Some days were more difficult than others, but once I started looking for them, I always found my three noteworthy good things. After the first week, the exercise became easier and by week three I didn't have to actively search anymore. I easily spotted positive things in many places throughout the day. After four weeks, the gray cloud had lifted, and though it still had a long way to go, Guangzhou had started to grow on me. I had also stopped feeling sorry for myself.

Another month later, on the plane to Hong Kong for a weekend of "rest and recreation," I was surprised to see that more than three quarters of the passengers consisted of Caucasian couples with Chinese girls. The girls all seemed to be between one and three years old and they were dressed in designer children clothing. Many wore headbands with little bows or colored clips in their hair. The parents were hugging and fussing over them.

"Hi, is this lovely girl your daughter?" I asked the woman across the aisle.

"Yes, this is Ellie Li," she said, swallowing hard. "We've carried her photo with us for over a year, but we only just met her in person a couple of days ago."

Ellie Li was a beautiful Chinese toddler, dressed in jeans and a pink sweatshirt that said, "I am cute." She kept her dark eyes fixated on her mother while we talked.

"Congratulations, how wonderful," I said. "Is she from Guangzhou?"

"No, we picked her up in the Nanjing orphanage, but we had to come to the U.S. Consulate in Guangzhou to get her immigration papers. And now she is finally coming home to Texas."

We kept talking and I learned that all U.S. adoptions from mainland China had to be finalized in Guangzhou and that Ellie Li was one of thousands of orphaned girls each year who was moving from abandonment to affection. For all of them, this plane ride was the first leg on their journeys home.

I felt my eyes swelling with tears as it dawned on me that I was surrounded by hundreds of miracles coming true right there, right then. I sat back in my chair and allowed the energy of care and compassion to permeate me. I had to chuckle at the thought that Guangzhou—polluted, crowded, noisy Guangzhou—of all places, had such a special meaning. How could I not be joyful in this place of answered prayers, of love, happiness, and new beginnings?

This insight profoundly impacted my perception of Guangzhou. I had not changed a thing about my environment. But I had changed the way I looked at it. And with it, my experience changed from a dreary and self-pitying existence to a vibrant and enjoyable chapter in my life.

~Rita Bosel

43

What's the Worst that Can Happen?

Only a few things are really important.
~Marie Dressler

"W hen did you lose your hair?" The question came from a woman sitting next to me in the oncology waiting room. Her husband was by her side.

The summer heat had killed any remaining vanity I had and my head was covered not with the expensive wig I wore to work, but with a do-rag so pink it would make a biker cringe. I'd convinced myself in the mirror that morning I looked cute.

I was about halfway through my chemotherapy treatments and the process had become routine. I'd even started to enjoy my day of forced reading time while I waited for the doctor, waited for my tests, then waited for the chemo to do its work. Best thing about cancer ever—you have a lot of time to read while you're waiting on the medical staff to save your life.

It wasn't the first time I had been asked that particular question. I was asked by co-workers, church members and even complete strangers while I shopped at Walmart. I even had a woman stop me one night while I was walking the dogs, wanting to share her daughter's struggles.

I could tell the woman next to me was just starting her journey. She had yet to travel through the maze of treatment that follows the diagnosis of breast cancer. For me it was surgery, chemotherapy and radiation. And I had viewed the treatment as a checklist. Mammogram—check. Biopsy—check. Surgery—check. Now chemotherapy.

My first visit to the oncologist changed my checklist view of my condition. I'd been sitting in this same chair that day, worrying about my hair. Looking at the magazines, seeing the ads for hats, head rags and wigs, my eyes filled with tears.

I had cancer and I was going to lose my hair.

I was in a strange town after living all of my life no more than thirty miles from the town where I was born. The only constant in my life was my boyfriend of seven years with whom I had packed up my life and moved 1600 miles to live closer to his folks. We were supposed to be here to take care of them. And I got cancer. It wasn't fair.

The pity party continued.

I returned to her question. When had I lost my hair?

At my second chemotherapy treatment, I'd been sitting watching the nurse hook up my newly placed port with the pre-medications that were supposed to keep me from rejecting the harder drugs to come. "You still have your hair," the nurse commented. She even pushed a wayward curl out of my eyes.

"I'm hoping it will stay," I confessed. My hair was long and curly. Finally after years of trying to mold the crazy curls into a straight style, I'd surrendered and I loved the way it looked. I'd bought a wig (check) but I still hoped I'd be one of the lucky ones who kept her hair during chemo.

The lady across from me in the eight-bed treatment pod laughed, overhearing our conversation. "It won't stay. I've lost all of my hair everywhere except a line down the front of both of my legs. So I still have to shave. It's not fair." She laughed again and returned to working on a photo album with her daughter.

The young man in the bed next to her chimed in on the hair subject. "One day I put shaving cream on my face and my beard just came off with the foam." Most people he ran into just thought he had a new hairstyle. Another place where men have the advantage; they can rock the bald look.

They were right. My hair started falling out right after that treatment. At first, my hair shorted into a curly bob, like I'd gotten a haircut. The next Monday, I showed up at work in my wig and people didn't recognize me.

Sitting in the oncologist's office that first day, losing my hair had been the worst thing that could happen. I'd been devastated at the thought.

That changed when the doctor told me a lymph node had swollen up after the surgery and was a new concern, possibly be a sign the cancer had spread.

Stunned, I asked about the next steps. He told me about the additional tests that would define my treatment. And if the cancer had spread, what did we do then? The look on his face told me the rest of the story.

Luckily after more tests, the doctors agreed that the cancer was curable and I was back on schedule for the chemotherapy and radiation.

The woman in the waiting room was still waiting for an answer. I took a deep breath, pasted on the smile, and gave her the news she didn't want to hear. "I lost it during chemotherapy but I was able to fight the cancer off, so it was a small price to pay."

I told her about my scare during my first appointment. I then went on to talk to her about my experiences and hoped that it helped her deal with the hardest part of cancer, not knowing the future or what to expect. I hope she understood that the loss of hair was temporary. I hope I helped her spirit deal with the fight she was about to undertake.

As I watched the woman and her husband leave with the nurse, I hoped she found a way to embrace the journey. Now, with my hair back and my year of cancer and treatment just a memory, I'm glad that I was able to learn that losing my hair could be the least of my problems. Now each day is a gift. Bald or not.

~Lynn Cahoon

44

86,400 Seconds

We often take for granted the very things that most deserve our gratitude.
~Cynthia Ozick

"Cars," my not-quite-two-year-old son Nathan said, pointing at the hanging display of Matchbox cars at our local grocery store. He smiled sweetly and said it again.

"Yes, I see those cars," I said.

But Nathan shook his head. "Need cars," he said.

"You already have lots of cars at home," I said.

Nathan shook his head again and said—quite loudly this time—"Mommy, cars!"

I glanced around the store and noticed a few people looking our way. But before I could even feel embarrassed, Nathan hollered again, "Need cars!"

"Nathan, we're not going to buy a car today," I said in my most soothing voice, "but you can play with your other cars as soon as we get home."

Nathan nodded and seemed to calm down. Satisfied that he'd understood me, I turned around to grab some chocolate chips. In that instant, Nathan decided to help himself to a car or two. He reached out to grab the coveted toys, but the plastic hanger they were on caught on a bag of sugar. Nathan kept pulling and ended up knocking three bags of sugar off the shelf. They fell to the floor where they—of course—broke open, dumping sugar everywhere.

"Uh oh," Nathan yelled. "Mess, Mommy! Mess!"

I think half of our town was at the grocery store that day and all of them were in the baking aisle, staring at me and the mess my son had made. A bag boy came over, saw the mess, muttered an expletive, and called for a "cleanup on aisle ten." It was beyond embarrassing. All I needed now was for an old boyfriend to appear and want to "catch up." That didn't happen—thank goodness—but the entire fiasco was bad enough.

When we arrived home from the grocery store—which I will not be going back to until after Nathan goes away to college—I put away the few groceries I managed to get before the sugar incident. I laid Nathan down for a nap, praying he would sleep for a long time.

Then I sat down on the couch and cried. I'm not sure why. I just did.

But just moments into my pity party, the phone rang. I sighed and muttered, "Why can't everyone just leave me alone?" I grabbed the phone and barked a hello.

"Um, Diane? It's Margaret from church. I'm calling because you're on the prayer chain."

Uh oh. Mid-week prayer chain calls always meant an accident or other emergency.

"What happened?" I said.

"Matthew passed away this morning," she said. Matthew's family attended our church. He was five and he'd been battling leukemia since before his second birthday. We'd all known he didn't have much longer, but still, the news hit me hard.

Margaret gave me the funeral arrangements as I choked down more tears.

When we finally hung up, I returned to my spot on the couch, crying once again. I cried for Matthew's parents. They were more acquaintances than friends, but my heart broke for them all the same.

My tears were sad, but they were also guilty. Guilty that just moments before, I'd thought I had problems. I'd been in a rotten mood because my son—my healthy, wonderful son—had embarrassed me at the grocery store. It was nothing compared to what Matthew's mother had been through.

In fact, she'd probably give anything to go through that experience, just to have her little boy back.

The funeral was heart wrenching. It was only the second time I'd attended one for a child and it hadn't gotten any easier. I was crying before we even entered the church. One of the pallbearers handed me a program. I glanced down and read Matthew's name, along with a quote by William Ward. It said: "God gave you a gift of 86,400 seconds today. Have you used one to say 'thank you'?"

Matthew's parents had chosen that quote because of Matthew's love of life and gratitude for every day he was here, no matter what that day brought.

I thought about my own life and how often I found myself in a bad mood over something relatively minor. I realized how little gratitude I felt for the many blessings in my life. All of my children are healthy, but I hadn't thought much about that. Instead, all too often, I focused on the small, but daily, frustrations of having young children. The messes, the temper tantrums, the noise. Never getting to hold the remote.

But when I think about Matthew and his family, none of that stuff matters. My kids are a blessing and I'm lucky to have them. No matter what.

So today, instead of becoming annoyed at them for leaving toys on the floor and arguing over the last fudge pop, I'm going to spend some of my 86,400 seconds being grateful for them.

And I'm going to spend even more of that time enjoying them.

~Diane Stark

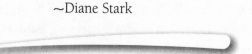

45

Entering the Thankful Zone

If you want to turn your life around, try thankfulness.
It will change your life mightily.
~Gerald Good

One by one we wrote upon the 3x5 index cards and then taped them to the closet door across from my husband's hospital bed. On the card at the top was written "God's Love," on another "Each New Morning."

It was Thanksgiving Day 2011, and my husband and I were celebrating the holiday alone in his hospital room. He had been admitted a couple of weeks earlier, after his AML (acute myeloid leukemia) had roared out of remission. Our adult children, who lived with us, were spending the day with friends in our town an hour to the north.

Earlier that morning, as I prepared to leave home and head to the hospital, I found myself grumbling about the fact that we wouldn't be together as a family; this would not be the kind of Thanksgiving we had hoped for. A specter of worry about my husband's health hung over the day. But then, I had an idea!

I raced about our home gathering supplies and printing things out on the computer. As I did so, I found my attitude changing and a sense of anticipation and gratitude replacing my darker thoughts.

Later that morning, I walked into my husband's room and pulled out a sign I had printed. I announced, "We are declaring this room the 'Thankful Zone.'" I taped the sign to the outside of his door, where anyone coming into his room would see it. It read, "You are now entering the 'Thankful Zone.' Admittance is an Attitude of Gratitude."

I handed my husband a pen and some of the 3x5 cards I had brought with me, and we proceeded to reflect on the things that we were most grateful for. The list grew as the day passed.

"Hope," "Faith" and "Love" were placed at the top of our list. "Good friends" and "Dear family" also held places of honor.

My husband, who could not leave the medical unit he was on, wrote that he was grateful for "Sunshine," for "Moonless nights, when you can see the stars" and for "The smell in the air after rain."

He laughed, but wholeheartedly agreed when I added "anti-nausea drugs" and the name of the sedation drug that he was given before each of his many bone marrow biopsies.

Something happened as we added each new item. We were able to step back from the horror of cancer and see that even in the midst of great adversity there can also be great blessings. Among the many blessings were "Laughter," "Music" and through it all "Each other."

Our changed attitude affected everything around us. We even found ourselves thankful for the delicious hospital dinner of turkey and stuffing and the hands that had prepared it. We recognized the blessing of the amazing nurses and doctors who were caring for my husband.

At the day's end, the closet door was overflowing with written reminders of the many things we were thankful for. No, we had not been able to spend a traditional Thanksgiving with family and friends, but we had experienced a day overflowing with giving thanks. Simple things such as "Warm showers" and "Dancing with the one you love" can make life an unexpectedly sweet journey.

~Jeannie Lancaster

46

Charmed

The robbed that smiles, steals something from the thief.
~William Shakespeare, Othello

The meat cleaver in his hand shone in the moonlight. "Don't come in." He sounded serious.

Arriving home, my husband Danny had unlocked the door. I thought he was coming back out to help me unload the children. What was he doing with that meat cleaver and why couldn't I go in?

A glimmer in the moonlight caught my eye. Shattered glass covered my back doorstep. Instructing our thirteen-year-old to watch the other children, I ran into the kitchen, rummaged through the first drawer and found what I needed. I clasped the steak knife as if I knew how to use it. After we called the police, we stood guard over our home and children.

Looking back, I'm not sure what we would have done had we confronted robbers. "Freeze or I'll cleave you." Come to think of it, we added a whole new meaning to cleaving to your spouse. Thankfully, the burglars were long gone.

Sirens blaring, the police arrived in less than five minutes. They were a dichotomy of tough, Texas men-with-guns and tender comfort to our trembling children—and their parents holding sharp objects. After they dusted for fingerprints and took their report, an officer helped Danny board up what had been our patio glass door.

Tiny shards of glass crunched under our feet with each step.

Everything had been turned upside down. Our jewelry boxes were missing.

My charm bracelet was gone.

I didn't wear it that often, but every time I saw it, I remembered my twelfth birthday celebration at my grandparents' house. After dinner, surrounded by my whole family, Pop sat in his overstuffed papa-bear-chair. His eyes twinkled as he patted his leg. "Come over here, li'l darlin'."

Almost too big, I obediently climbed into the cocoon of my grandfather's lap.

From beside his chair, his hand lifted a box. Not just any box. It was store-wrapped in fancy foil paper. The bow itself could have been a gift.

"Gorgeous!" A squeal of excitement escaped my lips as the deep maroon velvet tickled my fingertips. It opened with a hinge, like Mama's special box.

As I gingerly opened the box, every eye focused on me and everyone held their breath for the unveiling.

Pop lifted the treasure from the box, opened the clasp, and placed the chain around my wrist. I raised my arm and watched beams of light dance off the sparkling, grown-up, bracelet.

Mama and my grandmother buzzed around me, pointing out the ballerina explaining the tradition. "You add charms representing special events or trips."

Their excitement wrapped around me like a warm blanket. Pop's belly jiggled as he laughed with sheer pleasure at my joy. I knew he adored me, just as I adored him.

But he was gone and the bracelet was gone too.

I was angry over the next few months when my children were too afraid to walk through the house alone. I wanted to look those thieves in the eyes and let them know how they hurt my children... how they hurt me.

The bracelet was the thing that brought me the most heartache. It was all I had left from Pop. Every time I thought about it, I sunk deeper into a dark abyss, whining over the loss.

A wrestling match formed inside me. I knew I shouldn't whine. I knew how to think positively, but it didn't work. I reminded myself that the letter "I" was in the middle of the word whine, that whining was a symptom that my focus was off. It was on me, myself, and I rather than what was truly important. Sure that gratitude should trump grief, and recognizing it was all in my head, I counted and recounted my blessings. My head knew better, but my heart grieved for that bracelet.

Jeremy, our five-year-old son, must have heard my whining. One day he made a little bracelet out of pipe cleaners and proudly twisted it around my wrist. Dangling slightly off center was a construction-paper ballerina.

"See. She's smiling just like you used to."

Like I used to? Oh, my heart. Had I been so self-involved over a petty theft that I was stealing joy from my child? Kissing his forehead, I exclaimed over the beauty of his masterpiece.

Love and memories of love were what made that old bracelet have real value, just like this new one. The bracelets were only a reminder. Those thieves may have stolen my jewelry, but they couldn't steal the memories.

My smile was back.

~Tamara C. Roberts

The Power of Positive

The Power of Giving

Finish Lines

Most people run a race to see who is fastest.
I run a race to see who has the most guts.
~Steve Prefontaine

Alex started running competitively when he was a sophomore in high school. It was hard to imagine him on a cross country team—or any running team. He had such funny little running steps as a young child. It was one of those things you just had to see... he wasn't fast and looked suspiciously like a trotting cartoon character. But it all clicked as he ran through woods and obstacles that year. The runners on his team kept each other going, finish lines beckoned, and running became huge in Alex's life.

There's something about high school sports—the way seasons are determined by sign-ups, practices, and events. The crisp days of changing leaves, wooded trails, and pounding sneakers evolved to frigid winds and pungent odors at an indoor track, and finally to green grass and longer days. It was heaven to watch the last traces of a frigid New England winter dissolve into temperate breezes, determined buds, and spring track sign-ups.

Alex came blasting through the door, carrying his backpack and stories of the day... his unfair Spanish test, whatever they were serving up in the cafeteria that was taken from the biotech lab, and Special Olympics coaching. Special Olympics coaching? "I signed up to volunteer," he said. "It starts tomorrow. Sam's volunteering also. It's right before my track practice. And we get our athlete assignments tomorrow!"

I can still remember Alex's excitement the next morning as he rushed to grab his team jacket and get to the bus stop. "Today's going to be wicked cool," he said. "Ari's coaching too. A lot of us are." Cute girls. Of course.

"Good luck with your athlete," I said. "I'll see you after practice!"

I was in the kitchen trying to make a casserole out of droopy leftovers when Alex came home that afternoon looking like a typical high school athlete. His messy hair was soaked with sweat, and he had that energy I had come to expect in him after a good run. But before he could say a word, I knew something was bugging him. "Mom, I got Keith."

"Who is Keith?"

"At Special Olympics—my athlete is Keith. He's the same age as me, and he doesn't talk at all. He just makes noises. I don't think he understands anything I say. I can't get him to run, so I basically just stand there. I really wanted to do this! When I signed up, I even told the coach he could count on me every spring, but I don't know how to work with Keith. It's not fair. I better not get him next year."

Well this is going well, I thought. And I opened the fridge wondering what culinary perfection might suddenly materialize to salvage dinner. It was only the first day. Surely, by the end of the week, Alex would have a whole new perspective.

But on Friday, Alex came home from school and slumped down on the kitchen floor. "I don't like coaching," he said. "I can't get Keith to do anything. It's really awkward."

"Did you talk to your coach about it?" I asked.

"He told all of us that we are the coaches, so we need to be patient and encouraging. But this is impossible."

Days turned into weeks marked by Alex's track meets, goals, wins, and losses. Alex didn't talk too much about Special Olympics training, so I didn't push it; but I knew he was there each week trying to figure out Keith, and I imagined that Keith was trying to figure out Alex too.

Watching Alex's races was always amazing for me. At one meet, after his relay, he joined me in the grass. "That was a great race!" I told him, wondering when my little boy had grown into this runner with muscles and grace. "It's wild how we all push ourselves," he said. "I mean, we all get what we have to do, who we pass the baton to, what our goals are. It must be so hard for Keith—so scary not to understand what we're telling him or what a finish line is all about. I can tell what a lot of his noises mean, and I think he really likes to run. But he can't tell anyone too much about what he feels. His world is hard. Everything is so different for him."

Before I could respond, a couple of Alex's teammates whisked him off to watch the girls run. His fading sneakers neared the crowds just beyond the track and then disappeared into a sea of colorful feet—that rainbow of spectators waiting for action. As if on cue, the starting gun exploded, the crowd cheered, and runners took off in perfect rhythm.

The Special Olympics competitions were held at a local college campus, and Alex got up super early that morning. He grabbed his necessities—camera, cereal bars, and cell phone—and prepared to catch the bus that would bring him to this all-day marathon. He seemed nervous—preoccupied—as I watched him stuff last-minute items into his sports bag. "Are you excited, Coach?" I asked.

"Definitely," he answered. "I hope it's okay. I hope Keith stays on the track. That's the hardest thing—helping him to stay on the track."

I have to admit, I was anxious all day waiting for Alex to get home. I wondered how it was going, how Keith would fare against other athletes who were far more communicative and responsive… how Alex would fare with other student coaches who had made more progress and formed deeper bonds with their athletes. It felt like forever until I heard the creak of the garage door and Alex's familiar footsteps on the stairs. I braced myself.

"Hey," I said, waiting for Alex's familiar energy.

"Hey," he responded.

"So?"

"Keith did great," Alex said slowly. "I mean really great. He stayed on the track for almost a lap. He didn't cross the finish line, but today was his personal best. He got a medal. He wouldn't let go of that medal for the rest of the day—you should have seen him holding it! And he sat with me after… we just hung out. That kid has guts. He really does."

And with that, Alex brushed by me and headed upstairs. The breeze he created was gentle, like a changing season or the passage of time. "Mom," he called back.

"Yes?"

"I requested Keith for next year."

~Carol S. Rothchild

Happy Cancer-versary

How beautiful a day can be
When kindness touches it!
~George Elliston

My "cancer-versary" was two days away. The worst parts of treatment—the surgeries and four rounds of chemotherapy—were long behind me, yet I was miserable. Why? Because the part of breast cancer treatment that was supposed to be easy—just swallow a pill every day for the next five years to lower my risk of recurrence—turned out to be just as bad as the chemotherapy. The drug's side effects left me incapacitated on the couch.

The anniversary of my diagnosis was supposed to be a day of triumphant celebration and tranquil reflection on how far I had come in the past year. I had expected to spend the day being grateful for my life and health, grateful that I was still alive to parent my young children, grateful that my hair was growing back. I wasn't feeling grateful. I was feeling disheartened that the side effects were persisting two weeks after my oncologist had taken me off the drug. I had been a healthy, active person before my diagnosis. Was that never to be restored? I was sick and tired of being sick and tired.

The day before my cancer-versary, I took my seven-year-old daughter to piano lessons as usual. At the door of her piano teacher's house, an old friend and neighbor stopped me. He and I had served on the local church's council five years ago. I could always count on Jim to cheer me up with a funny story or news of a mutual friend.

"I need to tell you something," Jim said with an air of mystery. I sent my daughter on ahead with her piano books. "Do you remember Marcus?" Jim asked. My mind quickly scanned over our mutual friends, but I couldn't recall anyone with that name. Seeing my blank look, Jim continued, "He was the homeless man sleeping in the church garage five years ago."

Then I remembered. I hadn't known his name that Sunday afternoon five years ago when we, the church council, had learned that a homeless man was sleeping in the decrepit garage behind the church. He wasn't a nameless, faceless stranger; he was born and raised in our little, close-knit town. His mother still lived here, and many older residents remembered him as a boy. But five years ago he returned to the community as a broken man, homeless and addicted to alcohol. These are overwhelmingly complex issues, and we—the church council—felt inadequate in deciding the best course of action to take with the man sleeping in our garage. We wanted to be compassionate but not enabling. We wanted to protect him but also address the fears of neighborhood parents. We had no idea what to do, and we left the church meeting feeling at a loss.

"Remember how you left him your sleeping bag?" Jim asked me. I did. I remembered going home after our council meeting that Sunday and returning to church with a well-worn sleeping bag from our camping gear. It was winter, and a temperature of nineteen degrees was predicted for that night. I remembered stepping fearfully into that cold, dark garage and being horrified that someone in my own town would consider sleeping on that bare, oil-stained cement floor, under that roof so decrepit that it seemed only moss was holding it together. I remembered feeling relieved to see no evidence that anyone had been there. Maybe it was all a rumor, or maybe he had only been passing through on his way to adequate shelter. I left my sleeping bag with a note saying that it was from the congregation so that, if the man did show up, he would not feel guilty taking the sleeping bag. At the time, my act seemed shamefully inadequate, like a bandage on an amputation.

I was timid about following up on my meager offering, ashamed that I might have crossed a line of propriety either with the community or with the homeless man. But after several weeks, I peeked into the garage and saw that the sleeping bag was gone. There was no way of knowing if it had reached its desired recipient or had simply been removed by a zealous tidier. That seemed the end of the story, since I heard no more news of the man.

I had completely forgotten about the sleeping bag until Jim mentioned it. "Marcus came to church this Sunday and gave his testimony," he told me. Marcus is now sober and has a job and a home. He came to thank the church and the AA group that meets in the church building for their encouragement and support, for helping him turn his life around. "Marcus remembered the sleeping bag," Jim said. "He mentioned how much it meant to him and he thanked the congregation for it. Now, when he speaks at local AA groups to encourage others trying to recover from addiction, he tells them about the sleeping bag."

The day after Jim shared this story with me was my dreaded cancer-versary. Although I was still not feeling well, I did not spend the day dwelling on how harsh my life had been over the past year or how much I had lost to cancer. Rather, it was a day of rejoicing about how much has been unexpectedly gained. What a joy that a tiny act of kindness, forgotten over the intervening years, could have made a difference in someone's life. I hope I can meet Marcus some day and tell him how he returned the favor: just as I had the privilege of encouraging Marcus five years ago during his dark days, he unknowingly encouraged me during mine by sharing his story. Happy cancer-versary!

~Sharri Bockheim Steen

Staff Lunch

We cannot live only for ourselves.
A thousand fibers connect us with our fellow men.
~Herman Melville

The 100-year-old red brick building I worked in a few years ago was half a block long and two stories high, with twelve-inch thick walls. Our landlord Wilbur had owned it for forty years.

Several different businesses were renting space there then. There was the non-profit I worked for and a working art gallery with five artists. An electrical distributing company had a small space and there was an antique and collectibles store. The most profitable business was an interstate wholesale distributing company that sold products that outfitted hardware stores.

In the basement, with its massive wood beams, was Wilbur's workshop and spaces for folks to rent dry storage space. In a little space in the top of the building Wilbur had carved out a tiny apartment for his residence when he was in town.

As he grew older, folks noticed he spent more time at the building instead of his other homes. His grown children were suggesting that he consolidate his holdings and move to an assisted living facility. They were alarmed by his increasing health issues. They thought it would be easier to watch out for him if he lived closer to one of them, and they also wanted him to monetize his assets.

We folks in the big red brick building were concerned about

Wilbur too. His long distance family wasn't going to take better care of him or improve their relationship with him if he moved closer; they just wanted life to be easier. And what would Wilbur do without his beloved basement workshop?

Our answer came rather accidently. Wilbur usually "took his meals" at a local café. He had oatmeal for breakfast, a hot meal at lunch (it was called dinner when he grew up on the farm he told us), and a sandwich for supper. Often he would buy a large fruit pie and that was his meal for the day. Folks knew he wasn't eating well and would ask him if they could "zap" him something. Most often he would refuse even when he liked what was offered, which was puzzling.

One day several of us non-profit folks were sitting down to lunch. We had forsaken our brown bag lunches for what we found in the refrigerator. There had been a big event the night before and some sweet soul had wrapped up the leftovers. Wilbur happened by to use the copy machine, a first-of-the-month event that happened when he collected rent checks.

"Hey, Wilbur, we have leftovers from that big shindig last night. Why don't you join us for lunch?" It took a little arm twisting but by the time the food was on the table, Wilbur had washed his hands. "That workshop is a dirty place," he told us as we sat down. Lunch was delicious (probably because someone else made it). It was a pleasant forty-five minutes before Wilbur excused himself. "Got to get back to the workshop," he said, "there's a project calling my name."

Pretty soon our staff had Wilbur for "staff lunch" twice a week. Word got around the building and in no time the other businesses were asking him to join them for a noon hot meal. "Staff Lunch" became the code word for a hot meal with others. Wilbur ate with a different tenant each weekday. He would apologize saying he could eat with us only once a week. "You know, I can't disappoint them," he would say.

Once in a while Wilbur would throw his own hot "staff lunch" for the entire building. The grocery store had a little deli that helped. Of course he would have his "staff lunch" on Saturdays so everyone's family could attend. And that way he wouldn't have to disappoint anyone by missing one of his weekday lunches.

Conversation built community. Funny thing, Wilbur's health issues became less frequent and less severe when they happened. Folks traded recipes and clothes their kids had outgrown, vegetables and home baked goodies appeared and we got to know each other better.

It is definitely arguable as to who benefited most from those lunch relationships—Wilbur or people like me who worked in Wilbur's building—the building that had become his real home.

~Pamela Gilsenan

While I Wait

There is no hope unmingled with fear, and no fear unmingled with hope.
~Baruch Spinoza

Seventeen years ago I had a malignant tumor removed from my breast, and I did what I had to do in order to move on with my life. And I'm fine pretty much every day of the year... until test time. Then I start to worry. Mammograms. Blood tests. X-rays. The possibility of facing cancer again overwhelms me, and I get a sick feeling in the pit of my stomach. What if...?

Each day seems like an eternity when I am waiting for test results. What if...? When the "what if" questions start to surface, I have to work hard at getting beyond the fear that grips me every time I hear the phone ring or I see the mail carrier open the door of my mailbox and put an envelope inside. I have to concentrate on generating thoughts that will soothe my shattered soul.

The first thing I do when I wake up in the morning is listen. I listen to the chorus of birds chirping in the fig tree right outside my bedroom window. I love their voices. I listen to their perfect harmony and revel in the multiple melodies of song I can pick up on. At times I don't know if I hear one bird singing a lofty aria or many birds singing in concert all at once, but I am transported to another place, letting myself get caught up in their symphonies.

A mantle of peace embraces me as I recall a passage from the Bible. "Look at the birds in the sky; they do not sow nor reap, they gather nothing into barns, yet your heavenly Father feeds them. Are not you more important than they?"

As I make my way to the kitchen for my morning egg and toast, I pass through the family room where portraits of my children have greeted me day after day, year after year. "You are my joy and my life," I whisper into the morning light of a brand new day.

Even though my children are grown now, I can't fathom the thought of leaving them. What if they need me in the middle of the night and I'm not around to help them? What if they need a shoulder to cry on and I'm not there to comfort them? What if someone hurts them, and I'm not there to hold them? More "what ifs." It is in this "waiting period" that I need to keep myself busier than usual.

I like writing children's stories, so I pack my book bag with a sea of smiling fish, a lonely pumpkin that finally finds a home, and a fuzzy, yellow duck who loves splashing in her puddle. I head for a nearby elementary school or city library where I can share my make-believe characters with eager listeners. I soon find myself falling headfirst into the story right along with the children, hoping all the while that I am creating a world for them where they can be happy and safe and carefree for as long as they want.

On other days I leave my bag of make-believe characters behind and bring a box of writing activities with me so that the children can create their own stories. They write about colors and animals and what makes them happy and sad. And I am blown away by the beauty and sincerity of the words that flow so freely from their unbridled hearts.

"White is a page lonely without words," one student writes.

"And life is a page lonely without hope," I quickly write in my heart's journal.

I marvel at how well I feel at the end of my stay when I leave this world of imagination and inspiration. These children have lit up my soul with their enthusiasm and their gusto for living life in the moment—and I am reminded of the miracle of living life one new moment at a time.

And when the day is done and evening's shadows have faded

into the moonlit sky, I close my eyes and listen for the chirping of the birds in the fig tree right outside my bedroom window. The night is silent now. The choral performance will have to wait until morning when its symphonies once again will transport me to another place where I know all will be well.

"Look at the birds in the sky…. Are not you more important than they?"

As morning splashes its light on a brand new day, the phone rings and it's my daughter telling me of the day she has planned with her twenty full-of-life third graders. Or it's my son telling me he will be able to come home next weekend. And a quiet peace fills my soul.

I head for my mailbox where the mail carrier has put an envelope inside. My heart skips a beat as I tear open the letter, regarding this year's test results: "Everything is fine. See you next year."

And suddenly I feel like I can fly.

~Lola Di Giulio De Maci

What Is the Higher Response?

Never look down on anybody unless you're helping him up.
~Jesse Jackson

I was having lunch with a friend one day on the pier in Geneva, Switzerland. A summer crowd was relaxing, enjoying the sunshine and the view of the harbor when a very large, heavily tattooed punk rocker dressed all in black arrived and started challenging everyone to fight. My friend and I watched as the people he challenged backed down or did their best to ignore him, hoping he would go away. He even kicked one person a few times, trying to force him to stand up and fight. We were at the end of the pier so we knew he was going to get to us eventually.

As the man approached us, it became obvious that he was extremely drunk. I knew then that it would be easy to subdue him if it came to that. I was heavily immersed in martial arts at this point in my life and held black belt rank, but I wasn't sure whether to fight or to seek peace, as all true martial artists should.

The friend I was with was a peace-loving beatnik, a little like Shaggy from the *Scooby-Doo* cartoons. That's what I liked about him, actually, but I was fairly sure he wasn't going to be much help if I couldn't find a way to calm this beast down. This was a chance for me to be a big hero by humiliating the bully who was terrorizing everyone. I would probably get a round of applause, a free drink or two, maybe even the key to the city from the mayor. However, a question I had begun to ask myself with increasing regularity rang in my ears: What is the higher response?

The drunken man finally arrived at our table.

"What about you two sissies, eh?" he slurred. "Which one of you wants to fight?"

I didn't look up. He put his hand on my shoulder and pushed hard. Several dozen attacks went through my mind. It would have been too easy to hurt him, drunk as he was. He was painfully vulnerable. Then that pesky question popped into my mind again—what is the higher response? Or as some put it, "What would Jesus do?"

Knowing that the main thing a drunken man wants most is another drink, I said, "As fun as that sounds, I have a better idea. Why don't you sit down with us and have a beer?"

Confused, he scowled and asked, "What?"

I reached into the bag of groceries we had with us, pulled out a cold bottle, handed it to him and said, "Here you go. We can be friends, too, you know? Come on. Have a drink with us. It's a lot easier on the knuckles."

He stood there reeling for ten seconds or so, trying to figure out if I was serious. People who were close enough to hear the exchange waited, transfixed by the unfolding drama. Would he take the beer or start swinging? Finally, he said, "Alright." He took the beer, opened it and drank most of it one gulp. He started to walk away when I said, "You're welcome to join us if you want to."

He paused again and asked, "Really?"

"Sure," I said. "Sit down and relax a while."

We all sat quietly for a minute or so when I decided to push my luck and said, "So what's going on? Why are you beating up all the tourists?"

He looked at me with a little fire in his eyes. I knew right away that I had gone too far. I had to do something drastic to defend myself so I broke out the secret weapon. I smiled. A big, cheesy one. It was the equivalent of going "all in" at the end of a poker tournament. I was either going to draw the ace or bust. He looked more confused than ever but gradually, wonderfully, a smile spread across his face, too. Then I really started fighting dirty. I laughed. Not at him but as if we had just shared a secret joke. He was probably starting to think I was crazier than he was. My friend and the others nearby were, too. But then something truly magical happened. He started laughing, too. There was a collective sigh from everyone present. When we stopped laughing, he got up and stood looking out at the sea for a minute or so. I noticed tears forming in his eyes.

I said, "Something is obviously bothering you. Why don't you tell us about it?"

He sat back down and told us one of the saddest stories I had ever heard about horrific child abuse, addiction, untimely deaths of his loved ones, and all manner of mayhem. When he was done, he said, "Nothing good ever happens to me. Everything I love gets taken away. It just seems like I was put on this earth to suffer, like God hates me."

I wanted to tell him that we create our own reality by how we use or misuse our minds, and that it's how we react to the tragedies that inevitably befall us that matters, not the tragedies themselves. But I didn't. There's a time for philosophy and a time for listening. This man who had gone to such great lengths to look scary had become a lost child right in front of me, and I could tell by the depth of his emotion and the despair in his eyes that very few people were interested in taking the time to listen to him without trying to "straighten him out." I put my hand on his shoulder and said, "Well, it sounds like there's nowhere to go from here but up, right?"

"I hope so," he said.

We sat quietly for a while. I wrote down my name, address and phone number back in America, handed it to him and said, "If you ever need a friend, you can always call or write." He thanked me politely and walked away, quietly passing the same people he had been harassing earlier. When he reached the entrance to the pier, he turned around and waved goodbye, then disappeared back into his life.

To my great surprise, several months later, I received a letter from him. We corresponded for several years. These were the days before the Internet really took off and people still wrote letters exclusively.

Our letters were wild, rambling exchanges full of expansive soul searching. I shared poems and stories with him that had helped me at dark and difficult times in my life. His outlook seemed to improve with every letter I received from him.

I don't tell this story to attempt to take credit for how he turned his life around. He was the one who finally arrived at a place where he was sufficiently motivated to do the work. I tell this story to demonstrate what can happen when we act out of our higher nature rather than our lower instincts. If I had reacted in a violent manner to his harassment of me and others that day on the pier, everyone would have agreed he deserved it. But I am glad that I was able to show him that there was at least one person in the world who accepted and valued him, warts and all. I'm proud that I sought peace and won without conflict. And I had made a friend. A beating would have only deepened his anguish and further convinced him that he was put on this earth to suffer, as he put it. What he needed was a little compassion and I was able to give it to him because I asked myself a simple question... what is the higher response?

Many years passed and I stopped hearing from my friend. I lost the letters he sent me in a fire and his address along with them. But I always remembered his name so I recently looked him up on a social networking site on the Internet. It is an unusual name so he was not hard to find. That same big smile he gave me on the pier was his profile picture. I wouldn't have recognized him if I hadn't squeezed that smile out of him that day when we were both twenty years younger. It was a happy reunion, and I was very pleased to see that he has a good job, a wife and three beautiful children. He exudes joy right through my computer screen. Something good finally happened to him. God never hated him at all.

~Mark Rickerby

Baskets Full of Hope

Angels deliver Fate to our doorstep — and anywhere else it is needed.
~Jessi Lane Adams

A never-ending stream of flowers arrived for weeks after my cancer diagnosis — like ants to a picnic! There were pink roses, red geraniums, purple chrysanthemums, and my "favorite" — a white wicker basket of daisies with a "Get Well" sticker pasted on the front of the cellophane wrap. It must have been the special of the month because I received three identical baskets in the same week. Our house looked like a funeral home.

My wound was deep — not just physically, but emotionally and spiritually as well. I did all the right things: I didn't drink alcohol, didn't smoke, exercised every day, and ate tofu when no one else knew what it was, and still — at the age of forty — I heard the words no woman wants to hear "You have breast cancer."

Plain and simple: I was angry at God!

How was I supposed to work a full-time job, go through radiation treatments on my lunch break, and take care of our two boys — ages nine and fourteen — with all their afterschool activities and weekend sports?

As I swept the floor and picked up the rest of the dried rose petals, I burst into tears. Didn't anyone understand how I felt? Everyone's life went back to normal, but I was stuck in a room full of dead daisies and only half a breast.

The next day—my first week back at work—there was a "Welcome Back" sign posted on the lunchroom door and sitting on my desk was another bouquet of daisies in a white wicker basket with a smiley-face sticker that said: "Feel Better Soon!"

I forced a "thank you" and then politely excused myself—heading for the emergency exit for a much-needed coffee break.

Tears streaked down my cheeks as I made my way into the parking lot—letting the spring breeze cool my blotchy face. The April rain left a familiar earthy smell and the evergreen trees—lining the parking lot—swayed back and forth as if waving "goodbye." I took a deep cleansing breath and whispered, "God, please help me!"

When I returned to my desk, the office supervisor observed my mottled face and suggested, "Why don't you take the rest of the day off, Connie?"

I couldn't speak past the lump in my throat and simply nodded in agreement.

On the drive home, I cried—no—sobbed for twenty minutes until I reached the driveway to our house. Wiping away the tears with my shirtsleeve, I noticed Mark was standing in the doorway holding a basket.

"Oh, please, no more flowers," I murmured.

"No, honey," Mark blurted out, "I think you're going to like this!"

Through the cellophane wrap I saw a basket filled with delightful gifts: a pink-ribbon mug, herbal teas, fluffy pink socks, a lavender-scented candle, shower gel, bath crystals, and nestled at the bottom, a bathtub pillow and an inspirational, spiritual book.

"Who sent this?" I asked.

"It was on the back doorstep when I got home!" Mark replied.

I rummaged through the cellophane shreds hoping to find a clue, but there was none.

"Why don't you take a nice hot bath, while I fix supper for the boys," Mark suggested.

I made my way upstairs—swinging the basket in my hand—and plopped it down on the bathroom floor while I poured the salt crystals into the warm water, lit the lavender candle and blew up my bath pillow. The scent of lavender filled our tiny bathroom and I relished the luxury of the moment. While I lay there, I picked up the tiny book, opened it to the first page, and read the words, "I will never leave you or forsake you!" Tears trickled down my face while I let the soothing waters wash over me.

The very next day I called my friend, Sue. I had to know who sent the basket.

"Hi, Sue! Do you know anything about a basket that was sent to my house?" I asked. Sue knew everything about everyone—not in a busybody type of way—but she kept tabs on the neighborhood.

"Nope, haven't heard a thing about any basket," she said, gracefully. "How thoughtful though... I mean... anything is better than flowers—right?"

I called several friends and even queried a few local florists in the area, but no one knew anything about a "breast cancer" gift basket. It was as if it dropped right out of the sky!

For weeks I enjoyed its contents: sipping vanilla chamomile tea in my pink-ribbon mug, savoring the chocolate mint truffles that were hidden at the bottom of the basket, and slipping into a warm bath each night to the scent of a lavender candle. For a few brief moments each evening, I almost forgot that I had breast cancer. Long after the contents were gone, I had a mug, a beautiful wicker basket and a book of "God's Promises" which I read each day. I even started attending church services again!

Almost a year to the day that I received my cancer diagnosis, another basket was delivered to our home. There was message—printed on the front—that read: "Survivor Basket!"

Again, I called my friend, Sue. "Hey Sue, do you know anything about a basket that was delivered to my house?" I could hear her chuckle in the background.

"Why don't you just send them my way next time," she prompted. "I really think God's trying to tell you something. Maybe you should start your own gift basket company!"

"You know what, Sue?" I said. "I just might do that!"

It didn't happen overnight; in fact, it's been a little over seven years since I quit my day job and started Baskets Full of Hope for cancer survivors and their families. Hundreds of baskets have gone out to all parts of the country and each one with a special handwritten message.... "May this basket start you on a journey of faith, hope and healing!"

~Connie K. Pombo

The Strength of
Vulnerability

Nothing is so strong as gentleness, nothing so gentle as real strength.
~St. Francis de Sales

I have never used the words strength and vulnerability together before. Strength essentially means great power, and vulnerability is about being open or exposed. Somehow I had not thought the two words could go together, but recently I felt the strength of vulnerability through one simple act of kindness.

It was Thanksgiving weekend and my family had decided to have our turkey dinner on the Saturday night. I had to work until 7:00 p.m. so the plan was that my mother and husband would have the dinner timed for around 7:30 p.m. The mall was quiet that evening and I was able to lock the store right at 7:00 p.m. I gathered the garbage and as I looked forward to our family gathering, I did not even notice I had not taken my usual route to the garbage bins.

An agitated young man who had missed his bus stopped me. He needed a ride and if he waited for the next bus, he'd miss his curfew and his bed at the Salvation Army. He'd be forced to sleep outside and he didn't have a sleeping bag. He needed to get there before they locked the door.

The voice inside my head got very loud as the survival instinct kicked in and quickly reminded me of all the reasons why giving this man a ride was a very bad idea. My family was waiting, my cell phone had a 2 percent charge left on it, I might get mugged or raped and on and on. I asked him a few questions and even wished I had some cash on me, to send him off in a cab so that this problem would go away.

As these thoughts whirled through my mind, I looked into his eyes. I saw desperation, but more importantly, I saw a person. I saw him. I heard a small voice that quietly said, "He's someone's son." In that moment, I just knew I had to give him a ride. The embarrassing thing was that I couldn't even remember where the Salvation Army was.

He promised directions and offered to take the garbage bag I still held, while I called home to say I'd be another hour. As we drove downtown we chatted. He was trying to get clean and turn his life around. He got kicked out of the house he was living in. I told him to look into going back to school, unsure of what other motherly advice I could give him.

Eventually, he asked about me and found out that I was missing my Thanksgiving dinner in order to drive him. He began to cry. Perhaps his faith in humanity was restored in that moment; I don't know. All I could think of to say was "Don't cry for me, my dinner will be there when I get home and it's more important that you get your bed. If I was in your position, I'd want someone to help me."

Somehow I knew our roles could easily be reversed. His name was James. We made it to the Salvation Army on time and he had a place to sleep that night. I felt alive and our dinner was made more beautiful by sharing this story. Interestingly enough, if I had taken my usual route to the garbage, I wouldn't have this story to share.

I am not saying we should all run out and give strangers a ride. In this case, however, in finding the strength to allow myself to be a little vulnerable, I opened myself up to a life-changing experience. I made an important human connection that I wouldn't have made if I had taken the safe and fearful route.

~Mary Anne Molcan

Jet's Gift

Dogs are miracles with paws.
~Susan Ariel Rainbow Kennedy

It happened in the early autumn of Jet's first year. Our twelve-year-old daughter Joan had just been diagnosed with a rare and potentially life-threatening blood disease. In the hospital, bruised and weak from transfusions, she'd begged for a day's reprieve to go to the country with her parents and her black Lab pup, eleven-month-old Jet of Acamac the Third. After much deliberation, the doctor had agreed.

It was a gray September Sunday. We were packing to go home late in the afternoon when Jet, galloping joyfully after a squirrel, dashed into the path of an oncoming car. We heard tires squeal and the simultaneous screams from girl and dog.

When we reached the road, we found a deathly pale girl kneeling in the ditch, an immobile pup clutched in her arms. A distressed motorist stood over them muttering, "I'm sorry. He ran right out in front of me. I couldn't stop in time. Is he alive? Will he be okay?"

Jet was breathing, but just barely. We gently wrapped him in quilts and loaded him into the back of our station wagon. Joan crouched in the hatchback, holding the dog's head, whispering words of love and encouragement.

My husband kept glancing into the rearview mirror as we drove toward the city. Each time our eyes met, I knew we were both wondering what would happen to our fragile daughter if she lost her friend. The doctor had warned us against exposing her to emotional stress.

Sunday has to be the worst day of the week to find your vet. Ours was no exception. He was out of town, his answering service informed us. If it was an emergency, we were to call his retired predecessor.

That veterinarian was a kindly old gentleman. He took one look at our pup and declared there was no hope.

"Have Tom put him down when he gets back tomorrow morning," he said sadly. "It'll be best. He's paralyzed."

Joan expressed no emotion at his words, but her blue eyes turned sapphire hard. My husband and I both knew that look. She wasn't about to accept the diagnosis, not without a fight.

We drove home in silence.

"Put him on my bed," Joan said when we arrived. Her tone allowed for no argument or refusal.

When the pup was laid as comfortably as possible in the center of her bed, I turned to her.

"Honey, it's only for tonight. Tomorrow…"

"I don't want to hear it!" she cried, throwing up her hands to cover her ears. Her arm hit her bedside lamp and sent it crashing to the floor.

In an instant, Jet was on his feet, staggering, falling over the edge of the bed onto the floor. Leaning against the wall, his eyes glazed with shock, pain, and confusion, tongue lolling out of his mouth, the big pup stared up at us.

"He's not paralyzed!" Joan was on her knees beside him, kissing him, tears rolling down her cheeks. "He's going to be all right, I know it!"

An hour later, she was still cradling Jet in her arms when I gently broached the subject of her return to the hospital.

"Let me talk to Dr. Henry," she said. "He'll understand. He'll know I have to stay with Jet tonight."

Ten minutes later, she handed the phone to me.

"He wants to talk to you," she said, then hurried back to be with her pup.

"I've decided to let her stay home tonight," the doctor informed me. "She'd never rest away from him. But bring her in tomorrow for a blood test. I'm concerned about how all this stress is affecting her condition. And let's keep our fingers crossed for the pup. She can't afford to lose him at this point."

That night, girl and dog slept in a tangle of quilts and pillows on the living room floor. Early in the morning, we eased the big pup out of her arms and carried him out to the car. If he had to be put down, better to have it done before she was awake, before she had to say goodbye.

But our vet gave us wonderful news. After examining Jet, he told us he believed that with hospitalization and a lot of TLC, the pup could recover. How fully, Dr. Larsen couldn't be sure, but he believed the Lab deserved the chance.

Over the following months and years, the girl and her dog required much specialized care. There were lengthy periods of hospitalization for both. Jet lost part of one paw to infection and Joan needed multiple blood transfusions. Both had to take life much slower and more cautiously than the average girl and dog. But each time they beat their illnesses, life became just a little more precious to them. Struggling back to health, they were drawn inextricably closer in their quiet celebration of joie de vivre.

They even discovered there were pluses to their disabilities. At this reduced pace, they both had time to savor the hamburgers, to study the birds and flowers and bullfrogs along the way. Together they enjoyed summer showers, autumn sunsets, Christmas snowfall, and the first pussy willows of spring.

And what if one was a little too pale and the other walked with a limp? Their days were filled with the joy of lives full of precious moments, moments they might never have been granted.

Jet even managed to give Dr. Larsen a kind of partial payment for saving his life. As a result of his constant and compassionate care of the chronically lame Lab, our vet was given an award by *Pets Magazine* for outstanding service to a patient.

But that wasn't Jet's only gift to the humans in his life. His courage and cheerfulness served as a daily lesson on how to celebrate life to the fullest, no matter what its hardships. He and Joan linked their spirits in a desire to survive and celebrate life. And while we were busy pretending he was no different than other dogs, Jet was just as busy forever etching his memory into our hearts.

When he died at age sixteen, Joan, a young teacher by then with her disease in remission, was heartbroken. For days, tears and a crippling sense of lose overwhelmed her. Then a sympathy card arrived from a friend.

"That which you have cherished with your heart you can never lose," it read.

Joan recognized the truth in those words. Stoically she placed Jet's picture on her bedside table and found the strength to get on with her life.

She'd realized, like Ron and me, that although Jet was gone he'd never be forgotten. He'd been a joy and an inspiration all the days of his life. And he had helped Joan find an inner strength and positive attitude that I am sure not only led to his recovery, but also to hers.

~Gail MacMillan

Looking Out a Window

You cannot fully understand your own life without knowing and thinking beyond your life, your own neighborhood, and even your own nation.
~Johnnetta Cole

Following my mother's death after a long battle with breast cancer, my grief was so overwhelming that I stopped functioning for a while. At the same time, my husband's engineering business was struggling, and money was scarce. Christmas was approaching, and I wondered how we were going to buy gifts for our five children.

Two weeks before Christmas, my two walking buddies, Tami and Marian, showed up one morning with a beautifully decorated box. They urged me to open it right then. With trembling fingers, I did so. Inside I found treasure after treasure: exquisite handmade cards complete with stamps, a variety of fine chocolates, and two angel pins.

My eyes filled with tears as I took in the very personal gifts. Each was chosen with care, thought, and love.

The love my friends showed me during what had promised to be a dismal season reminded me that angels were watching over me. These angels appeared in the guise of friends.

Their loving gesture turned my attitude around. I found myself once again excited about Christmas, excited at the possibilities.

For the first time in months, I started looking outward rather than inward. My thoughts turned to others. What could I do to turn around the attitude of someone who was struggling just as I had been?

As my husband said, "You need to look out a window instead of in a mirror."

His words startled me. Was that what I had been doing? Staring in a mirror? Had I become so self-absorbed, so self-involved, that I had forgotten that others had problems?

The unfortunate answer was "Yes."

I resolved then and there to find what was positive in my life and to share that with others. I didn't have much money, but I did have time. I started to share that. I volunteered to take a seventyish widow in our church to doctor appointments and to the grocery store. I wrote cards to people who I knew were lonely and needed an extra dose of love.

My prayers were full of thanksgiving. I consciously counted my blessings and found them overwhelming. A husband who loved me. Sweet children who tried their best to help whenever they could. A group of devoted friends who were always there for me.

And then I did something that appeared to have nothing to do with building a positive attitude: I cleaned house. No, I don't mean scrubbing toilets (though I did that as well). I cleared out the clutter.

The clothes that no longer fit were sent to a charity thrift store. Books that had been read and re-read were donated to the local library for its yearly sale. Toys that the children no longer played with were given to a family with young children.

There was something freeing in cleaning out the clutter that had collected over the years.

Even as I was getting rid of unwanted items, I questioned my actions. Our family was struggling financially. Could we really afford to give things away? Should I save them for the garage sale I was always planning to hold? Shouldn't I be trying to make money?

The quiet peace in my heart was answer enough.

Cleaning out the physical clutter in my life prompted me to clean out the clutter in my heart. I made an effort to let go of old grudges and hurts. I worked to banish the obstacles that were holding me back from being the kind of person I wanted to be.

Can helping others and cleaning out clutter work for everyone in their quest of a positive attitude? Maybe. Maybe not.

But they, along with a pair of angels in sneakers and sweats, helped me find my way back to looking out a window rather than staring in a mirror.

~Jane McBride Choate

56

Unity in Goodbye

Only in the agony of parting do we look into the depths of love.
~George Eliot

When I learned that my story "Dry Her Tears" had been accepted for *Chicken Soup for the Soul: Family Caregivers*, I never dreamed that one of the main characters wouldn't see it published. Thankfully, I had given a draft copy to Lou to read before the submission deadline.

I felt so blessed when the story was accepted. It really struck me that a story is a legacy we leave to the world. I had not felt that connection on such a personal basis before. This particular story will always carry poignant memories for me. In summary, "Dry Her Tears" was about how Lou, my ex-husband, and I worked as a team to care for our twenty-three-year-old daughter after she broke both her arms and was unable to care for herself.

I am glad that my last written words about Lou reflected a caring bond not usually found among divorced couples. Interestingly enough, the story of our family in "Dry Her Tears" characterized the tone for how we would come together during the last month of Lou's life.

It had seemed like a coincidence—as I was leaving a regular medical appointment in late September, I ran into Lou leaving the urgent care facility, where he had been seen for horrible bronchitis and laryngitis. Over the next weeks, I often wondered how he was doing.

I was therefore surprised to answer the phone one day and hear a whispered, "Take me to the hospital." I didn't have to ask who it was. I jumped in the car, picked up Lou at his apartment, and raced to the hospital. In the emergency room, as scans and chest X-rays were performed, I promised Lou that I would not leave him alone. The chest X-rays revealed a large mass in his throat, and he was admitted to the oncology ward.

While we anxiously awaited the results, he gave me a look as if to say, "My lifestyle has caught up to me — I think my time is almost up." I will always remember the look of resignation in his eyes. I dreaded calling our son, Warner, who was already on his way home from Eastern Illinois to celebrate Rosh Hashanah, to tell him to come to the hospital instead of the temple.

Warner arrived just as the doctor was showing the results of the scans on a monitor. She told us that fast-growing tumors were compressing Lou's windpipe to a fraction of its normal size. This was why he could not talk and had such difficulty breathing. An oncologist and radiologist were immediately called in.

The doctor advised me to call my daughter Dani and her husband Craig in South Carolina and ask them to come immediately. The greatest danger was that the tumor would close the airway and Lou would require intubation, meaning we would not be able to communicate.

Later that evening, Warner gravely revealed to me that when I left the room, Lou quickly wrote out his last wishes. The last whispered words Warner was ever to hear were "I'm proud of you."

Dani and Craig threw clothes into their car and raced to Illinois. Lou's condition deteriorated during the night. He was given emergency radiation and breathing treatments and eventually his air pathway opened a little, but he was still critical. He clearly knew what was happening.

By the next afternoon, based on more scans, a biopsy, and two surgical consults, we knew that the cancer was rapidly spreading and the mass was inoperable. Lou was alert and we understood his decision to have only palliative radiation therapy. I called his office and the staff was shocked when they heard the news. He had been at work only a few days before and they thought he had bronchitis.

We made arrangements to move Lou to a hospice floor. Miraculously, although the diagnosis did not change, Lou seemed to rally and became more alert. He communicated more often by writing and sign language. Even though he was probably in terrible pain, he used pain medication very reluctantly so that he would be able to spend more waking time with us.

Just as when we had cleared our schedules to take care of Dani years before, we now closed ranks to form a tightly knit caregiving group. Warner took temporary leave from his teaching position and Dani and Craig took family leave at their jobs.

Lou was never left alone in the hospital. We all synchronized our schedules. I was so proud and grateful for the way Warner, Craig, and Dani worked together and shared responsibility for the myriad of details that constantly arose. We made sure that our visits overlapped and that we were all present at the hospital for dinner. At first it felt strange to be there as an ex-wife, but soon the title of ex-wife and ex-husband ceased to matter. My children's father was dying and I wanted to be there for all of them.

It had been years since we spent so much time together as a family group. It was an adjustment for me to let go of the reins and realize just how capable and grown-up my children had become. The circumstances that brought us together were undeniably sad, but what a gift we had been given to get to know each other in the intimate and close surroundings of a hospital room. How fortunate that we could let go of our past hurt in order not to lose any of the precious moments available to us.

Lou seemed to be at peace with his prognosis. For a while he was even able to eat. One night as we planned for dinner, he insisted that we go to his favorite restaurant, order what we wanted, and then bring back steak and lobster. He was not able to eat much of it, but the phrase "having a final meal" really took on a new meaning.

Lou was not a typical hospice patient and his relaxed, positive attitude, and sometimes bizarre jokes, helped all of us. Soon people from work heard that it was not depressing to visit and they stopped by often. One day Lou wrote that he thought people felt better after coming to visit him and I fully agreed.

During one of his visits the topic of writing came up with his co-workers. Lou wrote a note describing the story I had written about him and Dani, and that we were hoping it would be accepted for *Chicken Soup for the Soul: Family Caregivers*. He was very proud of the story.

It was twenty-three days from Lou's admission to his passing. Although we were sad to say goodbye to Lou, we were blessed to share the time together. We brought out the best in each other and ourselves as we adopted a positive attitude and forgave the past on this important family journey.

~Jean Ferratier

The Power of Positive

Chapter 7

The Power of Dreaming

Living Our Dreams

Nothing splendid has ever been achieved except by those who dared believe
that something inside them was superior to circumstance.
~Bruce Barton

By eighth grade, I still didn't know how to read. Putting a sentence together seemed like an impossible feat. My teachers gave up on me, writing me off as lazy or just plain stupid. I was told that I would never amount to anything, that I would end up living in a cardboard box and eating garbage for the rest of my life. I'm sure this was an attempt to scare me into trying harder, but all it did was add to my already horrible self-image.

Finally, while watching a movie about a boy who had dyslexia, I figured out what was wrong with me. I wasn't stupid after all! I just saw things differently from everyone else. All I had to do was train my brain to adjust what I saw, to the way the rest of the world reads. I saw all the symmetrical letters normally but I saw all the asymmetrical letters backwards. It was like going through life where everyone knew the secret code, and then suddenly figuring out the code on your own. It took me a few years to get used to it. Even now, in high stress situations, I still make mistakes.

By high school, I started working as a barista at Clarence Center Coffee Co. I thought it would be a cool, laid-back summer job. Boy was I wrong! The owner had traveled all over the world studying coffee, and she was going to make sure her baristas knew their stuff. We were given reading assignments and expected to pass weekly tests to keep our jobs! I was afraid my teachers were right. I would be fired from my first job because of my horrible reading comprehension.

Somehow I managed to pass her tests. Reading about coffee wasn't hard because I was interested in the topic! A few weeks later, I realized that I was the only one left from the original employees. For once I was good at something. It hit me one day while wiping down a table. "I could do this for the rest of my life and be completely happy!" I said to myself.

For the first time in my life, I set a goal for myself. I was going to own a coffee shop. Most people laughed at my pipe dream. I was used to being laughed at so I didn't care. I was going to accomplish this, or die trying.

At that time, the Internet started to become more accessible. Now that I knew how to read, I could search for anything I wanted! I noticed a hunger for knowledge begin to grow in my soul, specifically for coffee. Now that I knew how to read, I could go to college! That seemed impossible before. What would I major in? In 1998, the closest major to coffee shop management was hotel restaurant management. I applied to five colleges that offered the major, and I got into every college I applied to!

While attending Niagara University, I met my amazing husband. He had a dream of his own. He wanted to be a professional firefighter. He understood my passion and we supported each other at working toward our dreams.

As I went out for dinner or coffee with friends, they saw my attention to detail as I observed the quality and service experience. Most encouraged me to write, but I brushed them off. The thought of writing was impossible, especially the thought of being published!

By age twenty-six, I had an amazing job as a general manager running three hotel properties. My husband was the well-respected owner of a security company specializing in custom camera systems. We had a beautiful home, with the latest furnishings and electronics, drove fancy cars, dined at the finest restaurants, traveled frequently to exotic places, and all of our bills were paid!

Despite all of that, we were both miserable. We had become complacent. We were stuck in a lifestyle that lived up to everyone else's expectations, but not ours. Worst of all, we had given up on our dreams.

Spontaneously, we gave up everything we knew. My husband sold his business, I quit my job, and we moved to a different city to pursue our dreams.

Currently, we are the proud owners of Café Roche Espresso Bar in Winston-Salem, North Carolina. My husband is a firefighter for the busiest fire department in the Department of Defense.

After years of trying without success, within a year of our move, we were blessed with the birth of our first child and we are currently expecting another. Our dreams have come true, and we couldn't be happier.

I was asked to write for *Fresh Cup Magazine*, an international coffee publication! The fact that I am now respected among my peers as an industry expert, or that I could be published in an international trade publication, is beyond my wildest dreams.

~Sarah C. Hummell

58

I Have It

Dancing is like dreaming with your feet!
~Constanze

My sister had a small painted music box when she was little. It was white, with blue swirls along its edges and pink flowers in the middle. Inside the box, where no one could see, was a tiny dancer, one arm above her head pointing towards Heaven, the other resting on her white tulle tutu. I used to peek inside, opening the box just a crack to see if she danced while no one was looking.

At age ten, after years of begging, my parents signed me up for ballet class. The ballet studio was on the first floor of a historic two-story bank building on the main street of Fishers, Indiana. My classmates and I changed clothes in the old bank vault, hiding in the shadows of the foot-thick green metal door, propping our dance bags on the tilted, rusting safe. I wore black ballet shoes and a hot pink leotard that said "Ready, Set, Go!" on the front. It was not exactly a professional ballerina's attire, but I felt just as beautiful as the music box dancer.

Most professional ballerinas begin dancing at the age of three. By the age of ten, many are already doing triple turns and are wearing their first set of pointe shoes. I got nauseous attempting one turn and my splits were more like the width of a cartwheel (which I couldn't do either). But I loved the way the piano boomed from the record player, filling the small studio and my body with a beat. If I couldn't embody the music in my moves, at least I felt it, as if I too expanded to fill that wooden room.

We danced as the cars splashed by in the rain, as the snow pelted down, as the sun set behind the butcher shop across the street. After class, my best friend Cathy and I would wait on the sidewalk for our parents to pick us up. As the cars flew past unnoticing, we danced with the light poles as our partners, doing turning jumps down the sidewalk in the lamplight. I spun through junior high and high school.

After graduation I moved to New York City and stopped dancing. Well, I never stopped completely; I danced every night in my tiny apartment. The galley kitchen was long enough for an arabesque, the living room was wide enough for turns, the boxy white walls thick enough to hold my music just like my sister's white music box. I was the lone dancer inside.

I was intimidated to take dance classes in the big city, where there were bound to be professional dancers in class. I remembered stories I'd heard of New York classes: "In New York City classes, dancers will run right over you if you're in their way" and "Teachers in New York don't slow down to teach combinations, either you learn quickly or you leave." I didn't stand a chance. That's what I told myself, but nightly, in my dreams, I was dancing. Sometimes you pursue a dream; sometimes it pursues you.

When the planes crashed that September, less than a year after I moved to New York City, I rethought my policies on everything and wrote a "Things to Change" list. I had to dance. If the classes were hard, then they were hard. If the people were mean, then they were mean. I would go anyway, I would dance. I had to try, to dare to do in life what I did so easily in dreams.

I was nervous stepping into my first New York class, but when the music began to play I got that old feeling back — the studio was where I belonged. Much to my relief, the rumors were wrong about New York City classes — the dancers didn't run me over or look down on me; they were actually friendly. They were right about the teaching method though — the combinations were taught quickly and I struggled to remember the steps. I'd left my dance body back in the Midwest — my New York body was shaky, but mostly unsure — of my ability, my appearance, my strength.

I spent months feeling pathetic until I decided that after each class I would think of ten things that went right. My tendency was to think of everything that went wrong, in dance, in life, but I determined if I could think of ten good things, well, ten is a big number when you're used to thinking of zero. If I could come up with ten good things, then it proved that it was a good class. On the subway, I'd number them — be they minute or huge; I could always come up with ten.

But still I wasn't free — I was in the back of the room, fixing my eyes on everyone else, relying on them. I never felt confident enough to enjoy the classes the way I did when I was little, dancing in hot pink, not caring who noticed. That is, until one hot New York summer night. I was taking a class in a thunderstorm. The studio was not air-conditioned, so we threw the unscreened windows open and let the stormy air flow in. The combination was long and I, as always, was unsure of myself. We danced three at a time, me trying to hide my 5'8" average-build body behind the skinny, petite dancers in the front. I focused on them, the way their doll heads tilted, the direction their trained feet were taking. I barely heard the music; I was just trying to follow their movement. After we danced, the next group went on, and I went to the back corner of the room. I was annoyed at myself for having fat thighs and frizzy hair and never remembering the combination. My dance teacher walked to the back of the room where I was panting. She gave me the best advice of my life, saying, "You have it. You just have to believe that you have it." This took me aback. I have it? Me? Could it be true? As I listed the good things that happened that day, the first was, "I have it."

Since that class, I've tried to believe her words. I pried my eyes off the other dancers and instead looked inside. Most of life is spent trying. But sometimes I've had moments in class where I forget that there are other dancers, where my breath matches the beat so that when I'm done I believe "I have it."

I may never be a professional dancer, not even in the chorus, but I will no longer be a dancer in my dreams only. Nor will I confine myself to dancing in the tiny white box of my apartment. Now I believe that "I have it."

~Kerri A. Davidson

Pinstripe Dreams

Keep true to the dreams of thy youth.
~Johann Friedrich von Schiller

Ask a classroom of eight-year-olds what they want to be when they grow up and you'll hear they plan to become astronauts, professional athletes and scientists. Nothing is impossible to a child.

Ask the same question to a high school junior or senior and you'll get a much more practical response. Seems that getting older prompts us to reel in our dreams, trading them in for more realistic pursuits.

My oldest, however, a high school junior, is very specific about his career path. He intends to wear a pinstripe suit to work. No, he's not planning a career in business or law. He will complete his pinstripe ensemble with a pair of baseball cleats. He plans to play shortstop for the New York Yankees. He told me so when he was ten years old.

Therein lies my dilemma. At age sixteen, he's still a dreamer. Just like his mother.

At ten, it was okay to nurture those dreams with inspiration like, "You can be anything you want to be as long as you believe in yourself." At age twelve, you applaud all-star achievements and keep the scrapbook up to date. But somewhere around fourteen or fifteen, most kids begin to cut themselves from the team. They realize their limitations. Reality sets in. Sometimes, their parents even help them to this conclusion.

I started to question my eternal optimism and support for my son's dreams after I ran into a former Little League mom. She said that her son wasn't going to play baseball anymore. This was a kid I loved to watch. Not because he was the best on the team, but because he played like he loved the game. When I asked her why he was giving it up, she said she encouraged him not to play anymore. A loving and protective mother, she wanted him to pursue something that would enable him to enjoy more success.

When should a mom help redirect dreams, if at all? What if your child holds on to dreams well past the expected age? Do you protect him, as my friend was doing, or encourage him to go for it?

I knew early on that I enjoyed writing, and dreamed of bestsellers and book tours. I imagined myself signing stacks of books and being interviewed on talk shows. I knew the odds were against me. Everyone has a book idea. Few ever make it into print. And, the bestseller list? I'll probably win the lottery first.

But my parents always encouraged me. They were, and continue to be, my biggest fans. Their years of support gave me the courage to put myself in the vulnerable position of being rejected as an author. And I was, over and over again.

But guess what? One of my books did get published and the publisher sent me on a coast-to-coast book tour. They put me up in fine hotels and provided a driver and an author escort to each TV studio and radio station. The best part: writing my book led to an appearance on NBC's *Today* show. There I was, being interviewed by Katie Couric in Studio 1-A in Rockefeller Center. I was living my dream.

The bestseller thing is still probably out of the question. I mean, realistically, the odds are against me. But it sure is fun pursuing the dream.

Shortly after giving birth to my future Major Leaguer, I came across a powerful quote. It read: "Successful is the man whose mother is his greatest fan." I promised then to make that my motto.

I think I'll stick with it. Like my parents stuck with me. Next time my son looks to me for encouragement, I'll steal a line from Thoreau: "Go confidently in the direction of your dreams. Live the life you've imagined."

I hope my son makes the big leagues. If he falls short, well, so be it. It'll have been a great ride. If he makes it, I will revel in the missed opportunity to buy him a tie to go with those pinstripes.

~Kimberly A. Porrazzo

Postscript: The author wrote this essay ten years ago. Her son, now age twenty-six, never played baseball in college, but was hired by the San Francisco Giants in 2010 as a video scout. That year, his first year working in baseball, the Giants won the World Series and he received the ultimate prize in baseball: a World Series ring.

Open Your Books

Never, never, never give up.
~Winston Churchill

From the time I could line up my dolls on the sofa and play school, I wanted to be a teacher. "Open your books," I would instruct my teddy bear, dolls, and sundry stuffed animals. Then I would regale them with whatever new thing I had just learned. Every grade accomplished during my own education intensified that desire. From cursive writing to "new math," from home economics to world literature, I knew I wanted to join the ranks of the magical people who made the world come alive for me. I wanted to be a teacher.

The most inspirational teacher I ever had was my high school biology teacher, Coach Hogan. He was all business on the football field but pure passion in the classroom. Biology came alive in his class (no pun intended, though I think he'd like the joke). He opened my eyes to a world beyond the reaches of my troubled home life. He made me believe that science was fun and intended for everyone. I decided to follow him and become a biology teacher myself.

But how? Dreams and aspirations are one thing, money for tuition is quite another. My father was disabled so finances were challenging. Though I graduated seventh in my class of 400 and was accepted at a state university, I couldn't afford to go. In fact, no one in my immediate family had ever graduated from college. But I believed

I was meant to be a teacher. My heart and my childhood dolls told me so. I had to find a way to make it happen.

I won a partial scholarship but it wasn't enough to cover all the tuition. Then my parents offered me my portion of my father's Social Security disability. I could live at home for free and use the money to attend the local junior college. I was humbled by the depth of their sacrifice because the dollar amount was almost a third of their income. However, I still needed more to cover books and supplies. Undeterred, I found a part-time job and enrolled in classes, believing it was meant to be.

Before long, my life consisted of little more than school, studying and work. I decided to try and finish my degree in three years—the sooner to have a job and paycheck. So I took large class loads, sometimes over twenty credits per semester, and continued my studies through the summer sessions. I hid my textbooks under the cash register at work so I could study when there weren't any customers. Sleep deprived, I napped on my break. All the while I pushed forward, seeing myself in the classroom, imagining my interaction with students, and believing I could make it happen through faith and hard work.

Even dates with my boyfriend entailed trips to the library or studying at home. There was little time to waste. During spring break, the extra hours available for work were too precious to spend in the sun, though I lived in a coastal beach town known worldwide as a major spring break destination. When I graduated from junior college and transferred to a four-year university, the higher tuition meant I needed more funds. So I added a work-study regime to my schedule, cleaning test tubes and setting up labs in the science department. Sometimes I felt like a marathon runner without a finish line. But then I would remember that every dirty test tube I cleaned meant I was one step closer to my dream. I couldn't wait to start making magic in my own classroom.

Because of my student teaching requirement, my graduation month was December. I'd have a few months to work as a substitute teacher in the local area before the schools started hiring for the next academic year. It seemed a great opportunity to scope out the job market. I had never heard the term "RIF" before.

"County Teachers Affected by a Reduction in Force," read the local headline. In short, there was a drop in student population and many teachers were laid off. No new teachers would be hired until all those who lost their jobs were placed. I couldn't believe it. Disheartened but determined, I continued substituting, hoping a break would come my way. I took a long-term substitute position in biology at a private school and felt like I had found a home. When I learned they were planning to replace the biology teacher I had subbed for, I was sure the position was meant for me. I could see the pieces falling into place. I could see myself in the halls. I could feel the chalk in my hand. This is where my journey was leading. However, the principal had other ideas.

"You're too young," he told me during my interview. "This last teacher was young and had a lot of discipline problems. We want someone older — with more experience."

"I don't believe age determines how well someone can conduct a class," I responded quickly. "It's about technique and skill," I replied. And magic, I whispered to myself.

"I'm sorry," he replied. "My mind is made up. Good luck to you."

I cried all the way to work that night and was in the break room trying to pull myself together when a new employee walked in. Her name was April and it was my job to train her. We introduced ourselves and got busy learning how to take catalog orders over the phone. In the moments between customers I shared my feelings. I told her how much I wanted to teach. I told her how much I loved that private school and how disappointed I was to be turned down because of my age. I told her I was having a hard time believing I had worked so hard for my dream only to be denied. I told her about the magic.

A few nights later a man walked into the store and April introduced him to me as her father, Reid Hughes. We chatted about the store and how quickly April was learning her new job. He casually mentioned that April had told him I wanted to teach. I assured him that was true and shared some of my thoughts with him. He left after a few minutes and I thought April was lucky to have such a nice father.

The next morning my phone rang. It was the principal of the private school calling to offer me the biology position.

"Are you kidding?" I was dumbfounded.

"No," he assured me. "I'm not kidding. It seems you made quite an impression on the chairman of our Board of Directors."

"Who, h-h-how?" I stammered.

"His name is Reid Hughes, and he wants you to have this job."

I was speechless.

A few weeks later I stood in the door of my classroom, welcoming my students to their first day of school. When they were settled, I picked up a piece of chalk, walked to the board and wrote my name.

"Let the magic begin," I whispered to myself as I turned back to greet their expectant faces.

"Open your books," I said with a smile.

~Liz Graf

Living the Dream

You can have a laugh in Los Angeles, or you can weep in Los Angeles,
depending on your attitude towards it.
~Miranda Richardson

I was about ten years old. I spent a lot of time day dreaming, like most children of that age. One thing that fascinated me was California, particularly Los Angeles. Being from a small town in Nova Scotia, I was amazed at the big city, the fancy houses, and the celebrity lifestyle. I would look in the phonebook for country and state area codes — 323 was one of the area codes for Los Angeles. When nobody was around I would get on the phone and dial 1-323 then seven more random numbers. Sometimes the call would not go through but then I would try again until somebody answered on the other end. When the person said hello I would say, "Hi, is this LA?" They would say "Yes" and then I'd hang up.

Just knowing that for that moment I was talking to someone from Los Angeles made me happy. I made so many calls to LA that I remember one day when I was sitting at the kitchen table my dad walked in from work with papers in his hand, slammed them on the table and said "Angela, your calling LA days are over." Turns out that I had called so much it ended up costing my dad a lot of money. I don't know exactly how much, but obviously it was enough to tick him off.

I always imagined that when I got older I would "live in LA with the stars." A lot of my family knew this. They thought it was cute and sometimes they would even make jokes about it. I didn't know when or how I was going to get there. I just knew for certain that I was going to leave my small town and live out my dreams in Los Angeles.

When I was graduating from high school, one of the first universities I looked at was UCLA. I soon realized that going to a school in a different country was not going to be easy. The tuition was higher, the admission requirements were different, and things were a lot more complicated, so I ended up settling for a school close to home.

I did not know anybody that lived in LA and I did not have the money to take a trip there on my own, but I never gave up hope that one day I would get there. That day came when I was twenty-four years old.

I had taken a summer job in Vermont working as a camp counselor. My roommate, Diana, was from Hungary. Over the summer we became great friends and in September, when camp was over, Diana asked me if I wanted to join her on a trip to visit her friend in Santa Barbara. I was ecstatic. I couldn't believe that I was finally going to California. We would stay with her friend in Santa Barbara, then head to Hollywood for another week before going home. Well, that was Diana's plan (and the one I shared with my family and friends). I, however, had a different idea.

I told my family that I wouldn't be going home from Vermont and would be going to California for a few weeks. They were a little disappointed but were happy for me that I would finally get to see LA. What they didn't know was that I had only bought a one-way ticket to Los Angeles. I did not know what I was going to do when I got there, but I knew that I was going to stay there for a while.

California was everything I had hoped. I belonged here. I ended up landing a "dream job" as a nanny in a gated community in Calabasas, down the street from Jessica Simpson and Nick Lachey. I lived in a million-dollar home, drove Escalades and Mercedes, lounged in the amazing back yard with a pool and hot tub, ate at posh restaurants, had everything paid for — gas, food, vacations, etc. — and still got paid weekly. It was even better than I had imagined — except that the "dream job" turned out to be not so glamorous and only lasted seven months.

I went from living with the rich and famous to waiting on the rich and famous at various restaurants. I overstayed my visa (did I mention that setback?) and could not travel to Canada because I would not have been allowed to re-enter the US. Luckily for me, I met Ehab and we fell in love, got married, and fixed all the immigration issues. As I write this, my husband and I have been together for six years and married for three and a half. I've been calling LA "home" for seven years.

My life in LA has definitely had its ups and downs and it's not always glitz and glamour, but I am living my childhood dream. I wanted this with every ounce of my being and I made it happen, through a combination of hard work and a positive attitude. I always knew I would end up in LA and that it would be right for me.

~Ange Shepard

There's No Ceiling On Dreams

If you can dream it, you can do it.
~Walt Disney

I f you walked to the end of the hall last year and peeked into my classroom, you would have seen lots of clouds hanging from the ceiling. Suspended by fishing line and paper clips, they'd swing in the breeze. And on each cloud was a dream.

Oh, I admit, I stole the idea from another teacher. While attending a summer workshop at another school, I sat in the room and admired the paper clouds floating above us. Each one had "I dream of becoming a lawyer" written on it, or something similar, along with a student's name.

Visually, they were appealing. The blue marker outline of the puffy poster board clouds against the stark white added some colorful interest to the classroom. At times, they swayed and twisted gently. When the fan was clicked on, some of them rocked wildly back and forth, threatening to careen into each other.

As a third grade teacher, every year my room was decorated in a different way. Sometimes, the changes were subtle—a new motivational banner across a wall or a different bulletin board to display the students' work. Sometimes, the change was radical and encompassed the entire room. One year I transformed our classroom into a tropical rain forest. Vines hung from the fluorescent lights, a green "canopy" of trees hung from the ceiling tiles, and towering tree trunks were taped to the wall. The next year, we learned surrounded by the African plains.

Those puffy-shaped pieces of paper made me positive of one thing: when September hit, we'd begin the school year by publicly proclaiming our dreams. And I was determined those dreams would float us through the next nine months together.

During a class meeting in early fall, my third graders and I talked about their aspirations. We talked about what happens when people squash things—when we step on an ant, what happens to it? When someone puts the kibosh to our excitement, how do we feel? When people shatter our hope, does that help us reach our goal? Then, I asked the students to dig deep and unearth their dream. What did they want to be when they grew up? Where did they see themselves in twenty years? What did they hesitate to say out loud about their lives?

A couple of my kids wanted to be a doctor. One wanted to be a teacher. Several students voiced their desire to be a professional basketball player. Everybody got a piece of posterboard, and their wish was markered onto the cloud.

Even me. I signed my name under, "My dream is to be a published writer." It was a desire I'd had for over four decades. Besides, what kind of example would I be setting if my kids were expected to bare their souls, but not me?

There were times during a science or social studies lesson that someone would refer to the clouds, such as "My goal is to be a vet. Do you think Abe Lincoln dreamed of being president when he was our age?" We spoke of historical figures and the obstacles they faced when attaining their goals. In class discussions, we examined evidence of persistence in famous people. With classes in the past, when I sent off a writing submission and got a rejection letter, I would share it with my students, letting them know that those letters that said "no" were proof I had not given up. I was still trying. This group was no different.

In December, I got an acceptance letter. My picture book

manuscript was going to become a book. My story about a stray dog was going to be published by a small, independent press. I was beyond ecstatic. Sharing the news with my class, we all celebrated. It was as if the clouds were all connected; when one of us succeeded in reaching our goal, it formed a positive force field to protect all of our dreams.

Soon, the illustrator will be finished and the layout will be complete, and my book will be printed and bound. And when you see it on a bookstore shelf, pull it out, and turn to the page with the acknowledgments. Because there, you'll see all twenty-five of my students named, along with an expression of my gratitude.

We all had a cloud hanging from the ceiling. And I firmly believe that if I had failed to put my vision out there—alongside my class—I would have failed to reach that goal. You can't make it come true if you aren't willing to say it out loud.

~Sioux Roslawski

Lessons in Line

The indispensable first step to getting the things you want out of life is this: decide what you want.

~Ben Stein

Recently I was standing in line at the state university bookstore. I find myself there periodically for game gear and various sundry items I can't find elsewhere to cheer on the college team.

This day the line at the checkout counter was several people deep and into the aisle. I was in the middle of it. Ms. Perky Cashier had her fingers dancing across the keys of the cash register faster than my eyes could follow. They seemed to have a Caribbean beat as she punched in merchandise codes and prices for each customer. She was clever, witty and fast. She had the situation under control. She didn't need a second cashier. Although the people in line didn't talk much to each other, they smiled and seemed pleasant about the short wait till their turn.

Still several customers back, I was close enough to hear the conversation when a young man moved up to the counter with his dad. Ms. Perky Cashier took his purchases from his hands and set them on the counter. "You hardly seem old enough to attend the university," she said smiling. She had excellent customer service down to a science.

The young man was pleased she'd noticed. "Well actually I'm not old enough," he said. "I'm only a kid. But my dad here said that maybe I needed an incentive, you know, a carrot." He pointed to the quiet older man on his right elbow. "You see," the kid went on, "I am just in high school so I have two years left before graduation. I really want to go here after I graduate. My dad says I will have to work really hard to get in." Unlike his father, the kid had no clue as to the fight he faced.

The young man had tripped over the word "incentive" and it was clear he was not a high-performing student. This was not the class president, high school valedictorian, or some political or business go-getter. This was a regular kid who had been passed over a lot because he didn't sparkle. He gave the impression, though, that he was hard working and sincere.

Ms. Perky Cashier's fingers danced again across the keys as she typed in the codes and prices for his really nice T-shirt and a hoodie in the university colors. She hit the subtotal and the register added the tax for her.

"Is there anything else you need?" she asked as her fingers stopped. She made eye contact with both the father and son while noticing the customer line had lengthened considerably. "Well," said the father shyly as he slowly raised his hand from his side. "It's not so long until I will be needing this, so I will just get it right now." He laid a university car-window decal across the sweatshirt Ms. Perky Cashier had folded on the counter. The kid smiled so wide it seemed his face would crack. He must not have seen his father pick up the rear-window sticker while they were shopping for gear.

The people in line turned away, their eyes moist. Even if this kid didn't get into college he would always know his father believed in him.

Ms. Perky Cashier was also taken back by the tenderness of the moment. Her fingers moved slowly across the keys as she added in the additional purchase and called out the amount due. The cash register yawned open. She regained her composure and put the items in a plastic bag with the university logo on it. The dad handed her exact change that she put into the open mouth of the register and shut it.

Taking the handles of the plastic bag, she again made eye contact with the kid. "Well, young man," she said. "We will be seeing you soon then." She spoke as if she expected to see him later in the week to buy books for this semester's classes. The kid thanked her and moved towards the door with his father behind him.

"May I help you?" she said to the next customer. But no one moved up to the register. The line of people was staring after the father and son, sensing the price of their own goods had just included a free parenting lesson.

~Pamela Gilsenan

The Tunnel

There is light at the end of the tunnel.
~Proverb

When I was a young boy there was an abandoned train tunnel near our farm. It was a magical place to play.

The tunnel had been blasted through a granite hill in the 1850s so a narrow gauge train could reach the gold mines. The inside of the tunnel was black from years of coal smoke from the trains.

It could have been a dark, scary place but I knew every inch of it. I loved taking my friends to play in the tunnel because I was familiar with it and felt very brave.

"Don't be scared," I'd tell my friends in my most manly nine-year-old voice. "The tunnel is dark and long but as soon as you take your first step into the tunnel, you are already on your way out of the tunnel."

I didn't realize it then, but the lesson I learned about the tunnel would carry me through some dark, difficult times in my life. When a problem arises, as soon as I take the first step to face it, I'm already on my way out of the problem.

My family lived in bone-breaking poverty on a farm that was nothing but weeds and rocks. The old farmhouse was barely standing and we joked that the only thing holding it up was the termites holding hands. The roof leaked and every time it rained we'd have to put buckets and pots and pans throughout the house to catch the drips.

There were many nights we went to bed hungry.

I dreamed of growing up and buying a beautiful home for my mother and my sister so they'd never be cold or hungry again.

When I was twelve I promised my mother that when I was a man I'd buy a castle for her. I hung a picture of a castle next to my bed to inspire me. My dream had become my goal.

Only one person in my family had ever graduated from high school. No one had ever gone to college.

I was determined to be the first person in my family to get an education.

When I was seventeen I graduated from high school and enrolled at the local university.

I was a full-time student during the day and worked a full-time job at night. I was lucky to get four hours of sleep a night.

I went to a community college, using that as a springboard to go to two colleges. I then went to work for Wal-Mart for a year. I saved up enough to go on to get my master's degree with honors.

On Thanksgiving Day I had dinner with my mother and my sister and I walked through the train tunnel one last time. I packed my belongings, including the picture of the castle, into my twenty-year-old car and left for Seattle to make my fortune.

Jobs were scarce and instead of making my fortune I ended up working temp jobs unloading fish and cleaning offices. This wasn't my dream.

There are times in life when everything goes wrong. Just when I felt things couldn't get any worse, they got worse. It was as if one day I was on top of the mountain and the next day the mountain was on top of me.

The date on my calendar read March fourth. I smiled and took it as a sign. I'd gotten bogged down and discouraged but now it was time to "March Forth!"

I'd almost forgotten about the tunnel. I'd almost given up half-way through and stayed in the darkness.

I reminded myself that anything bad or negative that comes into my life today is already on its way out and problems have a life span... they don't last forever. No, not all problems are easily solved, all hurts are not quickly healed, but things change every day, solutions appear, answers are found and help comes from unexpected sources. Even though it is a cliché... there is light at the end of the tunnel.

I chose a new direction and became a realtor. In a year I'd saved enough money to send my sister to the university. She tried three majors, became the first female to get a stage-craft degree, and went on to get a master's degree herself.

I'd kept my promise to help her.

The picture of the castle still hung on my wall. I still had one promise to keep.

I worked harder but not for the money. I worked to buy a home for my mother.

I'll never forget the day I took my mother to the house I bought for her and handed her the keys. No, it wasn't a castle, but it was a beautiful home. She said it was the happiest day of her life.

I think it was also the happiest day of my life.

My mother and my sister now had security. Our family would never be hungry or live in poverty again.

I love my life. Every morning when I wake up I'm excited about the possibilities waiting for me. I know boyhood dreams can come true and the impossible is possible. I know the greatest motivation for success is to succeed so you can help others.

If you ever feel you are in a dark tunnel... just keep walking until you see the light.

~Aaron Stafford

The Power of Positive

The Power of Challenging Yourself

Oh Chute

You gain strength, courage and confidence by every experience
in which you really stop to look fear in the face.
~Eleanor Roosevelt

"Oh God, please don't let my kids see their mother go 'splat,'" I prayed, as I signed the waiver to release responsibility from the instructor, the pilot and the airstrip.

My co-worker Carly turned to me. "You know, we thought you might chicken out."

"Couldn't. Didn't rain, so I thought I should go ahead with this."

"Your fear of heights won't get in the way?"

"Nope." Yeah, that sounded confident.

Divorce, a forced job change, and moving in with family made me believe that my life was one big failure. And failure caused me to be fearful. Fearful to trust. Fearful to live.

Except where my children—my life's joy—were concerned. They inspired me to keep striving.

My teenagers, Toni and Andy, sat with me as I viewed a video on what to expect when skydiving, listened to an instructor, and walked through a dry run.

"Mom, can we ride in the plane?" Andy, my adventurous four-teen-year-old son, wanted to share in the glory. "Look, we can wear parachutes, too." He pointed to a sign that showed the rules and the rates for non-skydiving passengers.

I looked at my sixteen-year-old daughter Toni. "I don't want to jump out, Mom." She waved her hands in front of her like "no way."

John, my instructor, walked up, "Can't. Not legal." He turned to me. "They have to be at least eighteen to jump. But they can ride along in the video plane."

Andy jumped up and down a little. "Please, Mom? Please, please, please?"

How could I say no to an adventure for him when I planned to skydive? I didn't want the kids to learn fear, too.

Before the plane took off, John hooked his harness to mine. "I want to show you how strong these harnesses are." He placed his hands on the plane's open door frame. "Now, lift up your feet."

I resisted.

"Either trust me, or you can't go up."

I obeyed. True enough, I dangled.

"You need to trust that the harnesses will hold down here, before you trust them up there." He jerked his thumb up.

Plus, he had the parachute.

I looked out the small window as we climbed to ten thousand feet and thought about how pessimistic I had become after so many setbacks. Losing my parents. Losing my marriage. Losing my job. Losing my house.

"I can't give up now. I've got to show Toni and Andy that when life goes wrong, you can choose to make it go right." I wiped my sweaty palms on my jumpsuit. "I must conquer my fear."

The Cessna's engine roared and my focus turned back to the skydiving. I looked around the inside of the small plane. Old green shag carpeting covered the floor. Another instructor with his charge sat close to the wide passenger side door. I sat behind the only chair in the plane, the pilot's. John, my instructor, sat facing me. We didn't talk due to the engine's loud rumble.

So, I whispered a thankful prayer. "God, I can't believe I'm doing this."

A minute later, the wide-mouth door opened, and wind gushed

in. I shouted in my head a panic prayer: GOD, I CAN'T BELIEVE I'M DOING THIS!

The first team left without ceremony.

"Do you still want to do this?" John shouted over the engine's noise. Maybe he saw panic on my face. Maybe my face was pale.

To be honest, I did feel queasy.

My voice failed me, so I nodded vigorously. I put on my helmet and pulled the goggles over my eyes.

I then kneeled so John could hook up to me at the shoulders and hips. We then moved in tandem, on our knees, to the door.

"Oh my gosh, I see nothing but sky—don't panic now." I sucked in air and went swimmy-headed. "I can't quit now."

John motioned to put my hands next to his on the door's frame. After placing his left hand and foot on the plane's wing structure, he motioned me to follow his movements. Auto-obedience kicked in.

He motioned for me to pull my knees to my chest. Next, he wrapped his arms and legs around me.

I didn't see what happened next, because I had my eyes closed.

Then I thought about how I had saved for three months to pay for this adventure. I wasn't going to experience it blind. I opened my eyes and saw the plane fly overhead, then sky, and at last earth, as we rotated to be in the correct position. My arms and legs waved in the air as John released me from his grip.

In mere seconds John and I freefell 120 miles per hour. I could only hear wind roar past my ears. Ah, the freedom. While gravity pulled us to earth, I did not have the lose-your-stomach feeling.

John tapped my hand, signaling me to pull my arms in again. When I secured myself, he released the parachute.

The jerk of suddenly going from 120 to 80 miles per hour pulled hard on my harness. I had harness pain in places I care not to share.

However, peace replaced the pain in seconds.

I saw our plane fly silently far around us. There was no sound from the cars on the small freeway nearby. A bird flew past. The only noise was from the air filling the rectangular parachute's bafflers.

No other noise. Save for my heartbeat pounding in my ears. I could see the curve of the horizon. The air smelled sweet.

"So, what do you think of skydiving now?" John asked.

I couldn't speak. Overwhelmed by the total freedom and beauty in creation, I held up both thumbs.

He took my hands and placed them on the parachute handles. I pulled the right handle, we spiraled down right. Then spiraled left.

John's voice startled me out of my revelry. "Nancy, get ready to pull your feet up." His hands replaced mine on the handles. "Now, as I pull, lift your feet until I've landed."

I nodded. But then I jutted my feet out prematurely and knocked John off his perfect landing course. We went rolling in the mud. The parachute's cords tangled. We were muddied.

Toni and Andy reached us first and doubled over with laughter when we stood up with no injuries. My co-workers soon joined in with finger-pointing and good-natured ribbing.

I didn't die in a plane crash. I didn't go "splat." I didn't die of embarrassment. I didn't even wet myself.

In less than five minutes, I found courage and hope.

Even with a crash landing.

~Nancy Lombard Burall

We Talked Good

When we are no longer able to change a situation,
we are challenged to change ourselves.
~Victor Frankl

It was the last day of Philadelphia's *Evening Bulletin*. Once, nearly everybody read the *Bulletin*, according to a cartoon that ran for years in *The New Yorker*. On a grim day in February 1982, we milled around in the newsroom, saying goodbye to our fellow reporters and editors, telling each other we'd keep in touch, yet knowing it wouldn't be the same.

For twenty-five years my identity had been tied to my career. I was Gunter David of the *Newark Evening News*, *The Baltimore Sun*, *The New York Times*, for which I covered Newark and vicinity on weekends, and finally the *Bulletin*.

I had seen this day coming as circulation figures dropped. People were no longer reading two papers a day. They read the morning papers and got the evening news on television.

A year earlier I had begun looking for another job. But no newspaper wanted to hire a fifty-one-year-old man. Now here I was, with nowhere to go, nothing to do. The morning after the paper folded I woke up on time to get to the newsroom. My wife, Dalia, was leaving for work. Our daughter, Ronni, was heading for the school bus. I stayed in bed for a week.

Thereafter I got a job as a reporter on a new weekly paper. My former contacts in City Hall no longer returned my calls. The new editor had not been on a newspaper before. I had difficulty concentrating on my work. A story that once would take me an hour or two to write now occupied me all day.

I soon realized I was suffering from depression. I sought help from a psychotherapist about whom I had written an article some months earlier. She specialized in helping people with difficulties at work.

Once her interviewer, I became her patient. Matilde Salganicoff helped me cope with the enormous changes in my life, deal with what I considered a humiliating comedown. I had covered the Yom Kippur War of 1973, interviewed David Ben-Gurion, Israel's first prime minister, wrote stories that sent Newark's chief magistrate to jail, testified before a U.S. Senate subcommittee, and was nominated for the Pulitzer Prize.

With Matilde's help I saw the positives in my life—my wonderful wife of thirty years, my children, our friends, our home, and the years of joy that had been mine as an award-winning newsman. "Most men live lives of quiet desperation," Thoreau had written. I learned that despite what had happened to me, I was not one of them.

After several months in treatment, I had an epiphany while driving to my session. I burst into Matilde's office and said, "I want to do what you do!"

"You'd have to go to graduate school," she replied. "Then, if you get a job, you'll have to start at the bottom." Dalia and I talked it over. She agreed to support my decision. We would invest my severance pay from the *Bulletin* in my new career.

Matilde helped me get into Hahnemann University and Medical School in Philadelphia, where I was accepted even though I had never taken a psychology course. I enrolled in the family therapy program and would be awarded a master's degree at the end of two years.

On the first day, I attended an orientation in the school auditorium packed with new students. They were young, with fresh, shining faces. I had just turned fifty-three, yet I was one of them.

In addition to attending classes I was assigned to a clinic to obtain practical experience. For the first few weeks I "sat in," observing

Steve, my supervisor, at work. Abused women. Violent men. Major depression. Suicide attempts. Schizophrenia. Manic depression. Day after day I asked myself if I could ever help these people. Had I taken on more than I could handle? Would I ever graduate and get my degree?

So it was until Steve assigned to me the case of a woman, Millie—not her real name—who had been in treatment with him for a couple of years. He felt she had progressed enough that it was safe to transfer her case to me.

The chart said she was thirty-nine years old, although she looked considerably older. "You're new here," she said solemnly.

"I am new in the field," I replied. The words had slipped out of my mouth, even though Steve had told me to keep my background confidential.

Millie's face lit up. "What did you used to do?" she asked.

I told her.

Over the following months she told me all about her life—her alcoholic father who beat her mother, her alcoholic boyfriend from who she had run away more than once, her suicide attempts. Sometimes she cried, and I would feel tears in my own eyes.

We worked on straightening out her life. But there were some setbacks. A few times Millie was a no show. No appearance, no phone call. Under clinic rules I was not permitted to contact her. I sat soberly in my office and waited, wondering if I had failed her.

After a while the absences declined. Eventually it was time for us to part. I was completing my year at the clinic. Millie was making great progress, had broken up with her boyfriend, and had gotten a job for the first time in years. She no longer needed to be in treatment.

At the end of the final session she handed me a small, knitted white dog atop a crocheted blue pillow. "I made it for you," she said, smiling. "You and me, we talked good."

After graduation, the head of the program, Dr. Ivan Boszormenyi-Nagy, took me into his private practice. A few months later I was hired by Johnson & Johnson for the corporation's Employee Assistance program. I saw employees and their families, and at times, their supervisors. I served four different J&J companies in Pennsylvania and New Jersey. I also continued to work in Dr. Nagy's practice.

At times, in my sleep, I dreamt about the newsroom. When I woke up, it would take me a moment or two to reorient myself. At a *Bulletin* reunion one of my former colleagues asked how I was doing. "It's not easy, but I'm getting there," I said.

The years went by. I was fortunate in being able to help many people. Among them was an employee about to be laid off because of his poor work performance in recent months. After a few sessions I referred him to a physician, who discovered he had a brain tumor.

Now it was time to retire. Toward the end of my tenure, this man, tumor-free and newly promoted, arrived at my doorstep with a goodbye present.

Two golden pens and a small, round clock were attached to a base on which the following words were carved, "Thank you for being there. Nick."

They greet me daily when I rise.

~Gunter David

67

The Roller Coaster

Panic at the thought of doing a thing is a challenge to do it.
~Henry S. Haskins

My mother claims I was born with a positive attitude. My friends have called me Pollyanna and my husband says I am the most optimistic person he has ever known. There may be some truth in what they say, but what none of them realize is that maintaining a positive outlook sometimes requires a little self-imposed psychological warfare.

For example, when I had completed the required coursework for my doctoral degree, I still had a major hurdle to face before I could begin my dissertation project. I had to pass a qualifying exam. I learned in April my exam was scheduled for the first week of July.

This exam would be unlike any other test I had ever taken. The exam was designed to bring all of my coursework and experiences together. It would consist of three questions. On Monday I would report to the examiner's office. There I would leave everything I had carried with me: my purse, backpack, notebooks, everything. The woman proctoring my exam would hand me a sealed envelope and lead me to a room with a computer. The computer would not have Internet access. I was to open the envelope, read the question and type my response. I was allowed six hours for the first question. My assessors obviously expected a thorough answer. Once I finished my response, the proctor would print my file and seal it in an envelope.

Tuesday and Wednesday I would follow the same procedure, except these would be "easier" questions, requiring only four hours each.

My committee would then read my forty- to fifty-page exam responses. A few weeks later a hearing would be held and I would be required to defend my answers.

How do you prepare for such an exam? I began to doubt my ability to achieve my educational goals. Maybe I wasn't meant to enter the realms of higher education. Maybe I should give up. Those were not the thoughts of Pollyanna.

The test weighed heavily on me for the next few weeks. April's rainy weather yielded to the sunny, warm days of May, but my disposition remained cloudy and dark.

The first Saturday of May my husband and I traditionally took our three daughters to Kings Island, a local theme park, to enjoy the shows and rides. I would ride the merry-go-round or the tilt-a-whirl. If it was a hot day I could sometimes be coaxed into riding what my daughters called the "baby flume" but I avoided roller coasters.

As a child I had a very bad experience on a roller coaster. Up until this particular spring I had been able to avoid riding roller coasters of any size, since I could use the excuse of having a young child to watch. This year, however, even my youngest daughter had reached the magical height necessary to ride the major rides. I had no excuse.

As we stood in line at the park entrance, I realized my thoughts were not on spending the day with my family or the beautiful summer-like weather. Instead I was worrying about two things: the pressure I might face from my children to ride a roller coaster that very day, and the upcoming qualifying exam two months away. I was afraid of both. I made a decision right then to ride a roller coaster. If I could overcome the fear of the roller coaster I could surely overcome the fear of the exam.

"Other people ride roller coasters and live to tell about it," I reasoned with myself. "If other people can do it, so can I. And if other people can pass a qualifying exam, I can too."

That day I rode every roller coaster in the park. As I plummeted toward the earth on the last coaster ride of the day, I threw my arms up in the air. "I love this!" I shouted into the wind.

Two months later I walked confidently into the testing process. After the successful defense of my exam documents my advisor congratulated me. "You always seem so confident and positive," she told me.

"Not always," I smiled, but inside I was throwing my arms up in the air and shouting, "I love this!"

~Rebecca Waters

68

In the Cards

Confidence is contagious. So is lack of confidence.
~Vince Lombardi

I remember how I felt when the idea hit me: thrilled, certain and ready!

It was in algebra class, the spring of my junior year. Football season was long over, and a long way away. We had done well last season—qualifying for the playoffs for the first time in school history—and I wanted us to do even better next year, my senior year. But how? Then the idea hit me. I didn't wait till after school. During my lunch break, I drove over to a print shop and ordered business cards with a simple, direct prophesy—

"BOONVILLE PIRATES—1974 STATE CHAMPIONS!"

When the cards were printed, my teammates and I distributed them all over town. Teachers pinned them to classroom bulletin boards. Merchants taped them in store windows. Pretty soon those cards were everywhere. There was no escaping them, and that's what we wanted. We wanted our goal to be right in front of us, for all to see, impossible to overlook, no matter where we went.

Although we faced skepticism, it only served to strengthen our conviction to make our dream a reality. Our school had never won a state title in any sport—we were determined to change that history.

By the time football practice started in late August we were focused. That sense of direction and unity made us a closer team. From day one we gave more in practice, paid more attention to detail as we executed assignments sharply. With our goal imprinted in our minds and hearts—"BOONVILLE PIRATES—1974 STATE CHAMPIONS!"—we marched through the season undefeated and stepped into the playoffs with a sense of destiny.

The first playoff game matched us against a powerhouse team that was riding a twenty-eight-game winning streak. We knew we were in for a fight, but as the intensity of the game increased, so did our determination. We won, pulling away in the second half. That win brought us to the brink of our goal, a matchup with the defending state champions for the title.

We went into preparing for the big game with the same calm intensity and focus we'd shown as a team all season. Then it started to snow. A huge storm blew through and school was canceled, roads were closed, and transportation systems shut down. Still, every member of the team made it to the school gym and we practiced for the biggest game of our lives in tennis shoes.

Our coach received a phone call before practice the night before the game telling us that state officials were thinking of canceling the game and declaring co-champions because of the severe weather. We were asked if we would accept such a decision. "No way," was our response. This was our year. We were not going to get this close and not take a shot at the title.

On Saturday, we arrived at the stadium to find the field buried in snow. The goal posts stuck out above a six- to eight-inch blanket of snow. Someone asked if snowshoes would be allowed as legal equipment. Undaunted we dressed for the game and began our warm-ups.

Frustration grew as both teams struggled to a scoreless first half. Slip, slide, fall down, dropped pass, missed blocks, fumbles were all either team had accomplished. There was a growing sense of urgency that time was running out on our dream.

In the locker room at halftime, Coach Reagan reminded us of all we had been through to get to this moment. Then he reached in his pocket and pulled out the card. Right there in front of us once again was our vision. "Do you want this?"

Playing conditions were as tough the second half as they were the first, but our determination didn't numb out with our fingers and feet. We scored thirty-four points in the second half on the same field we couldn't score any on in the first half. Our yearlong dream became reality:

"BOONVILLE PIRATES—1974 STATE CHAMPIONS!"

And yes, I still have my card.

~Tom Krause

Captain Courageous

Courage is doing what you're afraid to do.
There can be no courage unless you're scared.
~Edward Vernon Rickenbacker

"My treat. Would you like to go with us to Maui?" It was a question along the lines of "Would you like a million dollars?" and, from George Clooney, "Would you marry me?" The answer, of course, should have been an immediate yes. Of course I would go to Hawaii with my mother and stepfather.

But... my mom wasn't proposing we take a ship from California to Hawaii. And the only other way to get there was by airplane, or as I'd taken to call it, "The Agent of Death." I'd been afraid of flying for the past twenty-five years, ever since I'd had a particularly turbulent flight on the way to London. After that, I'd watched the news of plane crashes with horror. I'd listened, alarmed, to my brother's story of how his plane plummeted thousands of feet. I'd made my decision. If I had to go somewhere, I would find some other mode of transportation, or not travel at all.

Sure, it made for a reined-in existence. But at least I'd be safe, right?

The truth was, my reluctance to fly was only part of a gradual shift in my life from being a typical fearless child to a scared adult. As a child and teen, I swam competitively, wrote and submitted stories, played tennis, attended sporting events and plays, and traveled extensively. I'd tried snow skiing, jet skiing, snowmobiling, and snorkeling. I'd spent time with friends, gone out to dinner and to parties. Now... well, I stayed home a lot.

Why had I become frightened to live my life? The reasons were plentiful. My parents divorced right when I was beginning high school, an already turbulent time. A couple of years later, our house was robbed twice, and I received numerous phone calls from a man saying he was "coming to get me." Like many women, I had trouble with relationships, and had a hard time finding that "special someone." Then I did find him, but he tragically passed away. I'd come to believe that good things just didn't happen to me and that the world was filled with danger and heartache. To avoid it, I would just stay home or do things which made me feel safe.

But here was the opportunity for something good, really good. I was being asked to go to Hawaii, one of the most beautiful and peaceful places on earth. So why couldn't I just say yes?

The next few months were fraught with indecision. I checked out books from the library about flying and how to relax on a plane. They just made me more anxious. My brother offered to talk me through exactly what happens and why air travel is so safe. This frightened me even more.

Then, someone tried to break into my bedroom while I was sleeping. I scared him away but it took me a number of weeks to recover from the shock. It was just another indication that the world wasn't safe.

Before I knew it, it was March, and the trip was just ten days away. Would I conquer my fear? Or would I just stay home?

Though not convinced I would be safe, I started acting as though I was going. I arranged the time off from work. I told friends and family I was going. I was going to do it.

The big day arrived. We had an early flight, so I got up at 4:30. We drove to the airport. We boarded the plane. My heart rate picked up, but I was still all right. Then the plane started moving down the runway, faster and faster. I held onto my mom's arm. We took off. I had done it!

Landing was even easier, as was the flight home—after a lovely vacation that I will never forget. I had conquered my fear.

Afterward, I was asked how I had, seemingly so easily, gotten over a fear I'd had for twenty-five years. The best answer I could give was the quote from Ambrose Redmoon: "Courage is not the absence of fear, but rather the judgement that something else is more important than fear."

It was true. I had found something more important than fear. And I knew then that I would carry that attitude through the rest of my life.

~Carol E. Ayer

70

How I Got My Wings

Our greatest glory consists not in never falling,
but in rising every time we fall.
~Oliver Goldsmith

An enormous black curtain hid me from a buzzing crowd. Artistic directors from ballet companies around the world, benefactors, parents, and supporters of the arts shuffled into the Peter Jay Sharp Theater, anticipating a spectacular performance. At seventeen, this night was the moment I had been training for my entire life. It was my first Workshop performance at the School of American Ballet and I had the honor of dancing a lead role. I stretched and warmed up my feet backstage. Beads of sweat trickled down my forehead. My heart was beating so rapidly I thought it would pop out of my chest. I said a little prayer as I heard my cue in the music.

A rush of adrenaline shot through my body as I bolted from the wings and took my place at the center of the stage, with the corps posed behind me. I told myself, "Just go for it," and started my first variation as the Russian Girl in George Balanchine's world-renowned *Serenade*. I pushed off the floor as hard as I could and flew into the air. I started to come down for my landing on one leg, preparing to jump again, but my foot slipped out from under me and I fell, face-first. The entire audience gasped as my body smacked the stage. Backstage, other dancers ran to the wings to see if I was hurt, if I was going to get up.

For a moment I couldn't move. I was utterly humiliated. My hands began to shake and I contemplated whether I should even get up to finish my variation. It seemed like I was lying there for ten minutes, but it must have only been a couple of seconds. Trained for thousands of hours over more than a dozen years, my muscles ignored the hesitation of my mind and I found myself back on my feet. I finished the variation and left the stage. Suddenly short of breath, backstage I tried to keep my balance. I was lightheaded and felt like a fifty-pound weight had been dropped on my chest. My friends rushed to my side to see if I was okay. I bent over a table, fighting back tears, trying to breathe. I didn't want to go back onstage to finish the last twenty minutes of the ballet. I wanted to take off my costume, hang it on the rack and leave the theater. I didn't deserve a lead role. I was a complete failure.

I slowly got enough strength back in my body to drag myself to the wings for my next entrance. As I wiped away tears, one of my best friends gave me a hug and said, "The worst thing that can happen on stage is to fall. You've gotten it over with, so what's left for you to lose? You have nothing to be afraid of anymore. Just go out there, give it your all, and live in the moment." At that instant, I realized that everyone falls down in life. If you dwell on the fall, you will be stuck on the ground and never get back up.

I went back onstage and completely let go of myself. I felt free, without a single worry. I just danced. I danced without holding any-thing back. I let the music grab my heart and guide me through the movement. This was a sensation I had never felt before. After the show, the exhilaration dissipated and my disappointment returned. I had fallen during the most important performance of my life. Then my mentor, the great Balanchine ballerina Suki Schorer, ran up to me and told me it was the best she had ever seen me dance. "Balanchine used to love it when his dancers fell," she said, "because that meant that they were really going for it."

I learned that day that falling is scary, and sometimes it seems like it is easier just to stay on the ground. But if we never get up, we never experience what it is like to fly. Now, as a Principal Dancer with the Los Angeles Ballet, I think about that performance every time I stand in the wings waiting for my cue. I want to be an artist who has no restrictions, completely abandoned to the passion that takes over my dancing. The fear of falling shouldn't keep us from living life to the fullest. We fall down when we try our hardest. There is no shame in that, only pride. And we can learn to get right back up.

~Allyssa Bross

71

Finding Myself on Route 50

Inside every older person is a younger person wondering what happened.
~Jennifer Yane

For a man, the "Big 5-0" is a wake-up call. It's the one birthday where he finally realizes that maybe — just maybe — he isn't going to accomplish all of the things in life that he had hoped. Personally, I'm still holding out for that NFL draft pick.

So there I was, with August 8, 2009 — my fiftieth birthday — staring me right in the face. I asked myself, "What can I possibly do to celebrate the 'Big 5-0'?" Then it hit me. How appropriate it would be to drive across the country on U.S. Route 50!

I began planning my cross-country drive in late 2008. It involved a lot of weekday evenings and Sunday mornings spent on the Internet, searching for every tidbit of information on Route 50 that I could possibly find. Eventually, I had to buy a brown accordion file to hold all of my data.

But, alas, men make plans and God laughs. In the middle of January 2009, my body had a train wreck that resulted in an agonizing stay on the couch for an entire week. Thinking that I just had a severe case of the flu, I remember very little of those seven days — except for constantly begging God to deliver me. Finally, I threw in the towel. Maybe... just maybe... this wasn't the flu after all.

I called Bill, a friend from the gym, and asked him to take me to the local emergency room. There, they discovered that my blood sugar level was 889 milligrams per deciliter! I was diagnosed with Type 1 diabetes, which normally manifests in childhood. More importantly, I had been within inches of a diabetic coma, or possibly dying from undiagnosed, untreated diabetes. I spent the next twenty-four hours in the intensive care unit, followed by four days in the hospital as they tried to rein in my runaway blood sugar.

I must admit that I was disillusioned. For all of my life, all I had ever heard concerning diabetes prevention was diet and exercise, diet and exercise, diet and exercise. That would fend off Type 2 diabetes, which occurs later in life. So I figured that I had diabetes licked because diet and exercise were my middle names! However, I never counted on Type 1 diabetes, with my body's immune system attacking my pancreas. The spring of 2009 can best be summed up in twelve words—a long, painful climb back to where I used to be. Thus, I decided upon an ulterior motive for my cross-country drive. I had to prove to myself that I was still a normal, healthy male capable of living a normal, healthy lifestyle.

On Tuesday, June 9th, I departed Hilton Head Island, South Carolina, in a rented Dodge Caliber with the following ground rules:

1. I would remain on U.S. Route 50 for the entire drive. I would not travel on an interstate highway, except for the beltways around Washington, D.C., Cincinnati, St. Louis, and Kansas City.

2. I would only deviate from Route 50 for short distances to see historical sites and unusual, off-the-beaten-path Americana.

3. To maintain my level of fitness, I would do a hike or a bike ride every day.

4. In accordance with my diabetes regimen, I would not miss

any of my twice-daily insulin injections, or any of my twice-daily finger pricks to test my blood.

5. I would not take a laptop computer or a cell phone.

6. I would not stay at a chain motel.

7. I would not eat at a chain restaurant.

The late morning of June 11th found me in Ocean City, Maryland, where U.S. Route 50 officially begins. Risking life and limb, I stood in the middle of four lanes of traffic on Route 50, faced west, and snapped a picture of a green sign overhead that read "Sacramento 3073 miles." Then I hopped into my rental car, said "Let the games begin," and put her into drive.

In the early morning hours of Saturday, July 4th, a thunderstorm rumbled through Nevada's Great Basin National Park. My pre-trip homework had told me how beautiful the night skies are at Great Basin due to the lack of human-produced ambient light, so I had nestled into my sleeping bag atop the picnic table, anticipating a classic display of stars. I interlaced my hands behind my head, looked up to the heavens, and said, "Okay, Nevada, show me your best!"

Just then, a thunderclap sounded over my left shoulder. I shook my head and said, "No way. This can't be the one night of the year when Great Basin National Park has cloud cover." Thunder sounded again, and then a single raindrop hit me on the forehead. Minutes later, I was forced to grab my belongings and scramble back into the Caliber as a magnificent thunderstorm raged through the park.

Curled up on the reclined driver's seat, I mumbled, "Jeeesh, I guess it can be the one night of the year when Great Basin has cloud cover." But I soon realized more than that, for this thunderstorm was far more spectacular than any display of stars I would have seen. As lightning flashed and rain pummeled the car, I felt so diminutive and insignificant. I also felt guilty. In this wonderful world that God had created, Type 1 diabetes was small potatoes. Certainly, it was a cross that I could bear.

Eventually, the morning of Tuesday, July 7th found me in West Sacramento, California. Again risking life and limb, I stood on the narrow right shoulder of Interstate 80's six lanes of traffic, faced east, and snapped a picture of a green sign: "Ocean City, MD 3073 miles." Mission accomplished!

I had driven across the country on U.S. Route 50 to celebrate turning fifty. I had followed every one of my self-imposed ground rules to the letter. I had proven to myself that I was still a normal, healthy male, capable of living a normal, healthy lifestyle.

~John M. Scanlan

They Said I Couldn't... But I Did

Your dreams can be realities.
They are the stuff that leads us through life toward great happiness.
~Deborah Norville

Rita walked out of my office and left me sitting there with my mouth hanging open. She had no idea that what she'd said would change my life.

"You're really good at this. If you ever get tired of accounting, you could make a full-time living as a writer."

Tired of accounting? I was way beyond that. I had totally hit the wall in my chosen profession. But my college education and years of experience were invested in accounting. I wasn't sure how else to earn a decent income, not to mention that I was raising a teenage son alone, and I had a mortgage to consider. I thought I was stuck.

For a couple of months I'd been helping out with the company newsletter, writing articles here and there. Right away I started getting calls from co-workers, telling me how much they liked my stories. I enjoyed the kudos, but the idea of making money as a writer never occurred to me. Then came Rita, with her kind words, and I could think of nothing else.

That very night I started looking into the possibilities. At that point I was just looking for a diversion and a little extra income. Other than writing novels, which didn't appeal to me much, or working as a newspaper reporter, which I did not want to do, I wasn't sure how to make as money as a writer. Maybe I could write and sell some articles to magazines.

I spent hours searching online, but back then, the resources for writers were sparse. I did learn two key things. First, I needed some published clips if I was to be taken seriously, even if the clips were small. Second, the best policy was to write what you know. Publishers want people who can write with authority based on experience and/or knowledge. The problem was, who wanted stories about the joys of a balanced budget or the naughty truth behind straight-line depreciation?

I kept looking. Then one Saturday I stumbled onto a new e-zine that wanted articles. It was called *Parenting Troubled Teens*. I glanced at my son, asleep on the couch at two in the afternoon, and I knew I had something to say.

I hammered out a story in only thirty minutes, edited it a couple of times and hit "send." Before the day ended, the editor had purchased it for twenty-five dollars. I was hooked. Not only was I getting paid, but people would read my article and may be helped by it.

I joined a local writers group and found a lot more resources. I loved telling them how I'd sold the first story I ever submitted, though never again would it be that easy. Even so, that first sell was enough to capture my heart and soul. It was also enough to help me sell a few more small pieces here and there. The money was puny and the "sales" were hard to come by. But eventually they added up, giving me some credibility with publishers.

I began to talk about my desire to someday quit my day job and make a full-time living as a writer. But everyone, including my friends with publishing experience, said it was a pipe dream. "Unless you're the next John Grisham or Nora Roberts, it can't be done." It's not like I was trying to become fabulously rich as a writer, though I wouldn't turn it down! I just wanted to leave my accounting job, write full time, and ideally, do it from my home.

I wasn't ready to leave my day job yet, but I believed with enough hard work, I someday would. I'd found a quote that drove me on.

"Luck is when preparation meets opportunity." So I prepared. I kept my eyes wide open for opportunities, and in time, I found more and more.

A content mill paid me to write ten articles a month for decent fees. In the time I worked for them, I gained hundreds more published clips, and built credibility on many different topics.

My biggest thrill came when I submitted a family story to a contest, and won five hundred dollars and the lead position in an anthology. Most of my writing was non-fiction, and I enjoyed that. But having a family story—a story close to my heart—published in a book felt like an enormous blessing.

I'd heard about a woman who edited for a living from her home, so this interested me. I checked with the local community college and found an online editing class and signed up. This way I could add to my writing-related skills, and possibly add another stream of income. If nothing else, it would improve my own writing. After I finished the class, I used my newly acquired knowledge to edit thesis papers for PhD students who couldn't afford an experienced editor. Later, I helped a psychologist edit a humor book.

My skills were building, and my clips were mountainous. Still, I wasn't ready to leave the security of my day job. Perhaps I never would have done that, until I was pushed. One day, my boss called me into his office to tell me my job was being eliminated. I was petrified. I had no way to fully replace that income. And the only thing worse than staying in that job was the fear that I'd have to start over elsewhere, still as an accountant.

As it turned out, the push was exactly what I needed. I got a generous severance package that gave me time to get my bearings. Out of fear, I did apply for available accounting jobs, but in spite of excellent qualifications, I never got a single nibble.

With time on my hands, I wrote and edited even more, preparing myself, and looking for opportunities. My Internet searching turned up an ad for a person with an unusual combination of skills. An online business newsletter needed someone with paid experience as a writer and editor. Nothing odd about that. But they also needed someone who understood accounting. Most accountants avoid writing, so this had been a hard position to fill. That is, until they found me. We were perfect for each other.

Not only did they want me to write and edit for them, but they wanted me to do it from my home, on salary, with benefits. They were headquartered three thousand miles away, but that was no problem since every employee worked from his or her own homes. As it turns out, that company and I were made for each other. That was eight years ago. I am still with them, as an author/editor, and I can't imagine a more generous, upstanding employer.

I also continue to write freelance in the evenings. I've been honored to have numerous family stories published in well-known anthologies and other publications. I'm not rich in dollar figures, but in the satisfaction of my work, I'm fabulously wealthy.

Everyone said I couldn't do it… but I did. Whatever your dream, hold tight to it. Figure out how to prepare, then watch for your chance, because "luck is when preparation meets opportunity."

~Teresa Ambord

The Power of Positive

Chapter 9

The Power of Self-Improvement

Saved from Myself

Make the most of yourself, for that is all there is of you.
~Ralph Waldo Emerson

I grew up in New York City. I was very shy and had no friends. One day, a new boy appeared in my same class. Butch was funny, and a mediocre athlete like me. We had fun and he made me laugh. I was only happy when we were together. The rest of the time I was miserable. Both my parents suffered severe mental illness, which was a tough way to grow up. My sister over-achieved, while my efforts seemed poor. I envied her, making matters worse.

It was the sixties, and soon Butch and I became potheads. Only his stuff lasted for weeks, while I consumed mine in days. I knew I had a problem. My parents found out and took me to my mom's psychiatrist. I stayed silent because I was afraid. By age sixteen I was a liar and thief. I was put in a drug program. I was glad to be out of school, but now my friend Butch was gone too.

A year later they packed me off to a place called Phoenix House. To me it was like prison. I was the only white Jewish middle class kid. Surrounded by a hundred hard-core heroin addicts, most of whom came from the ghetto. Phoenix House did "treatment" in group settings. There was an awful lot of screaming, cursing and crying. It terrified me. Without even trying, I'd get into trouble constantly, which made me the object of ridicule. After thirteen months I ran away, with nowhere to go. Humiliated, I went back home. Dad said I could stay if I went back to school or got a job. I chose going to work.

I landed a job at *Time* magazine as a copy boy. This was the lowest and least respected rung on their corporate ladder. So I made believe I was a staff writer, living a fantasy. Before long the drugs returned, now pills and cocaine were added to the alcohol and marijuana. *Time* paid me $165 a week, not enough for my habitual drug use. I figured out a scheme to embezzle a couple of hundred dollars per week. Naturally I got caught and unceremoniously dismissed. The parting words from the Assistant Managing Editor: "You're lucky I don't have you put in jail. Don't ever set foot inside this building again!"

The years flew by and I went from job to job, always getting fired for one reason or another. Simultaneously I moved through romances that never lasted long, and were defined by verbal abuse and neglect. It only got worse.

By 1980 I was homeless, living on the streets of New York. Begging for nickels and dimes, I'd buy cheap wine or beer just to get through the day. Sometimes I'd hang around a park or playground because I knew there were likely to be drugs there. Standing alone, many times a stranger would say, "Hey man, you want to get high?" It was like that in those days, and I'd quickly take advantage of anything offered. When darkness came I'd find a bench at a bus stop, making certain to be in a heavily populated area. But I feared closing my eyes in the city that never sleeps. If you've never been there, let me assure you, that's really true. It was also true that I was afraid of getting mugged or worse. The streets are violent and dangerous. Staying awake all night, sometimes I'd ride the subways, looking for a transit cop nearby.

By late 1986, the only thing I was sure of was my name, and Jay Berman nearly died. Not the first time either, because I'd overdosed or attempted suicide more than once. Quite a few trips to psychiatric hospitals, medicated to keep me under control, sometimes put in a straitjacket. Like all addicts, I was my own worst enemy. A most unoriginal phrase described my reality. In mid-winter that year I was dying of frostbite. My home was the street, with snow and ice on the ground. The temperatures had dropped into the teens, one of the worst New York winters on record.

Then something happened that I still cannot explain. A taxi driver I'd never seen before pulled his cab to the curb. He literally picked me up in his arms and put me in the car. The guy took me to his apartment, laid me on the floor upon a bedroll of blankets, and told his wife he'd be home after his shift. She fed me and gave me hot coffee. Then she disappeared into her bedroom, leaving me alone on their living room floor.

Fast forward to January 1987, the guy buys me a plane ticket to Fort Lauderdale- Hollywood airport in South Florida. I stayed clean for a while, got a job at *The Miami Herald*, did well at first, but fell back into my old ways. I wound up destroying two more romantic relationships, and what might have been a promising career. By 1992, I was back on the streets, homeless and helpless. Several more trips to mental wards took place until it finally came to an end. I was never a religious person so when people spoke about "angels" I thought it silliness. But who were that taxi driver and his wife, who appeared as if out of a dream? Now in Florida, how did my family, who I'd not spoken to in years, decide to get me the help I desperately needed? Rehab, total strangers at AA meetings, therapists and renewed family ties all came to my aid. They did so without my even asking!

I am now celebrating twenty years of complete abstinence. I am still Jay Berman, who couldn't look people in the eye, and today I share the gift of life with so many wonderful people. I have a son who makes me proud and fills my heart with joy. My residence is nice, safe, clean and filled with good neighbors. My days are spent reading and writing, going for walks, at the library, cooking, cleaning, and paying the bills on time. The evening is time for meditation, some exercise, and socialization with kind and loving people. Most weekends are spent with family. Now I know about "angels," and I know I've been blessed. Today my job is helping others, which in turn helps me. Do you believe in miracles? I do.

~Jay Berman

74

Maintenance Required

*Good for the body is the work of the body, good for the soul the work of the
soul, and good for either the work of the other.*
~Henry David Thoreau

The yellow light flashed on my dashboard, illuminating the
words: Maintenance Required. "I don't have time for this," I
stewed. "I've got two jobs, a family to take care of, dogs to
feed, exercise to get in, I don't have time for this. When can I
squeeze in a four-hour window without the use of my car?" I crumpled
the foil from the sandwich I'd eaten as I sped along the freeway.

For days I drove with the light illuminated and flashing.
Normally after a couple of minutes it would relent and turn off, as if
to say, "Okay you might not want to listen, but I'm warning you..."
But the next morning when I headed for my hour-long freeway drive,
the light came on and stayed on. It stared me in the face day after day
gloating, glaring, and never going away.

I felt frazzled, juggling a new job that had me driving all over the
city, eating in my car, and toting heaps of files with me. I was never
good with paper organization and now piles mounted and papers
slipped out of folders. Other piles accumulated and not just the lit-
eral ones, like bills and clothing, but the metaphoric ones as well. I
was drowning in my "to-do's" and this "Maintenance Required" was
putting me over the top.

I remember the last time I let the "Maintenance Required" light
flash a little too long and ended up stranded on the roadside, only to

be towed to the dealer and charged a whopping bill for repairs on an engine that could've been serviced by an oil change.

The light now had my full attention. It was obvious I was going to have to change my entire day. As a contract therapist, I am only paid for the clients I see, so canceling my appointments was going to cost me, but so would ignoring the light. As I searched for my cell phone to call the office, it rang from the depths of my purse. My client had called to cancel his appointment.

I made it to the dealer in time to drop off my car. I had at least four hours to "kill." And then it struck me, why would I ever want to kill this time? It was a gift I could never recover. I thought about waiting at the dealer, but that seemed like punishment. My car needed maintenance and so did my soul. I found out the dealer offered a shuttle ride that could drop me at a mall. Although I had no interest in shopping, I knew that the beach was about a mile from the mall. I had my sneakers, my iPod, and my phone so I set off on my adventure.

I discovered that everything, including waiting and distance, seems shorter and closer when I mentally use the word "only." It would only be four hours and I would have my car again. The beach was only a mile away.

I plugged in my iPod and grounded myself with the meditative chants from my yoga class. Then I listened to the self-help and motivational tapes that I'd heard before, but suddenly heard in a new way. As I walked, I dug my toes into the soft wet sand. I breathed in the salty fresh ocean spray. I felt the warmth of the sun and the gentle caress of the breeze. I was feeling so renewed and peaceful I almost felt guilty.

What a brilliant idea those carmakers have, I thought. "Maintenance Required." If only we came with such a light.

My phone rang. It was the dealer letting me know my car was ready an hour early.

"So soon?" I inquired. "Will it be okay if I come in a couple of hours? I'm still working on a little maintenance of my own."

~Tsgoyna Tanzman

75

The Day I Took Control

Dieting is not a piece of cake.
~Author Unknown

I tugged the jeans over my hips and yanked up the zipper, the effort leaving me practically breathless. Then I stood back and looked at my reflection in the dressing room mirror. Flesh spilled over the waistband. I checked the tag. The jeans were in my usual size. Probably just improperly cut, I reassured myself. Yet, when the zipper on the next pair of pants I selected would not so much as budge, I had to step back and admit the cold hard truth to myself—my weight was, once again, out of control.

My struggle with weight started long before, as my mother would say, when I was first introduced to cookies and milk. I mean, who could pass up something like that? A warm chocolate chip cookie straight from the oven washed down with a cold glass of milk? Or what about an oatmeal cookie filled with plump, sweet raisins? And don't even get me started on those brownies: plain, frosted, or the kind I had recently discovered behind the glass case at that specialty market, crafted with a soft peanut butter filling.

I just couldn't resist such goodies, though I tried. Many, many times. Through a combination of various diets and sheer willpower, I had dieted myself down to an acceptable weight a number of times through the years. Liquid, high-protein, low-carbohydrate, calorie counting, and point system diets, I had done them all. In fact, I was practically a weight loss expert.

What I wasn't, however, was a maintenance expert. After reaching my goal, the weight would eventually return. When I found my heart palpitating as I climbed stairs, or felt an ache in my knees, or was unable to pull up a zipper, I would revisit my cycle of diet and weight loss followed by overeating and weight gain. I knew this was a dangerous cycle. Yet while I had all the skills I needed to lose the weight, I lacked those I needed to maintain the loss. Invariably, it seemed, I always backslid in my efforts, lured by my love of sweets.

There in that fitting room, my flabby reflection stared back at me, disgusted. I huffed and puffed as I pulled off the jeans and put on my own clothes. I assessed what I saw above my double chin: dull hair, pallid complexion, circles under my eyes — all telltale signs of poor health. I looked bad. But worst of all, I felt bad inside and out. I lacked drive. Frequently I passed on social invitations because I didn't have the energy. And exercise? Forget about that. There was no cookie worth this, I thought, as I placed the cast-off clothing on the return rack.

That afternoon I went home determined to finally clear my cabinets, and myself, of all unnecessary excess. However, I'd be lying to say that this next step was easy. Tossing out each poor but tasty food choice was like letting go of an old friend. As I dropped each item into the garbage, I followed the suggestion of an article I had read in a woman's magazine: create a helpful mantra. With each piece of junk food I threw out, I chanted: "You don't rule me anymore. You don't rule me anymore, chocolate. You don't rule me anymore, cookies. You don't rule me anymore, cake." Though spoken half-heartedly at first, my mantra eventually took root in the deepest part of me. By the end of this exercise I discovered that tossing out the unhealthy foods helped me reclaim the upper hand in my quest for healthier living.

The next step on this journey was to further exercise my new-found authority over my body by finding a sensible lifestyle program. I started by visiting a bookstore and thumbing through some weight loss books. Soon, I found something I felt I could live with. No more being a slave to counting, measuring, or fasting — just good, healthy eating partnered with a moderate exercise program. With that selected, I went to the grocery store to gather the supplies I needed to see my new lifestyle through.

I began in the produce aisle and snaked my way through the store. With each good choice I made, I felt even more empowered. Then I rounded the corner toward the bakery aisle. There I stood, surrounded by my old friends: all manner of cookies, cakes, buns, and muffins. I glanced into my cart, filled with low-fat, low-sodium, and whole-grain provisions. I took a deep breath and struggled to repeat my mantra: "You don't rule me... you don't rule me... you don't rule me...." Then I picked up a white bakery box and looked longingly through its clear plastic window. Inside, a cake piled high with buttery, sugary, cinnamon-y crumbs winked at me. I swear, I think I actually heard it speak. "Take me home," it said. "Just a little nip now and then wouldn't hurt, would it?"

I held that box for what seemed like a long while, finally scrunching my eyes together and shaking my head to break its spell. "You do not rule me anymore," I said aloud. "I rule me." And I placed the box down hard, much to the surprise of the supermarket employees and other shoppers nearby.

"Really, honey," one grandmotherly woman joked in my direction, "you shouldn't be so hard on that. It's only a crumb cake." But she was wrong, I now realized. I did have to be hard on the poor choices I had allowed to control me for way too long.

That day the magnetic pull that sweets had over me for most of my life ended once and for all. Thanks to my newfound regime of healthy food choices and moderate exercise I am able to report that I have since reached my weight loss goal and maintained that weight for over ten years. I am more active in my middle-aged years than I was as a teen and no longer find myself huffing or puffing from everyday exertions. More importantly, though, each year at my annual physical my doctor confirms that I remain in tip-top shape.

I still hear the siren song of cake, cookies, and candies. Sometimes I even indulge. Just a little. Yet when I feel the urge to take that larger piece or go for seconds, I remind myself that I hold the power where my health is concerned and repeat the mantra that set me straight about the sugary foods that once held sway over me: "You don't rule me anymore." And they don't. Now I do.

~Monica A. Andermann

Who Wants Ice Cream?

*I doubt whether the world holds for any one a more soul-stirring surprise
than the first adventure with ice cream.*
~Heywood C. Broun

In minutes, my living room has become flooded with people. A giant man wearing black and yellow from head to toe presides in the middle, cradling my pink, wailing baby girl. Others look on. Bags and medical kits litter the floor as feet shift, faces move in and out of my sight.

While I focus on one.

"I have never held someone this small before," the big fireman says. His hard hat nearly brushes the ceiling. "How old is she?"

"Eight months," I reply.

The other two firemen, along with the three paramedics converse, then tell me what to do, where they will take her.

In another minute, like a vapor, everyone, including my child, is gone.

•••

The next nine hours bring a roller coaster of emotions ranging from fear to anxiety, anger to relief. But the next day, as the sun rises, I know the path of our lives has changed course. I'm unsure how to keep my baby safe.

The verdict? Food allergies. Lots of them: peanut, dairy, egg, tree nuts, sesame, and garlic. She'd eaten a tiny fleck of Swiss cheese that night. She'd found it on the floor, beneath my son's chair. Minutes later, her cries pierced the evening silence, reaching an unbearable pitch, like shattering glass. Breathing trouble ensued, along with a bold white blister on her lip.

I called 911 and the sirens came blaring for her.

It is one thing to hear an ambulance or glimpse its flashing lights on the road. It's another to hear the siren's cries, look out your kitchen window, and see the cars pull over for the red and white entourage of trucks, edging closer, the noise deafening, knowing they are coming—that you called them—for your baby.

$$\bullet\bullet\bullet$$

Once Audrey received her diagnosis, I too went without dairy, peanuts, nuts, egg, sesame, and garlic so that I could continue nursing her. During this transition time, I lost twenty pounds because I was scared and didn't know what to eat. Many of my favorite foods—peanut butter sandwiches, pasta, ice cream, cereal—were off the table. Unsafe. And I didn't know what to do. I was nervous around food, worried about remnants lurking on toys, grocery carts, and other people's hands. I suddenly felt closed off from the world I knew, where eating was enjoyable, a social event, a way to celebrate, and a comfort under gray skies.

On one of the many days when I felt sorry for Audrey and for myself, someone very close to me lamented, "And she won't be able to eat ice cream. That is so sad." Her pity only brought me down more.

With a diagnosis that eliminated any familiar means of comforting myself—no gooey doughnuts or cheeseburgers here—I felt lost. Alone, in a strange world, trying to navigate a new path for my daughter and myself.

Because her very existence depended on it.

Why Audrey? Why when no one in our family had allergies? And why so many allergies? Did I do something wrong during pregnancy? How were we going to live like this?

But I knew right away that I wouldn't stop nursing. My daughter had a dairy allergy, but, blessedly, she'd been drinking my milk from the moment she entered this world. My milk was safe. I wouldn't take that away. Not when so much had already been taken from her.

We would struggle together.

• • •

Shortly after the ambulance tore through the streets with our young daughter, and the reality of our new situation settled in, I could only see what we'd lost. The freedom to eat what we wanted; the freedom to move through playgrounds, stores, and life without a second thought. I thought we'd been robbed, and I could only see what was missing in our lives and how bleak things seemed to be with danger looming over every particle that passed Audrey's lips.

At one point, however, my attitude changed. On a visit to our newly allergen-free home, my mother-in-law spent the day playing with Audrey, reading to her, cuddling her, and spoon-feeding her. And then she touched my arm and said, "Audrey has food allergies. But she is an otherwise healthy, and very happy little girl."

And she is.

• • •

"Soy butter sandwich." My son, Aidan, glanced up from his coloring. "Please?"

About six months after Audrey's diagnosis, my husband and I, along with our two children, had settled into a new eating plan.

We said our goodbyes to such favorites as pesto, cashew chicken, pizza, Mexican food, grilled cheese sandwiches, microwave meals, and ordering take-out.

And we said hello to creative cooking. We found substitute ingredients that passed the taste test and helped us return to foods we'd always loved. We even made our own pizzas; we just left off the cheese. As Audrey grew, both she and her older brother joined me in the kitchen laying tomato slices and spreading onion slivers across the pizza dough. We found new joy in cooking together.

Everyone in our home eats Audrey-safe food. But it is not as difficult as first imagined. As a result, we are also eating healthier than ever—cooking our own meals, avoiding fast and processed foods, and branching out to foods we had never before tried—all positive results from what first looked only negative.

• • •

At two-and-a-half years old, during a typical midweek meal of burgers and chips, Audrey has already blown on the hot food and taken several bites before the rest of us have finished saying grace. Whether it's swordfish, coconut chicken, pancakes, risotto, or almost any other home-cooked meal, Audrey is usually the first to dig in and the first to finish, jump off her chair, and go play.

A few minutes later, I ask, "Do you want some more, Aud?"

She nods, then snatches a potato chip from my husband's plate.

"Very sneaky," he says.

Audrey grins.

When everyone finishes, I disappear for a few minutes before returning with a surprise. "Who wants ice cream?"

"Me!" my children both cry.

Audrey squeals as I dole out a big spoonful of cookies-n-cream coconut ice cream into her dish. It is her first time trying something she's only seen others enjoying.

Watching her eat—inhale—the ice cream makes my husband and me smile, grateful for our healthy, happy little girl.

There is nothing unsafe for Audrey on this table. We have adapted, we have grown and eaten healthily together, all as a family. The path, once again, looks bright. And Audrey, with her wide range of tastes, is quite happy indeed.

That night, with all the fervor of a two-year-old child, she licks her plate clean.

~Mary Jo Marcellus Wyse

77

How to Do Fine

Spirit has fifty times the strength and staying-power of brawn and muscle.
~Mark Twain

My mother called from Nashville to tell me my brother had died suddenly—at the age of forty-five—from what we later learned was a cerebral aneurysm. Our conversation was brief. Awkwardly, I asked how they were coping. She said the pastor was there and people from church had brought more food than they could eat. They were "doing fine."

At the funeral, a friend mentioned that my brother might have been genetically predisposed to the condition that took his life. "Early detection is key," he said. "You should have your brain scanned."

"Oh no, I shouldn't."

"It won't hurt," he said. My fear of needles was famous among my friends.

"I know it won't hurt," I said, "because I won't do it." In fact, I went to great lengths to avoid anyone in the medical profession trained to use a syringe.

"Look, Chris, the only thing worse than losing your oldest child is losing your youngest too," he said. "Do it. You'll be fine. And your parents will be relieved."

For weeks, thoughts of undergoing a complete diagnostic examination kept me up nights. I knew I'd run out of the clinic like a hysterical five-year-old the moment someone flashed a syringe. I was a coward and a wreck—which I'm fairly sure is the opposite of fine—but I knew my friend was right.

Eyes pinched shut, I trembled through the tests. As nurse after nurse approached me with one instrument more pointed than the next, I'd ask, "That's not going to sting, is it?" In the MRI tube, I kept waiting to be poked or jabbed or, I don't know, slapped maybe? It was all new territory. On one occasion, a nurse drew ten vials of blood before I told her feeding time was over.

The test results: Mr. Allen, you're a bit of a wimp, but you're fine.

"Whew," I said to myself, gave my parents the good news, and vowed to go on happily ignoring my health as I always had. All those brilliantly bland results confirmed the bliss of ignorance.

A year after losing her oldest son, my mother called me with more news: "I have breast cancer," she said matter-of-factly. She might as well have been telling me their car had broken down. She'd already lost a son. What could be worse? She was resolved and ready to stare down death. Within a few weeks of the diagnosis, she stormed through two operations to have both breasts and twenty lymph nodes removed.

"How are you?" I asked on the phone from Germany a day after the surgery.

"Growing older," she said, "is a pain in the behind." Then she laughed as she always did when conversation was getting a little sentimental. "But I'm doing fine."

"What's your cholesterol?" my father asked. He was on the other phone in his office.

"I don't know," I said. "That involves a finger prick, right?"

My mother, bandaged up and scheduled to start chemotherapy in a few weeks' time, laughed—at me, not with me.

I flew to Nashville to be there for the start of her therapy. My father and I—the support team—boldly accompanied her to the treatment room, which looked like a beauty salon except for the tubes attached to the women's chests. It was a gabby space with *The Price Is Right* dinging and screaming on the TV in the corner.

Armed with a smile and an enormous Hershey's chocolate bar, my mother made allies quickly. One woman's husband turned out to be an old army acquaintance of my father's. Soon the room buzzed with war stories, laughter and "Mmm-mmm, this chocolate's good!" But then a nurse entered with a cartoon-large syringe filled with a red chemotherapy drug that everyone called "the red devil." I suddenly needed fresh air—and maybe a stretcher. So much for the support team.

When I wobbled back in, the woman next to my mother was relating her decade-long battle with cancer. She'd lost the use of her left arm. Her speech was slurred, but she was smiling. The cancer had reached her brain but not her spirit. I looked around at the women in the room. They wore their beaming resolution like war paint. They would become my mother's real support team: a troop of women bound by a common disease—an addiction to chocolate.

An hour later on our way out of the clinic, I jokingly tugged on my mother's hair and said, "Hey, your hair's still there."

She laughed and said, "Yep. I'm doing fine. Let's go get me fitted for a bathing suit."

Of course she lost her hair but gained a hat for every day of the week. She bought a wig but never wore it. Hats and bandanas were quicker, and they were stylish without having to be styled.

Eventually I had to return to my job in Germany, but I called her often to see how she was. As always, she was "doing fine," which I found hard to believe. This insane positivity had to be a knee-jerk, Southern reaction, right?

"Define fine," I said finally.

"Well," she replied, "I still have shooting pains in my left arm where they took the lymph nodes out. The port in my chest is a little uncomfortable. It's hard to sleep, but I managed two hours this morning. My legs are cramping, and I'm nauseous as heck." She chuckled. "Oh, and taking that chocolate to my treatments was a mistake: it just makes me think of chemo now, so it makes me nauseous too"—another chuckle—"but I'm still here, so I'm doing fine."

"Really?"

"Really."

I waited for a laugh that didn't come. Whether she knew it or not (but I think she did), she was teaching me how to do fine. Doing fine is a decision to roll with the punches. With age, doing fine demands the stiff upper lip I sorely lacked, the boldness to face problems with a smile—with steely resolve and the courage to roll up your sleeve and make a fist. Doing fine comes with the realization that courage grows when it's tested, poked and pricked.

~Christopher Allen

78

The End of Excuses

Don't make excuses—make good.
~Elbert Hubbard

I was standing on a dumpster the day my life changed. I was twenty-five years old and had lived under the cloud of self-loathing for so long it felt normal. "Look at you," I would cry at the mirror in disgust.

I had been overweight for over half my life and although on the outside I seemed happy, when you loathe what you see every time you look in the mirror, it's hard to experience true joy. I punished myself daily for not being able to convert my low self-esteem into motivation. I yearned desperately for the strength to take care of my weight.

I found it on May 6th.

My husband was attempting his first marathon and I was there to scream wifely support and take photos. Family, friends, and onlookers, all with the same agenda, swarmed every inch of the sidewalk and I battled for space. I lugged my flabby, overweight body up onto a dumpster for better viewing, and after regaining my breath and balance, fixed my eyes on the deserted road ahead. My husband would be wearing a neon-pink cap and I had my camera ready. Within moments, the first athletes turned the corner, unleashing a wave of supportive cheers from the waiting crowd; I, however, stood speechless. There was no pink hat anywhere to be seen—there was, however, a sea of wheelchairs.

I watched one man in particular. His arms moved liked pistons in a well-oiled machine, his sculpted shoulders and bulging biceps compensating for the legs he didn't have. Grit and determination consumed his face, sweat drenched his red, white, and blue bandana, and his gloved hands spun the wheels like lightning. Some people would see an athlete, some a hero, some a paraplegic. I simply saw a man with no legs tackling a marathon. As I stood there, I had no words, just tears.

Within minutes, the next group of runners made the turn and the buzz of excitement intensified. My husband would be further back, but out of loyal support for my first-time marathon runner, I searched for his pink hat just in case. Within the sea of heads, a mass of striking gray hair caught my eye. He was taller and paler than the other runners, yet his long legs strode effortlessly. As he got closer, my jaw dropped. He had to be at least seventy years old. I was flabbergasted. How could this man almost three times my age be running a marathon, and be in the leader's pack? How could that be?

A lifetime of pathetic excuses overwhelmed me then. I had witnessed a man with no legs and a man almost three times my age competing in a marathon. My weakness disgusted me. I made a life-changing vow to those two strangers: I would commit to a new life of exercise and healthy eating. I wiped my eyes just in time to grab the shot of my pink-hatted hero as he ran by waving in frantic excitement — I was crying for the both of us.

The first time I ran, I thought my knees were going to explode and I was going to throw up right there on the track. I survived one pathetic lap before dragging my flabby, blotchy legs back to the car. Tears filled my eyes at the prospect of the huge struggle that loomed ahead: Eat less, exercise more.

I pulled myself together, ignored my throbbing legs, and rather than chastise myself for what I had not achieved, congratulated myself on what I had — I had run one lap. I had not gained the weight overnight and I would not lose it overnight, but every step was a step in the right direction. I refused to live the rest of my life under a cloud.

The next morning, I forced myself back to the track, parked, took a deep breath, and pushed my unwilling body out into the bracing winter air. After one painful lap, my heart raced, my stomach churned, and my knees still throbbed, but I ran a second lap. I knew that exercise had to become part of my life. Breathless and sweaty, I got back in the car, but this time I smiled; instead of feeling dread, I felt impatient to conquer three laps, then five, then ten. I knew what I had to do and I was ready. Driving home that day, I reflected on my two strangers and the dumpster. Was that the secret? Did everybody need an epiphany to "suddenly" start exercising and lose weight?

My professor was in her sixties, looked twenty years younger, and ran three miles daily. Inspired and intrigued, I shared my story then asked her what made her start running. Her response astonished me.

"I was out walking one day and it started to rain. I didn't want to get my hair wet so I ran home. When I got there and realized what I had done, I figured if I could do it once, I might as well do it again. That was thirty years ago." I laughed in disbelief; I had found my answer.

I did not lose my forty-five pounds of misery overnight but I did lose it, and I have kept the weight off for more than two decades. Lest you think I have extraordinary discipline or incredible willpower, I do not. What I do have is a regular exercise program, a healthy diet, some self-imposed rules, and a warning-bell weight just in case. And on the days when the going gets tough, two strangers who ran a marathon against all odds remind me of the one thing I don't have—excuses.

And for that, I am eternally humbled and forever grateful.

~Janey Womeldorf

79

Sock Puppets

Children are unpredictable.
You never know what inconsistency they're going to catch you in next.
~Franklin P. Jones

A few weeks ago, one of the neighborhood boys was playing at our house. He has ADHD and was being particularly impulsive. It seemed as if everything he touched broke. He was being loud and obnoxious. He wasn't doing anything horrible. It was just that he was full of thoughtless energy. It was so bad that even the kids didn't want to be around him.

He is one of those people that I feel God has put in my life to fight for and love. But this day, it was all I could do not to fight with him.

So I decided to leave the house to get groceries. I put my husband in charge of the kids.

When I got home I found my kids playing with handmade puppets. The neighbor boy was making puppets for each of them. They had props and were putting on an elaborate puppet show. They were having a grand time.

But, these puppets were made out of socks and they were not just any socks. They were our good socks. The ones that had just come out of the wash.

So, I let the kids have it. Everyone pointed to the neighbor boy. They said it was his fault. I proceeded to ask him if he knew how much socks cost. He said no. I told him we did not have the money to cut up the only good socks we had. I reminded him that I had told him this before and he was never to do this again. He said he was sorry as he handed my daughter her freshly made puppet.

Later that night, it hit me. I had put more value in those cheap socks than in one of God's prized possessions. And wasn't making sock puppets a wholesome way for a twelve-year-old boy to spend his time?

I went to the boy and told him that I really liked to see him and the other children being creative. I promised him a big bag of worn-out socks to use the next time he wanted to make sock puppets. The next day, in church, he beamed as he told the whole children's church that I was going to give him a bag of socks to use to make puppets.

And I was so glad that I did.

~Randi Sue Huchingson

80

Starting Fresh

Vitality shows in not only the ability to persist but the ability to start over.
~F. Scott Fitzgerald

A house fire had destroyed nearly everything we owned. Even my daughter's baby book was sodden with moisture and stained with soot. While I felt grateful that none of us had been hurt, the task of rebuilding our lives from scratch seemed more challenging than climbing Mount Everest.

With plywood nailed over the windows, our fifteen-year-old house now looked more like a story from the evening news than the place where our family had lived for the past nine years. My eyes filled as I waited for the contractor to arrive. How could this have happened? And how would we ever recover from it? My head spun with the enormity of it all.

An inventory from the restoration crew filled pages that needed to be checked and verified. How many sweaters did I have? What was in the top dresser drawer? What games did the children own? A family of four can collect a lot of things over the years. A mind numbing fog swirled through my brain, clouding my ability to think. Grappling with the list felt like taking a test for which I'd forgotten to study. Life as it used to be seemed more a fragmented memory than a reality. Tears spilled down my cheeks.

The sound of a car announced the contractor's arrival. He was kind enough to look away as I scrubbed a damp tissue across my face. Then he cleared his throat and gruffly spoke.

"Don't worry. We'll get the work done on your house as fast as we can."

I managed a weak smile.

"But where do we begin?"

"My crew will put a dumpster in the driveway. Once all the damaged materials are removed, we'll start to put things back together."

"So, we just wait until you're done?"

He shook his head at my question.

"You've got a lot of decisions to make. The carpet needs to be chosen and paint colors selected for every room. Then there's your wallpaper and plumbing fixtures. The cabinets and countertops are custom made, so you'll need to order them in plenty of time for installation. You'll have to replace your furniture and lights. Most everything will need to be picked out well in advance so it will be here when we're ready for it."

I gulped and wished I had a place to sit.

"How long do I have to do all this?"

"The process should take about three months. Considering the time it takes for ordering and delivery, if I were you, I'd get started right away."

Rebuilding and furnishing a house, plus replacing clothes and personal items for everyone in the family. Impossible. I could feel the blood drain from my head. My shoulders drooped from the weight of his words.

"I can't do it."

I blinked back more tears and the contractor reached out to pat my arm awkwardly.

"Ma'am, you need to start thinking about this project as an opportunity. Was there something about your house you wanted to change? Any remodeling you ever considered? Well, now's the time."

I chewed my lip and thought about it. We'd always lived in rentals or houses that had been designed by others. I wanted to change things to suit my own taste, but never had the money or time. As I contemplated the possibilities, a spark of enthusiasm began to push away defeat. A new idea emerged. I would focus on one room at a time, with the overall goal of creating my dream home. Suddenly the task seemed more manageable. Like fitting together the pieces of a puzzle.

A short time schedule meant that agonizing over every detail would be impossible. I resolved to go with my first instinct on every choice. A half dozen of my favorite decorating magazines became guides as I hacked my way through a forest of decisions. Choose a carpet color. Done. Pick out new cabinets. Finished. Light fixtures? No problem. I changed our great room to a design that would be more open. Dreary looking woodwork was transformed by white paint. Six-panel doors replaced the plain and dated construction-grade ones. Each item checked off my list brought me closer to my "new" house. It even surprised me that all traces of my usual wishy-washy decision-making style had disappeared.

A friend was awed by my prowess. "I can't even pick out one color to paint the bathroom. How can you make your entire house the way it used to be in only three months?"

Like everyone else involved with the project, she got my answer in a flash.

"I'm not resurrecting the old house. I'm creating a new one."

Nearly three months later, the final piece of furniture nestled into its proper place. I walked through each room inhaling the scent of fresh paint. My feet pressed into the carpet. I slid my hand over an oak table that gleamed in sunshine filtered through white wooden shutters. The house turned out as beautifully as I had hoped. Now a new chapter of our lives awaited.

Thanks to a simple change in perspective, I'd been pulled from a quicksand of despair. It gave me the energy and strength to do what I needed to do. And once every task had been completed, I realized it wasn't only my house that had changed. I'd been transformed, too.

From victim to victor.

~Pat Wahler

81

Focusing on What We Have

A happy person is not a person in a certain set of circumstances,
but rather a person with a certain set of attitudes.
~Hugh Downs

A s I entered the emergency room, she lay there motionless and vulnerable under a white sheet. The doctor turned around, introduced himself and said, "We think your mother had a stroke affecting her entire right side." My biggest fear was that she would have brain damage and not know who I was. I said, "It's Lisa" and held her left hand. She squeezed my hand tightly. We both cried as the priest said prayers over her partially paralyzed body. That night, feeling scared and helpless, I cried for hours until I finally fell asleep.

The next day in the ICU Mom began exercising her left hand, arm and leg in bed. She squeezed her hand open and shut, lifted her arm and leg up and down, all with a smile. Prior to her stroke, she took an exercise class at the local council of aging and knew that it was important to keep moving. Despite her limitations, she had a determined spark and it was contagious.

The neurologist told our family that she had a 30/30/30 chance. Broken down that meant a 30 percent chance that she would die, a 30 percent chance that she would stay the same, and a 30 percent chance of change. I remember thinking that was funny math. What was the other 10 percent for? I decided it was for miracles. And that was what I was going to focus on.

I focused on what we had rather than what we didn't. She could swallow, she was conscious, she understood everything going on, and she could write with her left hand when she had difficulties with speech. With rehabilitation, she learned how to feed herself and talk again. She regained a lot of her speech with only slight difficulties with finding the correct word or pronunciation. I prayed for my mother, gave her inspiring cards and read to her to maintain and support her positive mood. Most importantly, I was grateful that we still had each other.

One day I went to visit Mom at the skilled rehabilitation center and she told me she had pain and headaches every day but that she was at peace. I said to her, "How can you be at peace? You are in a wheelchair telling me you have pain and headaches every day and you need a catheter." She looked at me confidently and said, "I pray to God every day and thank him that I am alive." I had tears in my eyes because it was so beautiful that she could maintain such a positive and grateful attitude despite all the physical losses.

I thought when she was told her physical therapy was to end that she would have a setback, yet she accepted it gracefully. She understood that her right side was not regaining movement. She then focused on getting involved with the events at the nursing home. She circled events on the calendar and attended them every day. She was curious to find out what Chumba was and later told me that it was a chair version of Zumba exercise class. Using one arm and her head, she moved herself quickly from side to side and up and down, complete with imaginary music and a smile.

She did not allow the physical limitations to stop her. Although her body was handicapped, her will was not. One day, before I was about to leave the nursing home she wanted to show me how she could get to the dining hall. I said, "I will get you someone." She said no, "I'll do it myself." I stepped back and gave her some room. She used her left arm and hand to move the wheel of her chair and her left foot to propel herself forward. She got herself to the hallway where she pulled herself along using the handrails on the wall. It was a slow and steady movement. Some would say it wasn't perfect or smooth, but she was doing it. I'd say it was one of the best moments of my life. I watched proudly as she reached her intended destination.

Before she went to sleep at night, she told me that she rubbed her right arm and hand, believing that it would bring the circulation back into them and they would move again. Four months later, her right thumb did move. The last time she spoke with me, I asked her to show me. She lifted up her hand and thumb and I saw it move. I said, "It's a miracle" to which she said, "Yes."

After being through so much, I thought my mother would have felt angry, frustrated and stuck. Yet, she could not have been freer. She was grateful, happy to be alive, and easygoing. She was connected to her childlike sense of wonder, yet was still an adult woman who gave me wonderful advice.

Positive thinking, prayers and love did not change the experience or the aftermath of the stroke, but it certainly changed my life. My mother taught me to live in the moment. Her positive attitude helped me to keep going, to have faith and to remain connected to her, especially after her death. Everyone loved my mother. Who wouldn't? She was the one sitting in the wheelchair at the nursing home with a big smile on her face. I can't recall a time I visited her that she wasn't smiling.

~Lisa Hutchison

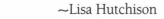

The Power of Positive

The Power of
Watching Others

82

Just a Kid

*A hero is an ordinary individual who finds the strength to persevere and
endure in spite of overwhelming obstacles.*
~Christopher Reeve

"Van, I can't move. Please get me off the ice."

"I wish I could Travis, but we need to stay here until the ambulance arrives."

And then we waited. "Of all nights for a snowstorm, why tonight?" I thought to myself as we waited what seemed like an eternity for the ambulance.

Hockey connects many different groups of people—players, referees, coaches, and even the off-ice officials. Sometimes there are events that draw together all of these participants as well as others from outside of the arena.

This story, although tragic, is a story of inspiration. In the 2000-2001 season I was coaching the Assumption Crusaders senior boys hockey team, a high school team from Burlington, Ontario. We were an average team that had shared some above average experiences. The previous spring we travelled to the Czech Republic, Germany, and Austria to play a series of games against European teams. This trip also enabled the boys to experience other cultures and take in the incredible sites of the Austrian Alps and surrounding regions. In the fall of 2000 we travelled by bus cross-country to play in a tournament in Dartmouth, Nova Scotia. The boys were a close team, a group of players bound together by hours spent in dressing rooms, working hard at practice, and competing in games, not to mention hours hanging out together outside of the arena.

In December of 2000 we were playing another local high school team. They were the dominant team in our league, and we knew we had our hands full just trying to keep the score close. Through two periods of play the score was 4-0. During the intermission our conversation was light as our coaching staff reminded the team that they were playing well and were only a "field goal" away from tying it.

At the start of the third period, our captain, Travis Colley-Zorrilla, broke in from the side boards at the blue line and went in on a partial breakaway. He made a wonderful move pulling the puck from his backhand to his forehand before shooting the puck past the outstretched glove of the goalie and into the back of the net.

What happened next took only seconds but its impact would last forever. Travis caught his foot on the goalie and that, coupled with the weight of an opposing player who landed on him after the goal, changed the direction of his fall from a gentle slide into the corner to an abrupt crash into the end boards. Not able to get his arms up to protect himself, the impact was absorbed by his head and led to a variety of horrific injuries including three broken vertebrae in his neck; specifically C4, C5, and C7. The most significant and sustaining injury was the crushed spinal cord that led to the paralysis of his arms and legs.

There are so many feelings and thoughts that went through me when I heard the doctor describe the extent of his injuries. Disbelief, shock, sadness, devastation, numbness, even anger. Travis, on the other hand, elected to be strong, resilient, optimistic, and uplifting to all who came to visit. While he remained in the ward recovering from his injuries and numerous surgeries, he never once questioned "why me?" or demonstrated any sign of self-pity. Early on he even commented, "I am glad that this happened to me and not anyone else, because I know I can handle this."

Travis was just a kid but he simply took this enormous challenge in stride and talked of walking again, going to college or university, and accomplishing all of his dreams in spite of this setback. I watched other patients in the ward who also suffered spinal cord trauma try to cope with the staggering news. They all had such sad stories of one wrong turn, or one bad decision, or being in the wrong place at the wrong time. Not all of them shared his strength of mind.

While Travis remained in the hospital, so many people in the school community pulled together to help. No one knew quite what to do, but we all tried to do something. Classmates, teachers, and parents all chipped in to prepare meals for his family, car pool for visits, and help out around the house to somehow make life easier for his family. In the meantime a committee was organized to fundraise. The reality of an injury like this is that modifications are required to all aspects of the home: kitchen counters need to be lowered, bathrooms need easier access, floor plans need to be altered, and all aspects of day-to-day living require greater accommodation. Transportation is another issue all together; a new van would be required to accommodate a wheelchair.

We decided a dinner-dance with a silent auction would provide the greatest return. Our committee reached out to everyone we could think of—local politicians, school community, local parish, celebrities, local businesses. We used our school as a depot for auctionable items. The outpouring of items was overwhelming. Sports memorabilia such as signed NHL jerseys and sticks came from teams across North America; Don Cherry provided all sorts of items but especially his genuine care and interest; PGA golfers like Fred Couples sent golf equipment and clothes to auction. We raised more than $100,000 through the generosity of our community—not just our local municipality but the hockey and sports community at large.

In addition to raising money, the local fire department stepped forward and offered to provide all the labour to customize Travis's house. A local building supplier (Home Depot) matched our efforts by providing an equal value in required building materials to every dollar spent in the store. It was a labour of love as every day a team of people showed up with tools and went to work on Travis's home. In total more than 100 workers would come over to the house, some immediately after their own twelve-hour shifts. The entire community was one big example of positive thinking and can-do attitudes.

It's been more than ten years since the accident. In that time Travis has dedicated much of his time to giving back to the community. He speaks to children in the community, both as an individual and for the Shoot For A Cure campaign, never shy about describing, in detail, his injuries and how his life has changed since that fateful game. He served as an ambassador for other fundraising ventures such as Wheels in Motion. He, along with friends and former teammates Chris Warren and Colm Rea, served as coach of the Crusaders lacrosse team for three years—teaching, instructing, motivating, and passing on skills that he is more than capable of providing.

Travis and I have always had a very close relationship, but in these past ten years we have become genuine friends. We live only blocks apart and find time as often as we can to catch a Leafs game on TV, travel to Cornell University to watch the Big Red battle away in the Lynah Rink, wheel around Glen Abbey Golf course and watch Fred Couples and other PGA tour stars shoot incredible scores trying to win our Canadian Open.

There are times when people will ask me how Travis is doing; I can't even get through a sentence without acknowledging that he's the bravest person I know, that he's my hero, and that he has demonstrated what it means to be a champion. A captain is expected to be a role model: mature, responsible, hard working, and dedicated to the goals of the team. Travis has maintained those qualities for life. Travis is truly an inspiration to all who know of his story and what he has overcome since that snowy December afternoon.

~Carl Van Landschoot

83

We Are Survivors

Man performs and engenders so much more than he can or should have to bear. That's how he finds that he can bear anything.
~William Faulkner

P icking up my eight-year-old son, Wes, from his counselor's office was something I never looked forward to doing. He often emerged silent, eyes downcast, with a "non-expression" expression. It was excruciating for me to watch my young son struggle with emotional pain—pain that no child should ever have to endure.

Wes was only four when our lives were turned upside down. I contracted a deadly bacterial infection, commonly known as "the flesh-eating bacteria." My battles with this disease, some physical some emotional, were hard fought, and I emerged victorious... I emerged with my life. But my victory came at a very high cost. This insidious disease claimed three of my limbs, and the left side of my chest.

The infection hit hard and fast. On February 13th, my life, as I had known it, ended. It began the same way as any other day. I felt fine that morning, but by evening I was not fine. And in the very earliest hours of the following morning, I was in the emergency room of a local hospital, fighting for my life.

Wes was in bed and fast asleep when I was rushed to the hospital. He could have never imagined that his mom wouldn't be home when he awoke the following morning. In all of his four years of life, Wes and I hadn't missed one morning together.

One hundred and sixty-one mornings passed before I once again walked across the threshold of my front door—a lifetime for my little boy. Walking on prosthetic legs and spending some portion of my time in a wheelchair, my presence in our home was dramatically altered. My losses were difficult and challenging, but my son's losses were profound.

It took months before Wes could sleep through the night. Often times I was awakened in the middle of the night by small ice-cold hands caressing my face. Wes, standing at my side of the bed, would look into my eyes, making absolutely sure I was awake. He very rarely uttered a sound. The only thing he needed to know was that my eyes would open, and that I was still present in his world. Once he was assured I was okay, he'd pad off to bed.

As heart-wrenching as these nightly visitations were, I believe they were necessary to my precious child's healing. Eventually, he began to trust that I would live through the night, assured that I would be where I was supposed to be in the morning. He began to sleep through the night once again.

Now, four years later, Wes was dealing with another blow. His dad, my husband Michael, was diagnosed with stage IV adrenal cortical carcinoma—a cancer of the adrenal gland—a cancer that carries a death sentence. Michael and I agreed that grief counseling was something Wes needed in his life.

After one of his counseling sessions, Wes slid into the back seat of my car. I quickly glanced in the rear view mirror to get a peek of his face. There were times after a session when he was approachable, and times when he was not. I took a deep breath and took a chance.

"Wes," I began.

He looked up at me. "Yeah?"

"When we get home, I need you to go over to Johnny's house and get Colin."

Wes's little brother, Colin, was playing at a neighborhood friend's house while we were at Wes's appointment.

"Why do I have to do everything?" he grumbled.

Oh great, I thought. Here we go!

I took another deep breath, gathered my thoughts and began speaking.

"I know that Dad and I expect a lot from you sometimes. And I know you think it's unfair. But Dad is sick and in bed, and I can't get up the steps at Johnny's house to ring the doorbell."

I went on to tell him that families were like a team. "When one of the team members can't do something, the other members will come to their aid and help out. That's what families do, Wes; they help each other out."

My words were met with silence, and then he started to speak.

"I'm so angry that those doctors cut off your legs!"

I had never heard my son speak this way before, and I was hoping he would continue talking. I needed to know how he was feeling as I was desperate to help him.

"I know, honey. It must have been very scary for you," I said, encouraging him to continue.

"I was sick too, when you were in the hospital."

"You were?"

"Yeah," he said in a small tremulous voice. "My head hurt, and my stomach hurt, and my heart hurt."

I fought back the tears, knowing from past experience that an emotional response from me would be the deal breaker for further communication. One shed tear and the door to any and every conversation would not just close; it would slam shut. I swallowed hard, shaking off the emotion, and began to speak.

"But look at us now, Wes! We're here, and we are strong. As a matter of fact, you are the strongest and most courageous kid I know!"

I glanced again in the rear view mirror, needing to see if he could hear my words—if they had landed where I had intended... directly on his heart.

I noticed a small transformation taking place. Wes was sitting up straighter, and a smile was beginning at the corners of his mouth.

"Yeah, I am strong, aren't I, Mom?!"

"You sure are, Wes. You are what I call a 'survivor.' You keep on going even when things seem scary and hard."

"That's what we are, Mom… survivors."

I nodded my head, again choking back my tears, unable at this moment to shrug off the emotion—unable, at this moment, to speak.

I pulled into the driveway. Wes unbuckled his seatbelt, jumped out of the car, and began loping across two lawns on his way to retrieve his brother. I sat there for a moment with my solitary hand still on the steering wheel. I could not believe what had just occurred—what I had just witnessed. I was in awe of the healing that had taken place in the small confines of the back seat of my car.

Both of my sons emerged from Johnny's front door, in a dead heat, racing for our house. Two little beaming faces lifted my spirits and melted my heart.

I shook my head, got out of the car smiling, and walked to my front door.

~Cindy Charlton

Two Strong Feet

I ask not for a lighter burden, but for broader shoulders.
~Jewish Proverb

No one can have it this hard, I thought, as I dropped my tired body onto the living room sofa. I checked the clock that ticked relentlessly above the television—almost midnight and still I could find no peace. I tried to quiet my mind, but thoughts of all the responsibilities that tugged at me daily as a caregiver, wife, and employee whirled around my head. And to make matters worse, chasing close behind, loomed a nagging case of self-pity.

I had been caring for my ailing mother for several years. Her condition had worsened steadily until she was wheelchair bound and now only able to leave the hospital-style bed I rented for her to go to the doctor, which happened up to four times a week. Lifting, positioning, cleaning up after her—she depended on me for all her personal needs. But my caregiving duties did not end there. There was my dad with his own host of health concerns to consider, and a disabled adult brother who also lived in the family home.

Through the kindness of a very understanding supervisor, I was able to cut back my work schedule a few hours a week so that I could get a head start attending to my family's needs on some afternoons. It helped, but not much. Even with those extra hours, I still could not shove everything I had to do into a day and make it back to my own home before 11:00 p.m. Upon my return home many nights, I would find my husband sitting quiet, alone. Even more nights, I would find him already sound asleep. I was neglecting my personal life in order to scrape together time to do all that was required of me. Yet, there was no other solution. There was nobody else available to help out. Surely, no one could have a life this hard, I thought again.

I flicked on the television, searching the channels for nothing in particular. Commercials, canned laugh tracks, music videos. I clicked around the circle of channels again. Then I stopped. There, I watched the screen as a young woman scooted around on a skateboard while she explained her duties as caregiver, wife, and employee. Her mother had a chronic illness and was nearing death. Her father had been diagnosed with dementia. Her adult brother was developmentally disabled. Her story was so close to mine, it was chilling. Yet there was one very important difference between us: she had no legs and I did.

This young woman went on to explain that a birth defect had left her without lower limbs. Finding a wheelchair too cumbersome to maneuver around tight spaces in her and her parents' houses, she quickly discovered that using her hands to propel herself on a skateboard was much more convenient in those places. I listened intently as she ran down her daily schedule: cooking, cleaning, grocery shopping, office deadlines, doctor and therapy appointments, all culminating in a late night arrival at her own home. It could have been me speaking, I thought. Though I wouldn't have sounded the same as this young woman. Because where I described myself as a victim of my circumstances, she spoke as a victor over hers. She counted her blessings and expressed gratitude for so many things that I had taken for granted: a good job, a kind husband, a roof over her head, a sharp mind, two strong arms. Finally, she gave thanks to whatever powers provided her with the strength to keep her family as comfortable and well as possible.

I watched until the final credits rolled. I couldn't help but recall the familiar saying: I cried because I had no shoes, until I met a man who had no feet. And finally, I understood. I wasn't alone. Everyone is struck with hard blows in this life. In fact, some people were hit even harder than me. But I could only be weighed down by these circumstances if I allowed myself to be. I took a quick inventory of myself. Just like that young woman, the Good Lord had given me everything I needed to make it this far and to go farther still. I decided I would drop the heavy burden of self-pity. Tomorrow, surely, I would emerge into the day lighter, get on my two strong feet, and hit the ground running.

~Monica A. Andermann

85

The Wounded Healer

We acquire the strength we have overcome.
~Ralph Waldo Emerson

As a marathon runner and regular gym groupie, physical fitness was my life. I would show up late for social engagements in order to get my run in. All that changed in May 1997. At thirty-seven years old, I survived a near-fatal car accident. I had no broken bones or cuts. I did, however, experience a traumatic brain injury.

After several weeks in a coma, I woke up with a raspy voice and no balance. My voice was hard to understand and my mobility was shot.

The week before the accident, I had opted for an easy running week. I only logged twenty miles in my running diary that week. Now I had to scoot around on my bottom until I learned to use a walker. Talk about a humbling experience. I had to relearn how to sit, stand, walk and move about. I didn't have to relearn to talk or eat though. That came pretty naturally. I promptly gained fifteen pounds.

My behavior was horrendous! My father says I used language that would "make a sailor blush." I'm guessing that is not a good thing. Since I have very little memory of that time, I have to base my facts on what family and friends have told me. People with traumatic brain injury go through several stages in their immediate recovery. It sounds like my potty-mouth stage lasted longer than the others.

Between critical care and rehabilitation, I spent several months in the hospital. That gave me plenty of time to reflect on how much rehabilitation it was going to take to get back to where I was before the accident. I prayed a lot, used my potty mouth a lot, and came home determined to fix it all.

Once a marathoner, I used to run on a treadmill when it was bitterly cold outside. Now I needed a treadmill to give me support while I learned to walk. Fatigue was a constant companion after my brain injury. When I wasn't sleeping, I was practicing walking on my treadmill. I was upset and baffled. Why had this happened to me? I had so much! Life as I knew it... was over. I knew it was an accident, but it was so hard!

Needing a walker was embarrassing beyond words. I was so ashamed. I had run marathons. Now I needed a walker to make it to the bathroom on time. Learning to live with this new body of mine was going to take time and patience. So seven years of physical therapy later, I began walking on my own. I walk slowly and haltingly. I keep a walker around for when I need to move quickly.

During all these years of recuperation, I remained a gym groupie. As I watched the personal trainers working with their clients, I knew I was as fit as they were. I didn't have to walk to write a fitness plan, or demonstrate proper use of exercise equipment. So I decided this would be my new purpose. I started studying for the personal training certification exam immediately.

My previous career as a pharmaceutical rep gave me an understanding of the body's anatomy and physiology, but memorizing new terms was very hard for me. My memory wasn't as good as I thought it was. Maybe my mind had become lazy from not studying for so many years. Whatever the reason, I had to take the exam twice before I passed the certification. Once I did, my health club immediately hired me.

However, if you don't obtain clients, you don't work. Who was going to choose me with a health club full of able-bodied trainers? My marketing background went right out the window. How do you promote a trainer with a balance and voice impairment? All that training and studying! Had I done the wrong thing? How could I promote myself? Seems the Lord had a different plan for me.

A woman from the Vocational Rehabilitation Office suggested I teach group exercise classes in senior homes. Voc Rehab even bought me a portable sound system with a microphone. The microphone helps the seniors to hear my soft voice over the oldies music I use in class. Over time, I've been able to add more classes. I started out teaching muscle toning and flexibility. Then I added more and more balance exercises. Balance work is so important for older people. And for me too! Now the exercises I teach are helping me as much as they do my class. The years as a physical therapy patient have given me lots of cues to use as I teach my classes.

A personal trainer—on a walker? It's not something you see every day. While my students aren't athletes or body builders any more, working with seniors gives me an audience that appreciates what I have overcome through regular exercise. I'm able to encourage them beyond what they thought they could do.

No longer do my disabilities embarrass me or make me feel ashamed. They have led me to a new purpose in life; inspiring and encouraging those I serve. Many times I hear myself using the same verbal cues with my classes that my physical therapists used while trying to get my body moving the way it did before my accident. "Elevate your rib cage." "Bring your hip bones forward." "Relax your shoulders." Sometimes I sound like a broken record!

My new purpose as a "wounded healer" uses the issues I've struggled with to motivate and encourage the seniors in my class. By showing them the exercises I've done to regain my mobility and strength, I'm showing them ways to maintain their own. To continue living independently, these seniors need to keep their bodies moving on a regular basis, just like I do.

I help them keep their bodies in proper alignment to make the tasks of everyday life easier. If caught slouching in my class, they are sure to hear me say, "Elevate your ribcage" for the fifteenth time.

Improved muscle tone and flexibility are not the only benefit of taking my classes. It's also a great opportunity for them to build camaraderie with the other residents. We share fashion tips, food recommendations and discuss current events, all the while commiserating about why we have to exercise. We laugh, joke, and truly enjoy our time together.

I've found my new purpose in leading these classes for seniors. I show them how to remain strong and flexible. They provide me a wonderful outlet for helping people again.

My days of being a long-distance runner are gone, but they led to a new and more meaningful purpose. My race time is slower now, but much more rewarding.

~Mary Varga

86

Moving Forward in Reverse

*The excursion is the same when you go looking for your sorrow
as when you go looking for your joy.*
~Eudora Welty

I was full of joy and caught up in my thoughts, so I didn't have time to react to the two girls who came sauntering around the corner, engrossed in conversation. I stumbled to my right, trying to avoid a collision. But I wasn't fast enough: our shoulders jostled and I staggered sideways.

"Excuse me," I called as I righted myself.

The girl I had bumped gasped and lifted one pink-manicured hand towards her friend for balance. "Ew!" I heard a voice cry behind me. I started to turn, curious what had caused her disgust.

"That man with no hands touched me!"

I froze. Her words seemed to reverberate towards me and through me. *I* was the thing causing her disgust, despite the appearance of the girls, with their bleached blond hair and overdone make-up.

Shrinking in on myself, I put my head down and subconsciously pulled my myoelectric hands towards my stomach. My emotions shut down. Sweat began to break out across my forehead. Fight or flight? Fight or flight?

I felt my heart race and dove for the sanctity of my office. The door was locked. I fumbled with the keys in my robotic hands. It took too many tries and too much concentration to single out the correct one. A screech like the yowling of a cat emanated from my hands with every motion of my fingers. I shied away from the sound, recoiling at the way it seemed to echo down the hallway. Once I had the key pinched between two fingers, I fought to navigate it into the keyhole and turn the lock. Without the use of a wrist, it was a trying feat on the best of days. And today was not the best of days.

Where had my confidence gone? I felt deflated and traumatized by what had just happened. I could feel the eyes of the other students on me, staring at my mannequin-like hands, judging me for my incompetence and handicap. I felt utterly inept and completely isolated.

When the key finally slid home and I managed to turn the latch, I rammed my shoulder into the door with unnecessary force. I stumbled across the threshold and quickly shut the door behind me, locking everyone else out.

My hands were shaking as I set the key on the edge of my L-shaped desk; my legs wobbled as I lowered myself into my chair. The only sounds were my panting and the creek of the hands as I laid them flat across my legs. I looked down at my lap, staring at the off-colored rubber that hid the metal fingers beneath. My handicap. Just when I thought I had made real progress in overcoming the hardships and self-consciousness having no hands or feet caused, something happened to knock me back down again. Hearing her words forced me to glimpse into the mirror reflecting my shattered self-image, and the broken figure I saw revolted me.

Maybe this is the new normal, I thought as I stared at the white, concrete wall before me. *The rest of your life is going to be spent as the object of other people's ridicule. Might as well get used to it, buddy. No one likes a handicapped person. Children gawk at you; adults avoid you; teens scorn you.*

I lowered my chin to my chest and closed my eyes against my unfair reality. From a successful collegiate soccer coach and player to this: Could life take any larger a turn for the worse? Six months ago I would have gone out to the soccer field to kick the ball around after something like this. But six months ago I had hands and feet and "the flesh-eating disease" was a term reserved for medical dramas. Now it was the illness that threatened to deprive me of the thing I loved most: soccer.

Playing soccer had been my greatest form of expression—my art form. A soccer field was like a blank canvas and the ball my brush. With them both I could create any masterpiece I dreamt of; I could funnel my emotions into the creation of my design and leave them on the field when I was done.

Now I couldn't even take the ball for a walk like I taught kids to do.

At least you still have a coaching career. This was true. I was still coaching and I still had my team. It seemed that was the only positive thing left in my life. But one positive is still better than none. As long as the players needed me—and hopefully wanted me—I would give them everything I had. Their canvas would become mine and I would teach them to paint like Jackson Pollock. If the rest of the university campus wanted to fear or ridicule me, so be it. I was a thirty-five-year-old man. I could handle a little bullying.

That was the last time I let myself think about the torments that threatened to pull me under. I put everything I had into developing the soccer program. I was able to recruit a few more strong players and implemented a new playing style to make up for our lack of a pure scorer. Long hours in the Soccer Office and as an Assistant Hall Director left me mercifully little time for self-pity and reminiscing.

It may have been avoiding a problem rather than confronting it, but I found that focusing on the good things I had going for me was better than worrying about the countless things stacked against me. Coaching was something I could excel at with or without hands and feet. As long as I was on the field or thinking about being on the field, I forgot that I had lost so much: I wasn't The Man with No Hands or severely handicapped; I was just Scott Martin, coach and mentor. The longer the hours I worked, the more time I was able to live as only Scott, and the less apparent my poor self-confidence became.

My dedication paid off when we cracked the Top 10 ranking

nationally that season and I was nominated for National Coach of the Year. I reveled in my team's success and realized it didn't matter if I wasn't the man I used to be on the outside, because I still had it on the inside. Life wasn't perfect: I still missed playing terribly and regularly dreamt I was running—more than once I woke after kicking the wall because I was playing soccer in my dream. In some ways, losing soccer was more devastating than the loss of my hands and feet. I could forget that I was handicapped at times, but I could never forget my longing to run the ball down field or the devastation at never being able to play as a part of a team again. But loss is a part of life and those who choose to focus on what is lost lose sight of what they have. And I still had a wonderful thing—myself.

~Scott Martin

Lightning Up My Life

*We can only be said to be alive in those moments
when our hearts are conscious of our treasures.*
~Thornton Wilder

In August of 2008, I was struck by lightning as I sat quietly and reflectively by a river not far from my home. It's something that happens to someone else, right? Still, it was me in the ambulance and in the ER, though nothing seemed real. As tubes went into my arm, scans were done of my head, and EKG readouts ticked by, I overheard the trauma surgeon say, "...back from the dead." Me? Dead? No, no! Impossible!

I don't remember being hit but I do remember vividly a desperate attempt to breathe—like coming up from a deep pool and struggling to reach the top to take in air. I remember a burning sensation throughout my body and an inability to see, hear or speak. As those senses gradually returned, the glimpse of blue sky and the sound of birds, for a moment anyway, completely numbed the pain. I was alive. I could take in the sweetness around me. I was joy!

Fully grasping what had happened, however, took place slowly and was laced over the next few months with tears, questions, fear, wonder and, finally... a journey into depths of gratitude and awareness that cannot be described with our limited vocabulary. I remember thinking to myself... "Who was the last person I spoke with?" "When was the last time I said I love you?" "When was the last time I said I was sorry?" "What do I do now?"

Throughout that first night in the hospital, I forced myself to remain awake, alert, and aware of every detail, every sound, every face, every smell and every thought. Just two weeks before I was hit, two young college students were hit just blocks from my home and both died. Visitors and nurses kept saying how lucky I'd been. "Lucky" didn't even come close to what I was feeling. Nothing would ever be the same again and whatever "luck" may have been associated with the event was partnered with a new sense of accountability for this blessing we know as life.

Drinking a glass of water felt like sipping from an ancient and healing biblical wellspring. Eating became sacrament. Walking felt like dance and the support of friends felt like the warm communion of angels. Waiting for test results and so many unanswered questions could have overshadowed the elation that I felt, but all of that didn't stand a chance. One chapter of my life had ended—literally and actually. I don't remember my "first birth," but I definitely remember the second.

Since that day, I cry easily and I laugh boldly and often. I've lightened (no pun intended) my "things" load by going through all of the stuff that crowded my rooms and shelves. How liberating it is to give away excess possessions and know that they will brighten someone else's life. Spending as much time as I can with family and friends is top priority. I don't text or tweet. Instead, I phone or visit. I hug openly and listen to the stories of others without judgment or critique. I watch wildlife and learn new lessons every day about patience, simplicity and community. When I see the sun rise or set, I wonder how many people at that very moment appreciate the miracle of each day. Each morning brings new meaning to the term "resurrection" as I wake from the little death of sleep. And, each evening there is so much gratitude when slipping into the night's dark mystery.

No one really knows the long-term effects of a lightning strike. My right shoulder will never completely heal and, strange as it may sound, I'm grateful for that. Its limitations remind me of the gift I've been given. I'm conscious of what I eat and how I honor this body-on-loan with exercise and rest. I take time to reflect and I pay more attention now to things I used to put on the back burner... sketching, writing, storytelling and music. Forever insatiable when it came to learning, I take classes and workshops more often and deliberately seek out those that will challenge my intellect, widen my world and deepen my understanding. I appreciate more than ever the multiple realities in our world and the richness they add to the expansion of our own humanity.

Volunteering has become huge in my life and my joy in it is boundless.

As with any life, be it the "first one" or one given in grace following a trauma, there are predictable moments of frustration, disappointment, loneliness, confusion, doubt, fear.... They're just part of the "human package." I feel those moments and the pain that comes with them. Are they any less painful since the lightning strike? No. Are they any less frequent than before? No. Nothing is numb and I never want it to be again. I don't know that I have ever before felt so completely "in my skin" and "in my heart and soul." How could there possibly be a turning back?

I have also discovered a place — a "room" — deep inside me that either went unrecognized before the strike, or that was added on afterward. It's a soulful room that I can visit in complete confidence. There is new insight there, and there is a peace that was not there before August of 2008. I find in that gentle room a broader capacity for compassion and patience. I find a warm reassurance that no pain lasts forever. I'm reminded in that special place that hope is accessible in any given moment, and that each moment of each and every life is a rebirth full of possibilities.

"Know that wisdom is such to your soul; if you find it, there will be a future, and your hope will not be cut off." (Proverbs) It would be great if gaining wisdom and awakening didn't necessarily mean getting fried! I wouldn't wish a lightning strike on anyone, but I am so deeply grateful for what I have learned as the result of my getting whacked. I recount the story and its lessons in workshops I give and it's been an inspiration for retreats I facilitate. I often get teased that I "probably don't need a lamp to light up a room!" My electric bill says otherwise. Nevertheless, "letting my little light shine" is a morning mantra!

Life is full of surprises. Some are little and subtle, others are enormous and can split a tree! Being struck by lightning, dying and being revived have certainly awakened me to the joy in life. I am more alive than I ever was before I died!

~Dale Mary Grenfell

88

Mr. Musau

Whether you think you can or think you can't—you are right.
~Henry Ford

I stared at the newspaper that lay on the table, idly drumming the red ballpoint pen in my hand against my coffee mug. I had been looking through the job vacancies but none of the openings appealed to me. I looked up and caught my reflection in the window—sitting at this desk, in my perfectly tailored charcoal gray skirt suit. What was I doing here? I didn't belong. I looked around at all the men's suits hanging neatly in rows, the expensive fabric almost shimmering under the lights that shone on them. I had recently found myself out of a job and had taken the position of store manager for this upscale clothing store as a temporary solution while I searched for work in the corporate world. It had only been a month and my frustration at not finding another job had been growing steadily.

My attention turned to a well-dressed woman who had just walked into the store, pushing a man in a wheelchair. At once, one of the salesmen rushed towards the man in the wheelchair to greet him. "How are you feeling, Mr. Musau?" he asked. The man stared blankly ahead of him as though he had not heard the question. He was well-dressed but he slumped in his wheelchair, and had on his face a look of resignation. I had heard about Mr. Musau from my co-workers—he was a regular customer at the store and a good tipper.

He had recently suffered a stroke and nobody had seen him for about six weeks.

The woman wheeled Mr. Musau over to the table where I had stood up from my chair, and said to me, "I'm going to pick out some new shirts for my husband. I'll leave him here while I look around." I nodded and smiled as she parked Mr. Musau's wheelchair at one end of the table. "Hello there, sir," I said as I sat down again. Mr. Musau did not respond. I was starting to feel a little uncomfortable. Silences made me uncomfortable and I usually ended up babbling away in spite of the lack of response.

"My father had a stroke four years ago," I blurted out without thinking. Mr. Musau continued to stare into space. "He had a blood clot in his brain which caused the stroke," I continued. "He was in a wheelchair too after that and had partially lost the use of his right leg. He also suffered memory loss. It was incredibly difficult for him to go from being the head of the household to being dependent on my mother and me. I think he even became depressed when he got home from the hospital, and wouldn't speak much for a few days. Then, as though something in his head had snapped, he began to behave differently. He wouldn't allow us to do anything for him unless he had tried to do it himself first. A couple of weeks later, he began to push himself to try and stand up from his wheelchair and walk a couple of steps at a time. He would sometimes fall down and we would have to help him up, but he always got right back up and kept trying. My father has always been a determined man. Every week, he would make it farther and farther from his wheelchair without losing his balance. Eventually, he did away with the wheelchair and was able to walk on his own without any assistance. He was back to being completely independent!"

Mr. Musau had not even glanced my way the entire time that I had been speaking. "It's incredible what the power of the mind can do, Mr. Musau," I added softly.

At that moment, Mrs. Musau walked up to us with a bag in her hand and said to me, "I hope he hasn't been a bother. Thank you for keeping him company."

"Not at all, ma'am," I replied. "Have a great day! See you later, Mr. Musau," I called out as Mrs. Musau wheeled him out of the store.

A few weeks after that meeting with Mr. Musau, I was offered a corporate job. I moved on and seldom discussed my short time as a clothing store manager. As for Mr. Musau, I had completely forgotten about him. That was, until one Saturday a year later, when I got an unexpected call from the new store manager at the men's clothing store. The manager said that a Mr. Musau had been asking for me for months and had finally persuaded the manager to retrieve my contact info from their system.

Bewildered and caught off guard, I agreed to speak with Mr. Musau. "Hello?" His voice was unexpectedly steady and strong. "Hi there, Mr. Musau!" I said, taken aback, "How have you been?"

The steady voice replied, "I have been trying to contact you for many months now," he said. "I need to tell you something. After my stroke, everybody around me, including my wife, was treating me like I was already dead. I prayed every night that God would take me and relieve me of my misery and the situation I was in. And then I met you. You spoke to me as though I still mattered, even though you may have thought I wasn't listening to you. You inspired me with your story about your father and how he used positive thought to reverse his disability. I would like very much to meet with you and your father."

With a lump in my throat, I said, "Of course, Mr. Musau. We can come and see you at home if you like — it may be more convenient for you."

His next words moved me a great deal. "My dear, I want to show you what your words have done for me. Thanks to you, I can now drive myself or walk to wherever it is convenient for you to meet! I want to thank you in person for helping me to realize that it was up to me to make sure that I did not waste away." As a tear escaped and rolled down my cheek, he asked, "Isn't it indeed incredible what the power of the mind can do?"

~Nafisa Rayani

89

What Doesn't Kill You Makes You Stronger

We shall draw from the heart of suffering itself
the means of inspiration and survival.
~Winston Churchill

I glanced at my best friend, Morgan, as she gave me a reassuring smile and said, "Don't worry honey. Everything's gonna be just fine." I smiled back weakly and once again began to stare down the door and check the time every ten seconds. Finally, the doctor came in.

"Let's take you back for some X-rays," he said.

I slowly followed him through the door and to a dark room where I was laid on a table.

"Okay. On three I need you to hold your breath for just a few seconds. You won't feel anything, so don't worry. Ready? One... Two... Three."

A few minutes later I was back in the examination room with Morgan and my dad. They both took turns telling me everything was going to be fine. I tried to believe them, but inside I had a feeling they were wrong. After what seemed like forever, the doctor returned and said three words that changed my life forever:

"She has scoliosis."

He lit up my X-ray film, which revealed my spine, which was in the shape of an S.

"Now the bottom curve is at thirty-five degrees, which is pretty significant, but they do not perform surgery unless it's over forty-five. I'm going to send you to a doctor in Denver, one of the best in the state."

When I heard I would not need surgery, I was relieved. Unfortunately, this relief didn't last long. My mom and dad took me to see the doctor in Denver a few weeks later. He took one look at me and shook his head in disappointment.

"That's not thirty-five degrees… that's probably closer to sixty… these are the wrong X-rays. We need to get one of you standing up."

So now I was in the same predicament. More X-rays. More waiting. More nervous feelings. When he came back with my new X-ray, I immediately felt my stomach drop.

"So… the bottom curve is actually fifty-seven degrees. And this top one is forty-three. And there's also this small one by your neck that's about ten degrees. Your only option is surgery."

After this, he said a lot more that I either didn't catch or just didn't understand. I was too upset. I was only fifteen years old, and I was going to have to go through one of the most intense surgeries possible. I couldn't hold it in any longer. I felt my eyes well with tears as they began streaming down my face. My mom hugged me close and whispered, "It's okay. We'll get you through this," as I cried into her shoulder.

Even more bad news. My insurance wouldn't cover anything if we continued to see this doctor. I had to switch to a new one in Colorado Springs.

That night, I looked at myself in the mirror with disgust. For the first time I noticed my uneven shoulders. My crooked back. There was no way I could get through this.

After a short visit to my new doctor in April, my surgery was set for July 26. Until then, I went to physical therapy once a week, and continued to participate in marching band at my school. Since I knew I would not be playing my flute on the marching field, I picked up playing the bells in the pit.

Surgery day came even faster than I expected. We got to the

hospital and I was put into a gown. I was terrified. After a few hours, I was wheeled into the operating room. The number of people and the amount of commotion going on in that room was what scared me the most. It seemed surreal to me. A mask was placed over my nose and mouth with a very sweet smelling gas. Before I knew it, everything went black.

I woke up eight hours later with two titanium rods, twenty-four screws, and a straight spine, with my parents hovering overhead. I had no idea where I was or what was going on. I didn't feel any pain, which I later found out was because of a nerve block. The two major curves in my spine went from fifty-seven and forty-three, to twenty and fifteen.

"Miranda? We're going to move you from recovery into your ICU room. Okay?"

I weakly nodded. My mouth felt so dry, I could not speak. That one nod of my head must have taken everything out of me, because I fell asleep again before I even got to my room.

I woke up again. Now I could talk.

"Mom? I'm thirsty," I said, as I once again noticed my dry mouth.

I was fed ice chips. Then a nurse came in and put a small device in my hand.

"If you begin to feel any pain, push this button for morphine. You can use it every fifteen minutes."

I nodded, right before falling asleep again.

I didn't wake up again until morning. After sleeping all night and not getting any pain medicine, I could now feel everything.

"This is it," I thought to myself. "I'm going to die here in this hospital."

I was given two units of blood. During the day I kept telling my parents, "I can't do this anymore… I just wish I was dead."

Later on the physical therapists came in to help me walk for the first time. I was not cooperative at all. I kept telling myself I couldn't do it. I needed help just to roll onto my side. But do you know what I did? It took time, but I got up. And I walked. Even though it was with the help of others, the feeling was indescribable. Those few steps around the nurses' station changed my mood from "I can't," to "I will."

After that day, I recovered at a surprising rate. I was expected to be in the hospital for at least a week or two. I was released after four days. I was supposed to be bedridden for at least six months. I went back to marching band practice in two weeks, and back at school part-time in less than a month. Every time I accomplished something, it raised my confidence. Once I stopped looking at the glass as half empty, and saw everything in a more positive perspective, I got better faster than anyone had ever expected. Recovery for scoliosis surgery is typically about a year, but in a few months, I felt on top of the world.

Today, I continue to heal and recover. I am beginning physical therapy to get some of my old abilities back. I participate in marching band and yoga. I will admit things are not always easy. My spine can no longer bend or twist. But I find my way around things. With a positive outlook on what I have, I now know that there is nothing I cannot do. What doesn't kill you truly does make you stronger.

~Miranda Johnson, age 17

90

Voice of Reason

Positive anything is better than negative thinking.
~Elbert Hubbard

"M ike, I need your help," said the physician at Ben Taub General Hospital as we were concluding a staff meeting. Everyone had just left, but he continued as we stood in the conference room. "I have a patient on another floor who suffered a stroke a week ago, and even though he could, and should, be doing so much more, he is merely lying in bed, not saying or doing much."

I thought back to my own hospitalization years ago after I was shot in the head. The expectation was that if I even survived, I would be a vegetable. Obviously, I proved all of those pessimistic people wrong. I had a long, painful, and grueling hospitalization, but I returned to college, went to graduate school, married my high school sweetheart, and with her had a daughter, lectured throughout the country, and worked at a trauma hospital. Sure, I still have many disabilities as a result of the shooting, but I survived, living a happy and fulfilling life.

I knew that the doctor wanted me to share with the patient the expectation that his life was not over. The doctor said, "He's so negative and I'm not sure if he'll even talk to you, but please try, as our goal for the patient is to get him to go to rehab. However, the way he is acting now indicates to all of us that there is absolutely no way he'll be able to qualify for the rehab hospital [where a patient must be capable of participating in three hours of rehab activity each day]."

I walked upstairs to the patient's room and introduced myself. "Hi, my name is Mike Segal from Patient/Customer Relations and..." However, before I could continue, the patient did something I could never have expected. He said: "Oh my God, your voice is even worse than mine!"

Was I upset by his remarks? On the contrary—I loved it! I quickly explained why my voice sounded as it did: I had been shot in the head, thereby affecting my vocal cords, and not allowing them to function 100 percent. I shared with him how difficult it had been for me after I was hurt, but I made sure that he realized that I am now happy—and I've been very happy for many years.

I told him that when I was hurt I was so angry and upset. "Before I was shot I could do 500 things really well, but now I can only do 200 things really well. For a long time, I was so negative and bitter over the many losses. But eventually I learned to focus on the 200 things I could still do well. I learned to focus on the positive and eliminate most of the negative."

I saw him thinking, reflecting on what I was telling him. I asked if it were okay if I saw him again, and he quickly replied, "That would be fine."

Through the next few days, I learned from the therapists (and from him when I would visit) that he was pushing himself to improve, trying to be positive. Now, he is at a rehab hospital where I continue to see him, and he's doing very well—not merely in his rehab, but also in his outlook on life.

Yes, I believe there are many reasons for his improvement, including his change from a negative attitude to a positive one. Perhaps, "my having a voice even worse than his" may have been just what the doctor ordered!

~Michael Jordan Segal, MSW

91

Dark Victory

The world breaks everyone,
and afterward many are strong at the broken places.
~Ernest Hemingway

I was twenty-three and pursuing a career in a city a thousand miles from home. I began to have disturbing health issues. I went from doctor's office to doctor's office, and my new friends thought I was a hypochondriac as weeks, and then months went by and no diagnosis was made. Finally, things came to a head. I was hospitalized for shock and released. The next day I made my way back to the doctor. I'll never forget sitting before the polished desk in his office, retching into a specimen cup he shoved in front of me. "I have a brain tumor," I mumbled into the Dixie cup. "It's a neurological problem... I have a constant headache; my handwriting's going; I'm beginning to walk sideways...." He cut me off.

"Seventy percent of my female patients are psychosomatic," he said briskly.

"I'm not one of them," I replied. "I need a scan."

"If you see a psychiatrist, I'll give you one," he said, ushering me out the door.

The next day, the psychiatrist said I seemed well adjusted. He watched as I staggered towards the front door, weaving down a long hallway. "Are you aware you're walking sideways?"

"Oh yeah, I have been for weeks now," I replied. By the time I got home, it was mid-afternoon. I seldom turned the television on during the day but for some reason I felt compelled to. *Dark Victory* was playing on Turner Classic Movies. Bette Davis was battling a brain tumor, and had all the symptoms I had been describing. I called my boss to take a leave of absence, packed a bag, and called a taxi to take me to the ER. An intern looked into my eyes and ordered a CT scan, which confirmed my suspicions. I didn't feel vindicated so much as grateful to have found a doctor willing to listen. Sometimes that's half the battle.

Since that fateful day thirty years ago, I have had fourteen major surgeries, either involving the brain, spine, pancreas, spleen, eyes, or kidneys, and will soon have a kidney transplant. In the intervening years I have learned—always the hard way—that no one knows my body as well as I do, and I must take control of my health. Because my cancer is a rare one, VHL (von Hippel-Lindau), and has so many varied symptoms, it is hard to diagnose. Medical knowledge is better than it was decades ago, but even today, too many doctors don't know much about it.

Everyone lives a complicated life, even without the variables of chronic illness. Those living with a very rare disease, however, have times when we envy those with a well-known and well-researched one. This multi-symptom cancer has no middle, just a beginning and an end. Symptoms come in spurts. Sometimes they crop up after years of inactivity. Sometimes they appear several times within a year. People die when their bodies become overwhelmed by disparate tumors and problems associated with the disease.

I survive episodes of illness, surgery, and recovery by remaining stubbornly fixed on the goal of getting back some semblance of a normal life. Throughout the years, it has been up to me to redefine "normal." I've learned what I can about the disease, joined an information and support group, and interviewed dozens of doctors to form a medical team. In the process, I've discovered fundamental truths about myself: I can stand up to doctors, technicians, and medical staff when I need to. When I take myself seriously, I gain more self-assurance, no matter what the trial. And I am incapable of using a bedpan, even if it means waiting ten hours before going to the bathroom!

I've lost friends and a first marriage to the cracking up—sorting out—coming-to-terms baggage that accompanies anyone who lives with chronic illness. Gone are the certainty of bearing a healthy child (with a 50-50% chance of passing VHL on, and not wanting a child to contend with a sick mom, I opted to have none)... the ability to continue the athletic pursuits I love... the ability to work full-time... independence and privacy... at times, personal dignity and modesty... and the luxury of what I call "false positives"—such as people taking for granted the fact they will wake each day and their bodies will work effortlessly. It's hard weathering things most people normally confront in old age—or, if they are lucky, not at all.

But self-pity to me is a bore. Even if I have to pretend a little, I force myself to re-engage in life and find things I can do. Soon I re-appreciate all I have and am able to do, and the activities and hobbies that keep me engaged fulfill me again. I resolve feelings of meaning-less and loss and move on. I reach out to others who are hurting or in emotional pain, and almost always feel empowered and relieved to get my mind off my own troubles.

Sometimes when too many surgeries (and too much pain) catch me up short, I still lose a sense of balance (it's called being human), and I become distraught and frightened. Sometimes I get caught up in my daily obligations and forget to nurture my embattled body. I do so want to be "normal" and keep up with the usual business of the world. But illness and fatigue intervene. And I realize that I have to put my own health first.

When I was first diagnosed with my chronic illness, the hope that sprang from within me was born of courage and determination—not just to survive, but also to prevail. I have prevailed and I have gained perspective over the years. My second marriage is a long and fulfilling one. My relationships with my family and friends are more authentic. I don't hold on to toxic people; I don't have time for them. I walk through fire, and am purified and humbled by the experience.

I know my willpower and inner strength are ironclad when I

must call upon them. My spirituality grows ever stronger. I'm constantly learning to appreciate, develop, and nurture this gift. And because the lessons are not learned easily, they are all the more precious. This disease has not only defined my life, it has refined it as well.

~Amy Gray Light

The Power of Positive

Chapter 11

The Power of
Changing Your Thoughts

The Book Shelf

Books can be dangerous. The best ones should be labeled
"This could change your life."
~Helen Exley

Tim sat behind the wheel of his yellow sports car. His brooding eyes stared straight ahead, seemingly unaware of me. I unbuckled and stepped out of the car, "Well, thanks for dinner, uh…" My wooden tone matched his wooden face. He nodded. "Yeah, sure." Then spun away. I watched the taillights become smaller. Another first date gone awry.

Later that night, I comforted myself with a book. I seemed to be on a mission to prove true the litany of my single friends, "All the good guys are taken." Unlike many of my middle-aged friends, I had not given up on love. I still longed for the marriage of my dreams. I saw marriages that were strong and happy. Couples who still held hands after decades together. The octogenarian couple who lived next door, and were often spotted walking arm in arm, chuckling over a shared story.

I dated here and there. Matt took me on grand adventures, but his penchant for dishonesty tore us apart. Roger was handsome and sensuous, but his angry outbursts shattered any hope for happiness. On and on it went. Soon, I was joining in the chorus of "All the good ones are gone."

Until one blessed day, I had an epiphany. Several women friends gathered for lunch at Mary's house. Our hostess was wailing, "I had the worst date last night! All he did was talk! On his cell phone! Over dinner! All evening!" We all commiserated. Soon bored, I wandered over to her bookshelf. What I saw, really saw this time, took my breath away. Book after book on bad relationships filled her shelves. (Fictitious) titles like: Men Who Hate Women; Women Who Hate Men; Women Who Hate Men Who Hate Women; 50 Ways to Leave Your Lover; How to Say No; Be Mean Today. Two entire shelves were stuffed with books on how to recognize and experience a painful relationship.

Mary was still in full volume with the "Life Ain't Fair" song. I knew the words of this sad song. I did not want to sing like this any longer. I turned again to her bookshelf. With rising dismay, I read more discouraging titles. While I was dumbfounded, I was also very excited. I knew I was on the edge of A Big Change. Excusing myself, I left lunch early.

I was thoughtful as I drove home. Coming into my quiet house, I ditched my winter coat on the floor, dropped my keys on the couch, and checked my own bookshelf.

How did those titles get there? Because the same titles, and more, were on my shelf. What's Wrong with Marriage Today? How to Be Happy and Single. Liberated Women Unite. The list went on.

I leaned my forehead against the cool wall. What had I created for myself? I had been surrounding myself with thoughts of bad marriages and poor relationships. How could these ideas possibly lead to a loving marriage?

I recalled the cold houses I lived in as a child, messy, empty of love. Many times I muttered as a child, "When I grow up, my house will be filled with warmth, laughter, clean furniture, plenty of delicious food and lots of loving."

The house I lived in now was a vast improvement in cleanliness and nice furniture. But emotionally, my home was empty. But what could I do to make my home and my life ready for love? I longed for a strong and happy marriage. Now I needed to match my environment to my desires.

I believe that all books, even bad ones, are sacred. So what I did next was near sacrilege. Heart thumping, peeking over my shoulder to ensure I was unobserved, I picked up every negative book on my shelf, and I threw them away! Yep, no recycling. This information was going to the dump.

My bookshelf was now nearly empty.

The next day I went to the used bookstore. My feet took me, as usual, to the relationship/couples section. I saw only the same old titles. At first. But this time I held my ground, and kept looking. A well-worn blue book caught my eye: *The Adventure of Being a Wife* by Ruth Peale. I paid my dollar and carried the book home.

Pouring myself a cup of fresh coffee, I sat in my comfortable green chair to read the table of contents. Warmth spilled over me like spring honey. My shoulders relaxed, as I read the intimate details of one marriage. The author's frankness and humor gave me hope.

I was happy. Then the dark voice inside me said, "Marriage for this man and woman perhaps, but not for you. You will never be happily married." I fought off the little voice, but only to the extent that I decided that even if I couldn't have my own happy marriage, I could take pleasure in the happy marriages of other people.

I finished the book, underlining my favorite parts. I returned to the bookstore and purchased at full price the hardcover book *The Good Marriage* by Wallerstein and Blakeslee. At home I read a story. And then another one, until I regrettably reached the last page.

I cheered as I read about challenges that couples had overcome. Sick siblings, the awful loss of a child's life, marital fights and marital make-ups. This marriage business was not easy, not by anyone's standards. With delight, I finished reading the book. Good marriages were possible for those lucky few. This was delightful news, and I was privy to it all.

A few days later I returned to the bookstore and purchased the book, *I Will Never Leave You* by Hugh and Gayle Prather. They were frank about their challenges. This kind of marriage would withstand time.

Over the period of several months, my bookshelf again filled. But this time, the titles filled me with hope and delight. Books on good marriages, including Dr. Gottman's *Seven Principles for Making Marriage Work*. This marriage business was a delightful thing, even if it wasn't going to happen for me. My heart filled with gratitude that I could read and vicariously enjoy the success of others.

Over the course of time, my mind changed and softened. I no longer took part in the sad litanies of "All the good men are taken." As I steeped my mind in happy thoughts, my attitude towards marriage changed. As my attitude changed, so changed my life.

In 2003, I met my beloved Shawn, the man I would marry. Last month we celebrated six years of married life. As we are well into our middle years, the adjustments continue. Best of all, the joy continues as well as the wonder. I am deeply grateful for the unexpected delight that my husband brings to my life.

Today, when I feel stuck in an area of my life, I review my bookshelf, which is now filled with positive titles. Are my finances in disarray? What thoughts am I entertaining? If my weight creeps up, a quick review of my bookshelf reminds me how I lost weight in the first place. A little mental check lets me know what I've been doing and thinking recently.

If you can dream it, you can achieve it. When I roll over in my sleep, and feel for the warmth from the large body that is my husband, I smile when I recall my "impossible" dream. And now, if you were to visit my home, you would find a new, growing collection of books on how to be a great grandparent.

~H.J. Eggers

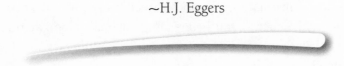

Insomnia

Don't fight with the pillow, but lay down your head
And kick every worriment out of the bed.
~Edmund Vance Cooke

Most people look forward to hitting the sack, but I dreaded going to bed—I associated it with thrashing around until the sheets were bunched up and wrinkled, and watching the minutes turn over on my nightstand clock. I flipped my pillow so often there was no longer a cool side.

"I'm so tired!" I would moan in the morning when the alarm went off.

My husband would snort. "It might help if you went to bed at a decent hour."

"But if I go to bed before I'm sleepy, all I do is toss."

Sometimes I stayed up till 2 or 3 a.m., but still couldn't count on falling asleep when I finally turned in. Every cell in my body screamed with exhaustion, but I couldn't lie still. I was so hot. Off flew the covers. Pretty soon, I was cold—time to bundle myself back up.

When it became unbearable, I would stumble downstairs for a cup of tea, a snack, or a book. After a bleary hour or so, I'd head back upstairs to try again.

I avoided caffeine in the afternoon. I prayed. I took hot showers. I actually tried establishing a "decent" bedtime. I drank soothing chamomile tea right before my decent bedtime—and then I had to get up to go to the bathroom a couple of hours later.

The worst were the nights when the worries surfaced—everything I'd managed to push aside by keeping busy during the day. My life looked bleaker, scarier, more hopeless at night.

"I have the worst insomnia," I would tell my friends. "I never get a good night's sleep. When I was a little girl, I never wanted to sleep. One night, my mom decided to call my bluff and told me just to stay up if I wanted to, because she was going to bed. So she turned off the lights and pretended to go to bed, but all I did was keep playing with my toys in the dark!"

When I was in elementary school, I went through a sleepless period that went on for months. I was obsessed with worries and fears, and the only way I knew to keep them at bay was to stay up and read or play with the lights on, until exhaustion overtook my feverish brain. My mother was so concerned, she took me to the doctor, who gave me "nerve medicine," which I now suspect was sugar pills. They helped a little, but she only gave them to me when absolutely nothing else seemed to work.

"I hate bed," I said now—the same way I did when I was seven or eight. "I just can't sleep."

One day, I ran across an article with "sleep remedies." I never passed up articles on insomnia, even though I already knew all the tips before I read the first word.

"Okay, let's see what this one says.... Good sleep hygiene, limit caffeine, blah, blah, blah..." Then, incredibly, I saw something new—positive self-talk.

Most insomniacs, I read, tend to tell themselves and others they "just can't sleep." Over and over, day after day, they go to bed saying, "I know I won't sleep." Even people who otherwise appreciate the power of positive thinking in their daily lives fail to apply it to their sleep habits. The author of the article had interviewed sleep experts, and several had seen significant improvement in patients who had decided to change their inner self-talk.

I was dubious... but desperate. I couldn't believe that just telling myself I could sleep would produce any dramatic results, as several of the article subjects claimed. After all, like Patsy Cline, I'd been "walkin' after midnight" for many, many years. But I had to admit, it certainly couldn't be helping me when I told myself over and over that I was a hopeless case. And, like several of the subjects interviewed for the article, I had already seen the power of positive thinking in other areas.

Could I change my thought patterns? All I could do was try.

When I went to bed that night, I smiled as I smoothed out the pillowcase and laid down my head. "I'm going right to sleep," I told myself with a confidence I was far from feeling. "I feel so relaxed. I'm so tired."

A worry tried to assert itself, but I just pushed it down and told myself, "I don't have a care in the world."

Miraculously, that very first night, I fell right to sleep! When I woke up the next morning, I felt a new sense of power—I could actually control this thing.

The next night, I repeated my new bedtime routine, despite a little lingering doubt. Maybe it had just been a coincidence. But once again, I fell right to sleep.

By now, I was beginning to believe what I had been telling myself. The following night, I repeated my routine with more confidence—and the same result.

After a while, I no longer even had to talk myself into sleeping. Of course, as time went by, I still had the occasional restless night. But they became the exception, and were no longer a way of life.

I'd never really realized the enormous power of our thoughts, even in controlling what seemed to be physical circumstances. I was sixty years old, and had struggled for so long—yet the answer to my years of misery lay right inside my own head.

~Susan Kimmel Wright

Fighting Cancer
with Attitude

When you treat a disease, first treat the mind.
~Chen Jen

On March 15, 2011, I sat in my living room with a few friends, celebrating my friend Sherry's birthday. We had both recently turned forty-four. Eventually the conversation came around to an acquaintance of ours who was dying from a very aggressive form of breast cancer. "Look around you, ladies," I said. "With the stats as they are, there is a good chance that one of us will get breast cancer." As if some creepy premonition were unfolding, I found it the very next day: a lump in my left breast. Life would never be the same.

Like most people who are diagnosed with a life-threatening illness, I underwent the typical stages of grieving: denial, anger, bargaining, depression and acceptance. I can almost pinpoint the exact moment that I transitioned from depression to acceptance. It was a beautiful day in October, six months after my initial diagnosis, and my body was under assault from a very difficult round of chemotherapy. I was lying in bed, looking through the upstairs window as my mother collected the last of the summer tomatoes from my greenhouse. It saddened me that I was not out there with her, enjoying the sunshine and harvesting the fruits of my labour. Life seemed so unfair.

While wallowing in self-pity, I realized that I had a choice to make in how I was going to face my cancer journey. I could choose to focus on the pain, suffering and utter devastation that is cancer. There is no denying that few things in life can rival a cancer diagnosis for the award of "worst thing that could ever happen to you." Cancer brings with it the terror of facing an untimely death; uncomfortable and painful treatments and procedures; loss of identity; coming to grips with a new body image; strained relationships; and financial setbacks or ruin. That is the reality of cancer.

Despite the ugly reality of cancer, I still had the choice of facing it with a positive attitude. It suddenly dawned on me that feeling sorry for myself was not going to help me get well. As a psychologist, I knew that positive emotions such as happiness and joy help to boost the immune system and enhance healing. Negative emotions such as anger and depression, on the other hand, have been proven to suppress the immune system. Since I needed a healthy immune system to fight cancer, a positive attitude was vital to my recovery!

I convinced myself that cancer wasn't that bad; hey it even had its perks. For example, since getting cancer, not once did I have to help with the dishes at big family dinners. That thought made me smile, and instantly I felt a little better. I then issued myself a challenge: if finding one perk could bring a smile to my face, I would find 100 perks of having cancer, and so a blog was born (www.perksofcancer.com).

Blogging the perks of having cancer has been instrumental in helping me to maintain a positive attitude through my cancer journey. Instead of focusing on all that cancer has taken from me, it allows me to see the gifts that cancer has brought to my life; gifts such as Perk #21: Cancer helped me find my soul mate. Perk #25: Cancer connected me to a powerful prayer network. Perk #28: Having cancer revealed to me a whole new side of my autistic son. Perk #34: Cancer made me realize my own strength. Having cancer forced me to evaluate my life and make some major changes. I ended some relationships that were not serving me well, and I put more of my energy into those which were. I identified work environments that were toxic to my spirit, and embraced a change in my career. I started to feed my body nutritious foods, and made exercise and meditation an important part of my day. As ironic as it may sound, this past year with cancer has been one of the happiest of my life.

Would I give up my cancer? Absolutely, in a heartbeat! However, I would not part with the changes that cancer has forced me to make in my life. Some say that a positive attitude alone cannot cure cancer. I agree. However, a positive attitude combined with positive action will give me the best chances of surviving this disease. If I live another forty years, it will be a wonderful thing if I can look back on this year and say that I lived it with happiness, joy and grace. If I live only one year, then it is even more important that I be able to say I lived it that way. For that reason, I choose to fight cancer with attitude—a positive attitude.

~Florence Strang

No More Bad Days

A cloudy day is no match for a sunny disposition.
~William Arthur Ward

At the classroom door a young mother tugged on her reluctant preschooler, who scowled at me, his nursery school teacher. Looking defeated, the mom apologized. "He's having a bad day." Within this apology was an unspoken warning: "Please, coddle my poor little child."

I murmured my standard line: "We'll make sure you have a good time at school, sweetie, and Mom, you have a good time, too." Sometimes this worked and the child soon could be seen happily engaged in the "free play" that began each morning. Often, however, the child sulked for the entire hour and a half of class while giving the assistant teacher and me meaningful looks that conveyed, "Don't mess with me. I'm having a bad day."

It hit me that particular morning this was occurring too often in our classroom. Further, not only were we teachers catering to bad moods, we were encouraging them by paying special attention to sulky children. The parents had condemned the children to a "bad day" because one or two things had gone wrong in the morning before school. We teachers, after an initial attempt to cheer up the child, allowed the black cloud to hover over that little person. No one, I mused, should consider him or herself destined to a whole Bad Day.

Conferring with my assistant, I changed the lesson plan. She went to the storeroom to find a large roll of paper while I called the children together for "group time." Instead of singing a nursery school oldie, "Good morning to you, good morning to you, we're all in our place with sunshiny faces," I sang out "Bad morning to you, bad morning to you, we're all in our places with mean, grumpy faces." The children laughed at this but they didn't think it a bit funny as I read their favorite book, Margaret Wise Brown's famed *Goodnight Moon*.

"Bad night moon, bad night room, bad night cow jumping over the moon…."

I read in a flat, sad voice. The children kept correcting me supplying "good" every time I said "bad." I knew I'd made my point when one sweet little girl, looking as if she were about to cry, pleaded, "Please say 'good', Mrs. Marks, please, please."

That led to a discussion of why we like to hear "the good word" more than "the bad word" and why everyone needs to have "good days as well as good nights." The children agreed we wanted happy faces and good things. My assistant had used the large paper to make a banner, proclaiming NO MORE BAD DAYS AT JACK AND JILL PRESCHOOL, which the children decorated with brightly colored markers. We posted this in the hall by the door for the parents to see at pick-up time. Each child explained the banner to the returning parent.

In the monthly newsletter for parents, I explained our new philosophy of not allowing our children or ourselves to wallow in bad moods. The parents readily accepted this, and in no time I saw more smiles on their faces and the preschoolers they brought to school.

Concurrently, I discussed what we'd done in our class with the whole staff. All agreed childhood should be a happy time and that our jobs included modeling positive attitudes. Preschool teachers are known for being cheery, but we agreed to make an extra effort to show joy in our interaction with parents, the children, and each other. Good days truly became contagious!

The success of our happiness initiative became apparent in the classroom when we sang an old favorite: "The Wheels on the Bus Go

Round and Round." In one stanza the children loved to sing, "The babies on the bus go 'wah, wah, wah… wah, wah, wah.'" A sharp little lad suggested, "Let's make the babies be happy." From then on, we sang, "The babies on the bus go 'goo, goo, goo… goo, goo goo.'"

Though retired from early childhood teaching for many years, I still make a supreme effort to avoid "Bad Days." As an aging senior, my days hold their share of "bumps and bruises," but I try not to let the bad moments override all the good ones so easy to find in any given day. When I start to feel a little down, I remember all those Jack and Jill preschoolers with their "sunshiny faces."

~Alice Marks

Adventure and Attitude Go Hand in Hand

*We live in a wonderful world that is full of beauty, charm and adventure.
There is no end to the adventures we can have if only
we seek them with our eyes open.*
~Jawaharial Nehru

I was born and raised in a small, rural community, and I planned to live out my life in the same county as my birth. I loved my hometown and was very close to my family. And though I intended to stay in South Georgia until my last breath, still, I daydreamed often of "seeing the world" and longed for adventure that would take me to distant shores.

I was an optimistic person, despite the fact that my family lived on very meager funds in an old, dilapidated farmhouse. I optimistically believed that we'd win the Publishers Clearing House sweepstakes, rescuing us from mountainous debt and enabling us to patch the leaking roof, insulate the leaky windows, and finally buy me a pair of shoes that were not, in the words of a fellow classmate, "the ugliest things she'd ever seen."

The summer after college graduation, I married my high school sweetheart and love of my life, and our journey as a couple began. I taught beautiful children from impoverished homes in the next county over while working on my master's degree in the evenings; David pursued a master's degree in entomology and worked as a graduate assistant.

I had absolutely no idea what my new husband planned to do with an entomology degree in Statesboro, Georgia, but I reminded him often that I didn't plan on going anywhere. He silently kept studying, but hinted occasionally that we might have to leave Bulloch County to find a job.

The closer he came to graduation, the more sullen I became. I realized that my address would soon change, but I thought if I had enough temper tantrums, I could somehow preclude that from happening.

My tantrums, though frequent, didn't earn him a local job, and he investigated a medical entomologist position with the United States Navy. Who knew that the Navy, which focuses on boats, would need bug experts? When he signed the dotted line that granted him a three-year tour of adventure—isn't that what the television commercials said?—I accepted defeat and started packing. For a brief time, I was miserable. But, my optimism kicked in, and I decided I could do this for just three years. David assured me that with three years of experience, he'd be able to find an entomology job elsewhere, and I kidded myself that what he really meant was, "We'll move back home in three years."

I made up my mind to have a good attitude about the move and look on the bright side of each situation. I really could do this... for just three years.

I learned to ignore the loud roar of the P-3's that flew directly over our two-bedroom base housing complex at Naval Air Station, Jacksonville, and instead enjoyed the beauty of Florida's St. John's River, visible from my front porch swing. With much prayer and time spent with new friends who also had deployed husbands, I tolerated the short, but frequent deployments required of a Navy medical entomologist.

I pushed aside my jealousy over my husband "seeing the world" without me, and I took interest in his adventures. On a couple of delightful occasions, I earned stamps in my own passport. We emptied our savings on a plane ticket for me; David took leave; and I met him, first in Barbados, where I ate fresh sugar cane, drank delicious fruit drinks, and saw spectacular shades of blues and greens in the Caribbean.

A year later, I joined him in Quito, Ecuador. I marveled at the Andes Mountains, suffered my first bout of altitude sickness, and stood in two hemispheres at once when I straddled the equator. We watched a Mestizo couple pick bugs from each other's hair in the park, then eat the protein snacks. I saw beautiful children in bright colored clothing with no shoes emerge from poorly constructed homes with patched roofs and gaping holes in the walls.

As the end of David's first tour of duty approached, he announced, "I think I'll sign up for just one more tour." I reluctantly affirmed his decision and kept my positive attitude. "I can do this for just three more years," I told myself.

Uncle Sam sent us to Camp Lejeune, North Carolina. I thought I deserved a stamp in my passport for this location too, but officials didn't agree. It was two hours from nowhere, a "cultural desert" as another military wife warned me.

I ignored the unwanted negativism others offered about our new home and determined to find the best. I welcomed new relationships with military personnel from all over the map instead, wonderful families on adventures of their own.

I went deep sea fishing, crabbing, and camping. I joined my husband in Israel and rode my first camel. I saw an olive tree that reminded me of Bible stories. I saw the Sea of Galilee, cringed at Golgotha, and scooped water from the River Jordan that, years later, flowed over my four children in baptism.

I trembled when an Israeli soldier cocked his machine gun. I trembled even more at an empty tomb. I saw beautiful people with empty eyes at the Wailing Wall. I wept.

My next plane ticket read "Puerto Rico," where I explored the El Yunque rainforest, with its captivating kapok trees and heard coqui frog serenades.

Prayers, my sanguinity, and my eighteen-month-old firstborn enabled me to make it through my husband's first wartime deployment. Operation Desert Storm separated my family for six months, but simultaneously bound us in a way that few circumstances can.

Post-war decisions signed us up for "just one more tour," where I looked past the smog, crime, and traffic of nearby D.C. to explore every national monument, admire cherry blossoms, and salute the known and unknown fallen soldiers.

God and Uncle Sam sent our family to the West Coast, where we landed first in California, then three years later, an hour ferry's ride from Seattle. I wished away San Diego's gray fog and hot Santa Ana winds and enjoyed the cold Pacific Ocean, giant sequoias and redwoods. I caught a tarantula and saw tumbleweeds.

I accepted the Pacific Northwest's constant rain and sunless days, marveling instead at the magnificent evergreens, Hoh Rain Forest, and snow-capped mountain views. I soared over Seattle in a seaplane, schlepped through banks of snow on a Christmas sleigh ride, and slewed through snow with sled dogs.

When our "three-year tour" ended twenty years later, I had more stamps in my passport and pictures in my albums than I ever dreamed possible. Life in the Navy was truly an incredible voyage for our entire family. Overlooking the negatives and capitalizing on the positives impacted our time at each duty station, bringing endless joy and a lifetime of treasured memories, especially for this small-town, country girl with big dreams of adventure.

~Julie Lavender

Yet a Word May Change Your Life...

Words are also actions, and actions are a kind of words.
~Ralph Waldo Emerson

I used to think that to make big changes in your life, you had to do big things. Harboring a bit of a defeatist attitude, I also assumed that big, scary actions would cost enormous amounts of money, which I didn't have. So, it became a self-fulfilling prophecy that I couldn't change my life and I stayed in my safe rut.

My optimistic friend Donna changed all that. A native Californian, she taught me the power of word choice. Reminding me that it was absolutely free, she took away my self-imposed economic barrier.

"Watch what you say because your subconscious hears the exact words, not what you 'mean to' say."

At first it sounded a bit "airy-fairy," but, with the proverbial nothing to lose, I decided to try it. Wow. This simple but potent piece of advice soon became a catalyst for all kinds of fantastic changes in my life, making me the most positive I have ever been.

Slowly I stopped using the word "can't," and that forced me to recognize that everything was a choice. Instead of saying, "I can't go with you tonight" I would say things like, "I wish I could go with you, but I already have plans and I don't cancel on my friends." I would try and remind my subconscious that I was choosing a different option; there is always another way. Sometimes it forced me out of old habits.

Instead of saying, "I can't, I have to work," I found myself asking my boss for a vacation day!

I began to think more about which words I selected, trying to be as specific as possible about what I was trying to express. The next word to go was "should." Says who? The word "should" symbolized something I felt obligated to do but I didn't want to do. Instead, I started doing what I liked.

Unfortunately, I was getting great offers to attend events and go out for dinner and my time at my health club was taking a back seat. That led me to working out in the morning. While I'll probably never be a morning person, it was a great way to ensure that I got my workouts in. Nora, a good friend I met when I changed my workout routine, explained this phenomenon to me.

"Early morning, before you head into the office, is the only time you own. After that, your job can easily take over." How right she was!

Then I got rid of "never," replacing it with "not yet," particularly when responding to a travel question. For example, when someone asked me if I had ever been to a remote island in the Pacific, I would proudly answer, "No, not yet." Instead of closing a door, this expands the possibility of at least going someday.

I kept practicing and paying attention to my word choices. Over time, they became automatic. My careful word choices, practiced for months, became habits... habits that had a profound effect and got me to a positive place.

My best example took place when I was traveling. I had gone to Córdoba (the second largest city in Argentina), to spend some time with my friend Monique when a friend of hers, Regina, walked in and joined us. We were quickly laughing like old friends. Regina was originally from Ireland but had been living in the United Arab Emirates (in Dubai and then in Abu Dhabi) for some time.

"Wow!" I exclaimed. "I would love to go there."

"You've never been to Dubai?" Regina asked.

"Nope. Not yet."

"Well, what's keeping you? Come visit! You can stay with me — I'd love the company!"

I was dumbfounded. Here was a free place to stay in an Arab country known for ultra luxury hotels with Rolls-Royces and helicopter landings. How cool would that be? Cool, yes. But, me? No. I was scared out of my mind at the possibility of how easily my dream could happen! Fear was holding me hostage.

So I looked for an out. "You can take it back," I said. "I'm a backpacker without responsibilities and with a bunch of frequent flier miles, so I could come and visit you. Easily."

Regina, a wonderfully optimistic person, looked at me and shook her head.

"Darling, I'm a very straightforward person. I invited you, so I mean it. You're welcome to come and stay with me. Just tell me when."

One look at my doubting face and she added, "I'm not going to un-invite you. I'd love to show you around. We'd have a blast."

"But you barely know me!" I protested.

"We get along great. I have an extra couch and time off. We can visit Oman. Have you ever been there?"

I was too shocked to even spit out my classic, "No. Not yet."

"Where else is on your bucket list?" she wanted to know.

"Egypt. I would really love to see the pyramids."

"FlyDubai. They're a great budget airline and you can find ridiculously cheap airfares there. Of course, Egypt is pretty close."

I was too terrified to act that day. Eventually, thinking about how much fun it would be, I gathered my courage. Less than a year later, I cashed in a bunch of frequent flier miles and went to visit Regina in Abu Dhabi. She took me to amazing places and we had profound discussions on changes we wanted to make in our lives. Before I knew it, it was time for my side trip to Egypt.

When I checked into a hostel in gorgeous Alexandria, the owner triple upgraded me, saying that I was the only person to have ever written my request in more than one language.

He added, "I would like to make your dream come true." Was I dreaming?

He walked me to an ocean view room with a private bath, and breakfast included! All for twelve dollars U.S. Knowing I was on a budget, he carefully explained how to take public transportation to Cairo. With the word "Great Pyramids" written in Arabic, I hopped from one small bus to the next. I will always remember my first glimpse of that Wonder of the World.

Returning to Abu Dhabi, my eyes filled with tears when I told Regina about my adventure. I thanked her for making such a difference in my life.

True to her word, she was the perfect hostess: we went all over and she became one of my dearest friends. And still is. We're trying to figure out where to meet up next.

All because I used the words "not yet."

~JC Sullivan

Making Peace

Change your thoughts and you change your world.
~Norman Vincent Peale ·

As soon as I turned the corner onto my street and glimpsed the ruddy brown shipping container with the three-letter word ZIM written in white capitals, I started to shake. It was a Thursday afternoon in mid-July, six weeks before our move date, and I wasn't ready to watch the bulk of our belongings being loaded onto that forty-cubic-foot container bound for Israel. I wasn't ready for our house to become an empty shell. Parking my car across the street, I sobbed while six burly men went in and out of our front door, laden with sofas and tables, boxes and beds. Finally, when I could no longer tolerate the oppressive New York heat, I got out of the car, walked down the driveway and entered the side door. My husband greeted me.

"Ça va?" he asked gently, opening his arms to hold me.

"No. I'm not okay. I know this is probably the happiest day of your life, but I can't share it with you," I said, crying into his chest.

Over the course of my life, I have made at least thirty trips to Israel. While I was there during my early twenties, I unexpectedly met and then married a Jewish Frenchman, Philippe, a new immigrant whose dream was to claim that country as his own. Even though I liked visiting, living there brought out the worst in me, making me act and react aggressively, whether I was changing lanes on the highway or waiting in line at the grocery store. But I fell hard for Philippe's accent and worldliness, and for his ability to make me laugh. When, five years later, we left for Philippe to study abroad, we agreed to eventually return. A decade passed, and we stayed stateside, for me, because I didn't want to raise my three children in a country where I didn't feel comfortable. But when Philippe suggested a one-year sabbatical in Israel, I was interested, thinking that it would make mid-life more exciting.

In the spring of our year away, Philippe announced that he wanted to stay. I balked, ill prepared and unwilling to extend our time. He was furious that I was so close-minded, and I felt betrayed that he wasn't sticking to our plan. We fought for months. Finally, I held out an olive branch: if he would agree to return to the U.S., I would consider coming back to Israel permanently after our eldest had graduated from high school.

But I didn't really mean it. Secretly, I hoped that Philippe's desire to move back to Israel would wane. When it didn't, I knew I had to concede. I wanted to stay married to the man I loved. I agreed to go.

Initially, our plan to move back was all just talk—before bed, during date nights, in therapy. And then, as the time approached, I moved from denial to reality.

During our therapy sessions, when I cried about leaving, our therapist told me repeatedly, "You're going to lose things—your friends, community, yoga students, house. You need to acknowledge the loss and let yourself mourn. Start now so it doesn't hit you after you've gone."

The first time I knew I had internalized her message was during my drive up Interstate 684 to yoga. I glanced at the trees. The colors of the leaves were so stunning—eggplant purple, fiery red, burnt orange—that I welled up with tears, trying to memorize their intensity, knowing I would no longer witness them every fall. I shared my sense of grief with my yoga students. With a shaky voice, I closed my eyes and described the colors. As time went on and each month passed, I began to acknowledge and accept my losses and all the lasts: snow days, yoga classes, writing group meetings.

Then, in early July, as our packing intensified, I fell apart.

Philippe was away, and I needed a friend. By the time I arrived at Laurie's house, my eyes were swollen and red.

"What's wrong?" she asked as I wept.

"I don't know if I can move. I'm so scared of the what-ifs."

"Like what?"

"What if our kids hate it there and want to come back, but there's nowhere for them to come back to? What if I'm miserable and want to leave? What if Philippe refuses to leave with me?"

"Stop!" Laurie pulled away to look me in the eyes. "I've known you for ten years, but I've never seen you like this before. Just stop, or you'll make yourself sick." The force of her words struck me. Strong and calm, Laurie had recently held herself and her family together for eighteen months while her husband was unemployed, only to be diagnosed with an autoimmune condition. I wholly believe in the mind-body connection; I feared the burdens she shouldered had made her ill.

"You can't play those what-if games in your head. Let them go," she said firmly. I wiped my eyes, listening to her every word. Unlike Laurie, I had a choice not to stress and obsess about difficulties that might or might not arise in the future. I had moved—counties, countries and continents—more than anyone I knew. Each time I had found my way. That wasn't the last time I wept for what I was losing, but it was the last time I let myself be swallowed by fear. I knew that Philippe and I, together, would determine the best place to live, as we had for the past twenty years.

Then, shortly before our departure date, I called Verizon to disconnect our Internet. When the woman tried to tell me their services were available elsewhere, I told her we were moving abroad.

"That's so brave! It's great to live in a different country with kids, to see everything through another lens." Those were the exact reasons we had decided to spend that sabbatical year in Israel. I appreciated the reminder and thanked her.

All along, our friends and family and community had been telling us how much they admired our ability to pick up and move and adapt to other cultures, but I was finally ready to hear it.

We have been in our new Israeli home for six months now. In that short time, I have found a friend with whom I go to the movies on Saturday mornings, opened up my own yoga studio and joined a writing group.

Friends who knew about my struggle with the move call and e-mail, asking the same question, "Are you happy?" Happy isn't the answer, I say. Rather, I am calm inside; I don't second guess myself, blame Philippe or play the what-if game. I have chosen instead to be content, to accept my life as it is.

Bolstered by everybody's words of support, I have come again to this extraordinary country with my eyes wide open, determined to see the bad and the good. This time, I packed everything I knew I needed to bring—wrap sunglasses, SPF 60+ sunscreen, a Nook—along with the things I'd never brought to Israel before: a sense of humor and an open heart.

~Jennifer Lang

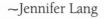

A for Attitude

Four things for success: work and pray, think and believe.
~Norman Vincent Peale

English was always my favorite subject. I "got" it, unlike math. In my freshman year of high school, I could write a killer composition and diagram a sentence with surgical precision. In my sophomore year, my teacher allowed me to give spelling tests to the class. I have wonderful memories of my junior year. Mrs. Alexander appointed me to sit at her desk and present the lesson when she had to leave the room. My senior English class was distressing, as it was very small and we had a teacher right out of college who stated that she expected college-level work. Every student received a C or D grade the first quarter. She wanted us to work hard for our grade, and we did. But English was still my subject.

I graduated high school, married early, had children and raised a family. I composed long letters and beautiful poetry. I wrote complaint letters to corporations that got results. I helped my kids with their compositions and English homework and I did my former husband's college-level English assignments. After all, English had always been my best subject. I was an A student, I told my family. Why, my teacher allowed me to take over her class when I was in high school!

Fifteen years later, I went to college, and because I had been an A student, I remained an A student. I lived up to my own expectations.

Recently, decades later, I was rummaging through old papers when I discovered my high school report cards. Holding that bundle of report cards brought back the smell of waxed hallways, chalk dust and Miss R's flowery perfume. I remembered sitting in my advisor's office explaining that I had always excelled at English, complaining that I did not deserve a D from that inexperienced teacher my senior year. The counselor empathized but was unable to change a grade.

Flipping through my old report cards revealed something else too. I wanted to shred them or at least hide them. I was not an A student in high school English! Somehow, I had convinced myself of this, when the grades clearly reflected an average student with an occasional A or B, but mostly C's.

Had I lived up to those grades and defined myself based on those letters, I would have never confidently pursued my successful freelance writing career. I would have ridiculed myself: "Who do you think you are calling yourself a writer? Actually submitting to publications?" Had I believed in my early grades instead of myself, I would have allowed my fear of failure to defeat my enthusiasm and paralyze my creativity. Instead, I viewed my younger self as an A English student. Except for that one undeserved D.

~Linda O'Connell

A Different Point of View

My sister taught me everything I really need to know,
and she was only in sixth grade at the time.
~Linda Sunshine

I used to adore walking home from school. I remember the first time my mother let my sister and me take the mile and half walk on our own. I felt so grown up. Ready to take on the world—to prove to my mother that I really was capable of taking care of myself. I hated being young, and more than anything, I hated taking care of my older sister. She was different, and at the time we didn't have a name for it. We didn't discover until my teenage years that she was autistic. Our classmates would constantly ask what was wrong with her, why she looked the way she did, why she never spoke. I didn't have any answers for them. How could I when I didn't even have the answers for myself?

In every school there is a mean group of kids—kids who rule the schoolyard and bully their way through lunchrooms and swing-set lines. At our school, they relentlessly tormented my sister and it enraged me. They would follow us home and throw things at her as we walked. On several occasions my mother had to call the police because they had followed us to our front door. Why did it matter that she was different, why did they care? She wasn't their sister—she was mine. As angry as I was, a part of me, I'm ashamed to admit, was embarrassed too.

I wanted so badly to just walk by myself. To be left alone with my thoughts and not have to listen to the things they shouted at her. Even then I felt like I was growing up too fast, that because of her I was being robbed of my own childhood. I resented it, and I resented her. I used to beg my mother to pick her up from school and let me walk on my own, just once, but it never happened. They needed me to help take care of her. To make sure she made it home safely. To their credit, they had no idea what they were asking of me.

Every day after school I would meet my sister at the library where we would walk home together. One afternoon, after a particularly bad day, she wasn't there to meet me. I checked inside the library, her classroom, the front office, but she was nowhere. I became frantic asking anyone who knew us if they had seen her. Finally, one of the teachers told me that she saw her leave with a group of her classmates. I knew there was no way she left with anyone, let alone a group of kids. I immediately started running.

I ran so fast and so hard I thought I would pass out. My sides were on fire and screaming at me to stop but I kept going. I pushed my way through the sidewalks, rushing through groups of children, trying to spot her in the crowds. I ran so far that I nearly made it all the way home when I finally saw her. There was a busy street underneath a freeway overpass that we had to walk through every day. There were large embankments covered in ivy that flanked each side of the bridge. My sister was sitting on the overpass, legs dangling over the busy road below, her face completely devoid of emotion. Her back faced the busy freeway traffic and her hair was blowing from the force of the moving cars behind her.

Underneath the bridge was a large group of kids on bikes making figure eights, taunting her. Some even sat on the embankment itself, throwing what was left over from their lunches at her. Hitting her face, her body... I screamed at them to stop. Some of them actually did, startled by my yelling, a look of shame coming over their youthful faces. I was in a state of utter panic, unmatched even now into my adult life. I did everything I could think of to get them to stop. I threw my backpack at one of the older boys, pushed another to the ground, and frantically yanked another from his bike. I was trying to hurt them, make them pay, not just for today but every other day before. If I had rocks, I would have thrown them. If my nine-year-old body were stronger, I would have fought them. Forced them into submission. In the end, all it did was make them laugh. She was four years my senior and these kids were her classmates, they weren't going to listen to me — a small, fourth grade girl.

Finally, it occurred to me there was nothing I could do to make them stop. Not just today, but any day. I had a moment of complete clarity when I realized that every day for as long as we went to this school, maybe any school, we would have to deal with this. We would have to endure it together. I picked up my bag and slowly climbed the steep embankment to my sister. I walked along the narrow ledge and silently made my way to her. I sat, legs dangling, hair blowing in the wind and looked at the world from my sister's point of view. I saw blue sky, feathery clouds, and the tops of blossoming trees all around us. The noise from the traffic made it impossible to hear the crowd below and we just sat, quietly together. I reached down to hold my sister's hand and for the first time, she squeezed back. Something passed between us on that bridge, something akin to understanding. That moment has lasted us a lifetime.

I never again felt ashamed or embarrassed to have her in my life. I am immensely lucky to have viewed the world from her eyes and my life is better because of it. Those kids never did leave her alone but it didn't matter anymore. We learned something from them and they showed me how to be stronger. How to recognize when something is bigger than I am. It's a lesson I have tried to teach my own children and something I hope to instill in all of you. See the world from a different angle and sometimes, just sometimes, everything changes.

~Audrey Clearwater

The Excited Mark

You will find more happiness growing down than up.
~Author Unknown

My six-year-old grandson Cade was preparing to attend the birthday party of a very pretty girl in his class. He and his parents picked out a present and wrapped it. Once it was wrapped and decorated to his satisfaction, he asked his dad to write on the card for him, since he was just learning to write. Daddy dutifully sat down and wrote as his son dictated. When they finished his dad showed Cade the card and asked: "How's that?"

Cade frowned and said, "You forgot the excited mark, Dad."

After his dad and mom recovered from their laughter, his mom asked, "Do you mean an exclamation point?"

Cade thought about it and said, "Yeah, that's it."

Leave it to a child to show us a new way of looking at our world. I laughed for some time after she shared this story with me but it reminded me that we take so many things for granted as adults. Doesn't an "excited mark" sound like so much more fun than an exclamation point? I think so. I will never be able to see an exclamation point the same again.

Lord, give me the heart of a child to see things in a new and refreshing way in the world around me!

~Sandy Stevener

The
Power of
Positive

Meet Our Contributors
Meet Our Authors
Thank You
About Chicken Soup for the Soul

Meet Our Contributors

Christopher Allen splits his time between the UK and Germany, where he teaches business English. In 2011, Allen was a finalist at Glimmer Train and was also nominated for a Pushcart Prize. In his spare time, Allen travels obsessively and blogs about his travels at www.imustbeoff.com.

Teresa Ambord writes business articles from her home in rural Northern California. Teresa is fully owned by her dogs, who inspire her writing and decorate her life. She volunteers as a foster parent for animals at AnotherChanceAnimalWelfareLeague.org. E-mail her at ambertreespublishing@charter.net.

Monica A. Andermann lives on Long Island with her husband Bill and their cat Charley. In addition to many credits in the *Chicken Soup for the Soul* series, her writing has appeared in such publications as *Skirt!*, *The Secret Place*, *Ocean*, and *Woman's World*.

Carol E. Ayer's publishing credits include *Woman's World*, *True Story*, *True Confessions*, and other *Chicken Soup for the Soul* anthologies. Visit her at www.carolayer.com.

Syndee A. Barwick is a freelance writer and purveyor of positivity. A published author of the nonfiction story, "The Wisdom of Socrates," in *Chicken Soup for the Cat Lover's Soul*, and an agented writer of a young adult fantasy that is on the road to publication. E-mail her at syndeebar@gmail.com.

Garrett Bauman is Professor Emeritus from Monroe Community College in Rochester, NY. His textbook on writing is currently in use at eighty-seven colleges and his writings have been in *The New York Times*, *Sierra*, *Yankee*, other *Chicken Soup for the Soul* books and many other publications. E-mail him at Mbauman@retiree.monroecc.edu.

Toni Becker received her Bachelor of Arts degree from Lakeland College, Sheboygan, WI. She works for Sheboygan County Health and Human Services, managing two senior centers and doing home outreach to the elderly. In her spare time, she enjoys freelance writing for local and regional publications. E-mail her at lynn-be@hotmail.com.

Jay Berman is a retired florist, working on his first novel; he volunteers for three non-profits, assisting with newsletters, solicitations, and peer counseling. Jay has one son currently attending college; and has family in New York, Texas, and Florida. His hobbies include: Yankee fanaticism, baseball memorabilia, reading, and creative writing.

Rita Bosel, a native of Germany, has lived and worked on three continents. Now residing in Palm Coast, FL, she enjoys life in the Sunshine State and capturing—and thus reliving—the defining moments that shaped her life's stories.

Allyssa Bross grew up in Charlotte, NC. She is currently a principal dancer with LA's professional ballet company, Los Angeles Ballet. She loves being an inspiration to others to follow their dreams. E-mail her at allyssabross1@gmail.com.

L.R. Buckman graduated from Mission College with an A.A. degree in English. She is pursuing a degree in nursing. She loves working with older people, but actually she would rather write, write, write.

She is a member of South Bay Writers club and Romance Writers of America and blogs at bayareawriter.blogspot.com.

Throughout **Nancy Lombard Burall's** life, she has walked through many heartaches, trials and new beginnings. From the death of her parents when she was a teenager, to being a single parent, to the breakdown of her health, Nancy has learned to trust God. She writes from her experiences with humor and encouragement.

Sally Willard Burbank received her medical degree from the University of Vermont. She is a practicing internist. She is married and the mother of two college students. Sally enjoys writing, reading, gardening, and bicycling. To read other stories by Sally, visit her blog at patientswewillneverforget.wordpress.com.

Lynn Cahoon found her true calling while examining life's highs and lows. She realized her happiest times surrounded writing and telling stories. Since that commitment, Lynn's sold her first book. She lives in St. Louis with her husband and three fur babies, but calls Idaho home. E-mail her at lynncahoonauthor@gmail.com.

Sara Celi is a TV anchor at KFOR/KAUT Freedom 43 in Oklahoma City, OK. She graduated from Western Kentucky University in 2004 and since then has traveled all over the country for her journalism career. She also enjoys running, hiking, and volunteering with the Junior League.

Cindy Charlton, professional speaker/author, brings her message of hope, inspiration, and gratitude to everyone. She survived a life threatening illness, losing three limbs in the process, but feels lucky to be alive. Cindy writes personal essays for magazines and a blog, thesurvivorshandbook.blogspot.com. Cindy welcomes e-mails at cindycharlsky@gmail.com.

Jane McBride Choate is the author of thirty-two books and over 400 short stories and articles. Being published in the *Chicken Soup for the Soul* series is a dream come true for her.

Audrey Clearwater is earning her B.A. degree in creative writing from Southern New Hampshire University. She resides in Nevada with her husband and two beautiful daughters. Her passion is writing stories that inspire others and she endeavors to become a novelist specializing in creative non-fiction. E-mail her at aclearwater@live.com.

Harriet Cooper is a freelance writer and has published personal essays, humour and creative nonfiction in newspapers, newsletter, anthologies and magazines, and is a frequent contributor to the *Chicken Soup for the Soul* series. She writes about family, relationships, health, food, cats, writing and daily life. E-mail her at shewrites@live.ca.

Gunter David was a reporter for major city newspapers for twenty-five years and a Pulitzer Prize nominee by the *Evening Bulletin* of Philadelphia, before obtaining a master's degree in family therapy. He has had numerous stories and memoirs published in literary journals and anthologies.

Kerri A. Davidson holds a Bachelor of Arts degree from Otterbein College. Upon graduation, she achieved her childhood dream of moving from Indiana to New York City and is currently writing a memoir about her adventures. In her free time, she loves to dance. E-mail her at 3kerri@gmail.com.

Lola Di Giulio De Maci is a regular contributor to the *Chicken Soup for the Soul* series. She also enjoys writing children's stories, some appearing in the *Los Angeles Times*. Lola has a Master of Art's degree in education and English and writes from her loft overlooking the San Bernardino Mountains. E-mail her at LDeMaci@aol.com.

Linda C. Defew calls writing her therapy and her sole purpose is to stay busy inspiring others. Linda writes for her local paper and numerous magazines such as *Christian Woman* and *The Writer*. She and her husband live in the country where they surround themselves with family, friends, and dogs. E-mail her at oldwest@tds.net.

Hollye Dexter is co-editor of *Dancing at the Shame Prom* (Seal Press), and author of two memoirs. She teaches writing workshops for adults and at-risk teens. She lives in Southern California with her husband and three children, where she hikes, plays music and blogs about living an authentic life at www.hollyedexter.blogspot.com.

Gary Duff is the CEO of xQ Public Relations, as well as an award-winning journalist, producer and talk show host, whose ideas have led to magazine publication and appearances on television and radio. E-mail Gary at Gary.s.duff@gmail.com.

H.J. Eggers is delighted to have her sixth story in the *Chicken Soup for the Soul* series. Life with her beloved husband Shawn is a blessing and education. Son Michael and his new wife Rose add even more joy. Gardening, quilting, fishing, camping, yoga and of course writing fill her heart and days. E-mail her at hjs01234@aol.com.

Terri Elders, LCSW, lives near Colville, WA, with two dogs and three cats. Her stories have appeared in multiple editions of the *Chicken Soup for the Soul* series. Terri is a public member of the Washington State Medical Quality Assurance Commission. Contact her at telders@ hotmail.com or visit her blog at touchoftarragon.blogspot.com.

Jean Ferratier is a heart-centered archetypal coach, helping people link their synchronous moments to their life's purpose. Her recent book is titled *Reading Symbolic Signs: How to Connect the Dots of Your Spiritual Life*. Jean loves to dance and share information on her blog at synchronousmoments.blogspot.com. E-mail her at jferratier@gmail. com.

Pamela Gilsenan has five adult children whose names begin with the letter "S." She graduated from Stephens College and plans to pursue a law degree.

Liz Graf is a retired high school biology teacher with three grown children. She and her high school sweetheart are now settled in Palm Coast, FL. Liz loves seeing and translating the world through the written word. She strives to make every day a Sunshine Day. E-mail her at linesbyliz@gmail.com.

Dale Mary Grenfell is an educator, writer and storyteller. She teaches in Colorado, conducts workshops and recently completed her first manuscript on a new look at grief in western culture. She also delights in hosting foreign students who enrich her appreciation of our marvelous multicultural world. E-mail her at grenfell@q.com.

Pamela Hawken has lived and worked in Europe, Africa, Oregon, Colorado and California. Retired from a career in business, she enjoys photography, music, travel, gardening, and being a grandma. Pamela has recently written a book titled *Angel on a 747* based on her travels and life as a single mom. E-mail her at pamestla@aol.com.

Sue Henninger lives in the Finger Lakes region of New York State with her husband, three sons, and some pets. She's a full-time freelance writer who enjoys boating, waterskiing, and tubing with friends and family in her spare time. Visit her website and blog at www.fingerlakeswriter.com.

Allison Howell is a homeschooling mother of seven children, two of whom have cystic fibrosis. She enjoys reading, crocheting, hobby farming, and hiking. She and her husband Ken have been married for twenty-two years. Allison blogs at www.northerncffamily.blogspot.com.

Randi Sue Huchingson lives in Florida with her husband and four children. She is a pastor's wife and a homeschool mom. She enjoys writing short stories about how God speaks to her through her daily life. She also enjoys teaching and making music with her kids. E-mail her at dickandrandisue@gmail.com.

Owner of Café Roche Espresso Bar in Winston-Salem, **Sarah Hummell** has devoted her life to coffee and café culture. She received her Bachelor of Science degree in Hotel Restaurant Management in 2004 and writes a coffee blog at www.caferoche.com. In her free time, Sarah enjoys traveling, and spending time with her husband and their two children.

Besides penning thank you notes, award-winning author **Jeanette Hurt** writes about food, wine and travel. Her latest book is *The Complete Idiot's Guide to Sausage Making*. She lives in Milwaukee with her family. Follow her on Twitter, visit her website, www.jeanettehurt.com, or listen to her on NPR affiliate, WUWM.

Lisa Hutchison is a writer, licensed mental health counselor and holistic educator in Massachusetts. She leads therapeutic and expressive therapy groups for elders in a partial hospitalization program, and has a private healing practice in which she teaches clients to empower themselves through the written word and educational seminars.

Jennie Ivey lives in Cookeville, TN. She is the author of numerous works of fiction and nonfiction, including stories in several books of the *Chicken Soup for the Soul* series. Visit her website at www.jennieivey.com.

Karen Lewis Jackson holds a master's degree in computer science from Syracuse University. When her family moved to Canada she retired from programming and has since been busy writing and volunteering. She also enjoys recreating the role of an 18th century fifer at historic sites. E-mail her at karenlewisjackson@yahoo.com.

Linda Jackson, a wife and mother of three, makes her home in Southaven, MS, where she writes full-time. More information about her writing may be found at www.jacksonbooks.com or on her blog at www.writersdolaundrytoo.com.

Miranda Johnson is currently in high school and will graduate in 2014. She is involved in marching band and plays piano, flute, is learning alto sax, and is also interested in art.

Tom Kaden is a graduate of Messiah College and Asbury Theological Seminary. He is vice president of Someone To Tell It To, Inc., a non-profit counseling service. Tom is married, the father of four, and he is an avid New York sports fan and outdoorsman. E-mail him at Tom@ someonetotellitto.org.

Tom Krause was a team captain on the Boonville Pirates 1974 State Championship team. He is now one of America's most quoted motivational speakers. Tom currently lives in Nixa, MO, with wife Amy and sons Tyler and Sam. Learn more at www.coachkrause.com.

Sheila Seiler Lagrand lives in the foothills of Orange County, CA, with her husband Rich and three dogs. By day, she works as the operations manager for a registered investment advisory firm. Otherwise, you'll find her boating, cooking, enjoying her grandchildren, and blogging at godspotting.net. E-mail her at sheila@godspotting.net.

Jeannie Lancaster writes from her home in Loveland, CO. She believes that even in the most challenging of situations, there can be moments of immense joy, which lead one to a sense of deep gratitude. It is from reflection on these moments that her most important writing emerges.

A freelance writer, **Jennifer Lang** has been published in *Parenting*, *Real Simple*, *Yoga Journal*, *Parents* and *Natural Solutions*, among others. Her essays have appeared in the *South Loop Review* and *San Francisco*

Chronicle, as well as on ducts.org. Most recently, her story appeared in *Chicken Soup for the Soul: Here Comes the Bride*.

Julie Lavender is married to her high school sweetheart David and together they have four wonderful children: Jeremy, Jennifer, Jeb Daniel, and Jessica. She is a homeschooling mommy, and enjoys cooking and traveling. Julie writes for her local newspaper, and has written books, devotionals, and articles. E-mail her at lavenders@bulloch.net.

Amy Gray Light writes animal and human-interest essays for regional, local, and national publications. A former editor for a design magazine and an international nonprofit, Amy now lives on Wye Mountain in Arkansas, where she and her husband, Excy, run a wild mustang sanctuary. Learn more at wingspur.org.

Sarah Darer Littman wrote *Confessions of a Closet Catholic*, 2006 Sydney Taylor Book Award, *Life, After*, a 2011 Sydney Taylor Honor book, *Purge* and *Want to Go Private?*, a 2012 YALSA Quick Pick for Reluctant Young Readers. She's an award-winning columnist for CTNewsJunkie.com. Contact her at sarahdarerlittman.com and Twitter @sarahdarerlitt.

Gail MacMillan is the award-winning author of twenty-six published books and numerous short stories and articles published in both North America and Europe. She lives in New Brunswick, Canada with her husband and three dogs. Contact Gail through her website at www.gailmacmillan.ca or by e-mail at macgail@nbnet.nb.ca.

Conny Manero is an executive assistant by day and a writer after hours. She has written two novels, *Voice of an Angel* and *Waiting for Silverbird*, and a children's book called *Kitten Diaries*. When not writing, Conny is an active fundraiser for the Toronto Cat Shelter and is an avid ten-pin bowler.

With degrees from the University of Wyoming and the College of St. Catherine, **Alice Marks** taught preschool for over thirty years in Minnesota and Texas. Upon retirement, she joined a writers group in Port Aransas, TX, which she now leads. E-mail her at amarks001@ centurytel.net.

Scott Martin and Coryanne Hicks are co-authors of the inspirational memoir *Moving Forward In Reverse*, available exclusively on Amazon in late 2012 and various other retail outlets in 2013. This story has been adapted for the good folks at Chicken Soup for the Soul and you, the reader. Visit scomartin.com to learn more.

Sara Matson lives in Minnesota with her husband and twin twelve-year-old daughters. Her stories have appeared in four other *Chicken Soup for the Soul* books. E-mail her at saramatsonstories@hotmail. com.

Catherine Mattice is president of Civility Partners, a consulting firm focused on helping organizations build positive workplaces. She became interested in the power of positivity while working with targets of workplace bullying, and her accident allowed her to experience this power firsthand. E-mail her at Catherine@CivilityPartners.com or visit www.NoWorkplaceBullies.com.

Audrey McLaughlin lives in Pittsburgh, PA, with her husband Tom, spending her winters in Florida. She retired after working twenty-seven years in early childhood education. She enjoys writing and sharing what she has learned from working with young children, their families, and her personal life experiences. E-mail her at audreylengyel@comcast.net.

Mary Anne Molcan is currently a fine arts student at North Island College on Vancouver Island. She has published poetry in a local magazine and plans to continue sharing her words and artwork so that others can learn about themselves. Mary Anne can be contacted via at faerie.artiste@gmail.com.

When **Gail Molsbee Morris** isn't chasing rare birds, she pursues God's heart. She writes for the Fort Worth *Star-Telegram* and can be reached through her blog, www.godgirlgail.wordpress.com. She continues to edit her book, *Finding Light in the Darkness*, an uplifting autobiography about alopecia and cancer. E-mail her at godgirlgail@gmail.com.

Carine Nadel has been writing features for *The Orange County Register*, *Orange County Jewish Life* magazine, More.com and many other publications. She has a humor/lifestyle blog at www.carine-whatscooking.blogspot.com. Her favorite stories come from her husband, Steve, of over thirty years and her grown children and grandkids. E-mail her at 4thenadels@cox.net.

Linda O'Connell, a seasoned preschool teacher from St. Louis, MO, enjoys a good laugh, dark chocolate and long walks with her husband. Her inspirational stories have been published in fifteen *Chicken Soup for the Soul* books and many other publications. Linda blogs at lindaoconnell.blogspot.com.

Dorri Olds is a Manhattan-based award-winning freelance writer who has written for a variety of publications including *The New York Times*, *The Jewish Daily Forward*, is a weekly contributor to NBC's Petside and a web designer/social media consultant. She is a member of American Society of Journalists & Authors and Graphic Artists Guild.

Galen Pearl leads retreats and discussion groups based on her program to develop habits to grow a joyful spirit. She writes a blog and is publishing a book about her program, titled *10 Steps to Finding Your Happy Place (and Staying There)*. E-mail her at galenpearl@gmail.com.

Award-winning columnist/novelist **Saralee Perel** is honored to be a multiple contributor to the *Chicken Soup for the Soul* series. She lives on Cape Cod with her husband and her perpetually increasing family of pets. E-mail Saralee at sperel@saraleeperel.com or via her website at www.saraleeperel.com.

Shirley Dunn Perry is a nurse and author of *Ten Five-Minute Miracles: How to Relax.* Her work has appeared in many publications. Biscuit making, hiking, world travel, watercolors, and enjoying her family and grandchildren add zest to her writing adventures. E-mail her at sdunnperry@gmail.com or read her blog at shirleydunnperry. wordpress.com.

Connie Pombo is an inspirational author, speaker and freelance writer. She has contributed several stories to the *Chicken Soup for the Soul* series. Connie is the creator of Baskets Full of Hope, a gift basket company for breast cancer survivors and their caregivers. She can be reached at www.basketsfullofhope.com.

Kimberly Porrazzo is a writer and editor with five essays published in the *Chicken Soup for the Soul* series. Her husband and two sons love baseball; Nick played Jeremy Giambi in *Moneyball*, and Anthony currently works for the Anaheim Angels. "Positive thinking" plays a big part in their lives. E-mail her at kimberlyporrazzo@cox.net.

Nafisa Rayani, a previous contributor to the *Chicken Soup for the Soul* series, is a young Kenyan woman who only recently discovered her passion for writing, but has been using the "Power of Positive" in her life for many years now. E-mail her at lucid.dreamer.ke@gmail.com.

Mark Rickerby's writings have been published in three previous *Chicken Soup for the Soul* books. He co-wrote his father's memoir, *The Other Belfast*, about growing up in Northern Ireland. His most recent project is a CD of fifteen original songs for parents titled *Great Big World*. To learn more, visit www.markrickerbymusic.com.

Tamara Roberts is CPO of Bring Your Own Tiara. Continuing to cleave to her husband of over thirty years, Tamara is an award-winning author and speaker. Besides enjoying tea parties with her six grandchildren, she has a passion to empower and encourage people. E-mail her at Tamara@tamroberts.com.

Sioux Roslawski is a third grade teacher in St. Louis, a teacher consultant for the Gateway Writing Project, a wife, a mom, a grammy and a rescuer of Golden Retrievers. Sioux enjoys reading, eating chocolate and napping on Saturday afternoons. Learn more at siouxspage.blogspot.com.

Carol S. Rothchild has her master's degree in writing from Johns Hopkins. A freelance writer/editor, she contributes to education, media, web, marketing, advertising, anthologies, and magazines—complete with celebrity interviews and backyard fashion shoots. E-mail her at carsusnh1@comcast.net.

John Scanlan is a 1983 graduate of the United States Naval Academy, and retired from the Marine Corps as a Lieutenant Colonel aviator. He currently resides on Hilton Head Island, SC, and is pursuing a second career as a writer. John can be reached via e-mail at ping1@hargray.com.

Michael Jordan Segal, who defied all odds after being shot in the head, is a husband, father, social worker, author (including a CD/download of twelve stories entitled *Possible*, as well as working on an autobiography entitled *A Shot of Inspiration*), and an inspirational speaker. To learn more visit www.InspirationByMike.com.

Ange Shepard was born and raised on the east coast of Canada on Cape Breton Island but currently resides in Los Angeles with her husband. She enjoys writing, donairs, 90s music, and of course Chicken Soup for the Soul therapy when needed. E-mail her at angeshepard@live.com.

Former public defender and prosecutor **Mickey Sherman** is a criminal defense lawyer in Greenwich, CT. He has served as a legal commentator on most every TV network except The Food Channel. His first book, *How Can You Defend Those People?*, has been universally acclaimed by the legal and literary community. E-mail Mickey at ms23@aol.com.

Aaron Stafford received his business degrees from Missouri, Hawaii and Arkansas. He lives and sells real estate in the Seattle suburb of Kent, Washington. He enjoys computer games, humor and reading as many books as he can find, especially those with a positive outlook. E-mail him at aaronts@hotmail.com.

Diane Stark is a former teacher turned stay-at-home mom and freelance writer. She is a frequent contributor to the *Chicken Soup for the Soul* series and loves to write about the important things in life: her family and her faith. She is the author of *Teachers' Devotions to Go*. E-mail Diane at DianeStark19@yahoo.com.

Sharri Bockheim Steen, Ph.D., is a freelance medical writer in New Jersey. She kept a blog about her experience with cancer (burnishingbrightens.blogspot.com) and is grateful for her fully restored health. Sharri thanks her wonderful husband Bob, her two children, and all her family and friends for their support and encouragement.

Sandy Stevener and her husband are involved in full-time missions work. They live in Mississippi and travel often to Central and South America. Sandy is involved with many local ministries and is an aspiring novel writer. You can follow Sandy at billandsandystevener. blogspot.com and sandy-stevener-mystery-writer.blogspot.com or e-mail her at sandy@stevener.org.

There is a famous quote that scars (both emotional and physical) remind us where we've been but they don't have to dictate where we are going. **Sidney Anne Stone's** "scars" made her who she is today and she wears them like a badge of honor but she never hides behind them.

Florence Strang is a registered psychologist with more than twenty years of experience in the fields of education and psychology. She has also been trained in mindfulness meditation, reiki, horticultural therapy and angel therapy. Her blog, 100 Perks of Having Cancer, is soon to be published as a book.

After discovering a secret "reset" button, **JC Sullivan** is re-living her twenties, confident that she's having more fun this time around. Having fled the cubicle, she seeks adventure. Not independently wealthy, she takes odd jobs — to backpack the world. She's been to over 120 countries and every continent. Visit her blog at www.backpackingpoet.com.

Annmarie B. Tait resides in Conshohocken, PA, with her husband Joe Beck. Annmarie has stories published in several *Chicken Soup for the Soul* volumes, *Reminisce* magazine, *Patchwork Path*, and many other anthologies. Annmarie is a current nominee for the 2011 Pushcart Prize. E-mail Annmarie at irishbloom@aol.com.

Tsgoyna Tanzman's career spans from belly dancer to speech pathologist to fitness trainer to memoir teacher. Writing is her "therapy" for raising her adolescent daughter. Published in nine *Chicken Soup for the Soul* books, her essays and poems can be read at More.com, mothering.com and in *The Orange County Register*. E-mail her at tnzmn@cox.net.

Nina Taylor is the editorial director for Pneuma Books, the book producer for Chicken Soup for the Soul. In between raising her husband, three teenage sons, and a toddler, she edits and ghostwrites books, and dreams of finding the time and energy to write young adult novels. E-mail her at nina@pneumabooks.com.

Carl Van Landschoot is the Head of Business Studies and the Director of Sports and Business Management at Corpus Christi High School in Burlington, Ontario. Carl is married to Jane and they are the parents of five children—Alex, Joseph, Katie, Thomas and Claire. E-mail him at vangolfinc@hotmail.com.

Mary Varga is a fifty-two-year-old single mother living in Louisville, KY with her family of origin. Her son, Andrew lives in Little Rock, AR with his father. She is an ACSM Certified Personal Trainer, teaching exercise classes at several senior homes/centers. Fitness is her passion!

Pat Wahler is a grant writer by profession and writer of essays and fiction by night. Her stories have appeared in multiple national and local publications. A life-long animal lover, Pat ponders critters, writing, and life's little mysteries at www.critteralley.blogspot.com.

Rebecca Waters received her undergraduate degree from the University of South Florida and graduate degrees from the University of Cincinnati. She is a professor of teacher education at Cincinnati Christian University and a writer. Rebecca loves spending time with her family. She may be contacted at rwaters.author@gmail.com.

B. Lee White has been a licensed practical nurse for twenty years and a writer since she could write her first words. She currently takes care of our wonderful veterans and in her spare time is working on her third book in the *Soulfinder* series. She enjoys reading, writing and singing.

Angela Winfield graduated from Barnard College and Cornell Law School. She is an attorney, life coach and motivational speaker. She delivers addresses at school assemblies and corporate events and helps groups and individuals "O.P.E.N." doors to reach their highest potential. E-mail her at angela@MyBlindFaith.com or visit www.AngelaWinfield.com to learn more.

Lisa Wojcik teaches literacy and art to low-income elementary grade children through a Florida public library system. Degreed from the University of New Mexico, Lisa is a science researcher, artist, and writer. Her short stories, poetry, children's literature, and research work can be seen at www.t4studios-bd.blogspot.com. E-mail her at lisawojcik@hotmail.com.

Ferida Wolff is author of seventeen children's books and three essay books, her latest being the award-winning picture book *The Story Blanket* and *Missed Perceptions: Challenge Your Thoughts Change Your Thinking*. Her work appears in anthologies, newspapers, magazines, and in her nature blog feridasbackyard.blogspot.com. E-mail her at feridawolff@msn.com.

Janey Womeldorf is a freelance writer who loves laughing, strong coffee, elastic waistbands, and travel. Born in England, she now lives in Florida where she scribbles away about the lighter sides of life. She also hopes to make a clay vase one day. Feel free to e-mail her at jwwriting@live.com.

Susan Kimmel Wright lives in a western Pennsylvania farmhouse with her husband and an ever-changing assortment of animals and adult children. She has authored three children's mystery novels and has had many stories published in the *Chicken Soup for the Soul* series. E-mail her at wereallwright@gmail.com.

Mary Jo Marcellus Wyse earned an MFA degree in writing from Vermont College of Fine Arts in 2006. She loves Yours Truly for Tofutti non-dairy ice cream cones and hoards them in her freezer. Mary Jo lives near Boston with her husband and two children.

Meet Our Authors

Jack Canfield is the co-creator of the *Chicken Soup for the Soul* series, which *Time* magazine has called "the publishing phenomenon of the decade." Jack is also the co-author of many other bestselling books.

Jack is the CEO of the Canfield Training Group in Santa Barbara, California, and founder of the Foundation for Self-Esteem in Culver City, California. He has conducted intensive personal and professional development seminars on the principles of success for more than a million people in twenty-three countries, has spoken to hundreds of thousands of people at more than 1,000 corporations, universities, professional conferences and conventions, and has been seen by millions more on national television shows.

Jack has received many awards and honors, including three honorary doctorates and a Guinness World Records Certificate for having seven books from the *Chicken Soup for the Soul* series appearing on the New York Times bestseller list on May 24, 1998.

You can reach Jack at www.jackcanfield.com.

Mark Victor Hansen is the co-founder of Chicken Soup for the Soul, along with Jack Canfield. He is a sought-after keynote speaker, bestselling author, and marketing maven. Mark's powerful messages of possibility, opportunity, and action have created powerful change in thousands of organizations and millions of individuals worldwide.

Mark is a prolific writer with many bestselling books in addition to the *Chicken Soup for the Soul* series. Mark has had a profound influence in the field of human potential through his library of audios, videos, and articles in the areas of big thinking, sales achievement, wealth building, publishing success, and personal and professional development. He is also the founder of the MEGA Seminar Series.

Mark has received numerous awards that honor his entrepreneurial spirit, philanthropic heart, and business acumen. He is a lifetime member of the Horatio Alger Association of Distinguished Americans.

You can reach Mark at www.markvictorhansen.com.

Amy Newmark is Chicken Soup for the Soul's publisher and editor-in-chief, after a 30-year career as a writer, speaker, financial analyst, and business executive in the worlds of finance and telecommunications. Amy is a *magna cum laude* graduate of Harvard College, where she majored in Portuguese, minored in French, and traveled extensively. She and her husband have four grown children.

After a long career writing books on telecommunications, voluminous financial reports, business plans, and corporate press releases, Chicken Soup for the Soul is a breath of fresh air for Amy. She has fallen in love with Chicken Soup for the Soul and its life-changing books, and really enjoys putting these books together for Chicken Soup for the Soul's wonderful readers. She has co-authored more than four dozen *Chicken Soup for the Soul* books and has edited another three dozen.

You can reach Amy with any questions or comments through webmaster@chickensoupforthesoul.com and you can follow her on Twitter @amynewmark.

Thank You

W e owe huge thanks to all of our contributors. We know that you poured your hearts and souls into the thousands of stories and poems that you shared with us, and ultimately with each other. We appreciate your willingness to open up your lives to other Chicken Soup for the Soul readers and share your own experiences, no matter how personal, in order to help other people. As I read and edited these stories, I was truly inspired, excited by the potential of this book to change people's lives, and impressed by the self-awareness you showed and your unselfish willingness to share what you learned about yourselves and the power of positive thinking.

We could only publish a small percentage of the stories that were submitted, but we read every single one and even the ones that do not appear in the book had an influence on us and on the final manuscript. Our assistant publisher D'ette Corona read every submission and pared the list down to a thousand semi-finalists. Then D'ette worked with the finalists, obtaining their approvals for our edits and the quotations we carefully chose to begin each story. Our editor Kristiana Glavin chose most of those quotations, adding so much richness to the stories. And editor Barbara LoMonaco performed her normal masterful proofreading and helped us get the book to the printer on time.

We also owe a very special thanks to our creative director and book producer, Brian Taylor at Pneuma Books, for his brilliant vision for our covers and interiors.

~Amy Newmark

Improving Your Life
Every Day

Real people sharing real stories—for nineteen years. Now, Chicken Soup for the Soul has gone beyond the bookstore to become a world leader in life improvement. Through books, movies, DVDs, online resources and other partnerships, we bring hope, courage, inspiration and love to hundreds of millions of people around the world. Chicken Soup for the Soul's writers and readers belong to a one-of-a-kind global community, sharing advice, support, guidance, comfort, and knowledge.

Chicken Soup for the Soul stories have been translated into more than forty languages and can be found in more than one hundred countries. Every day, millions of people experience a Chicken Soup for the Soul story in a book, magazine, newspaper or online. As we share our life experiences through these stories, we offer hope, comfort and inspiration to one another. The stories travel from person to person, and from country to country, helping to improve lives everywhere.

Share with Us

We all have had Chicken Soup for the Soul moments in our lives. If you would like to share your story or poem with millions of people around the world, go to chickensoup.com and click on "Submit Your Story." You may be able to help another reader, and become a published author at the same time. Some of our past contributors have launched writing and speaking careers from the publication of their stories in our books!

Our submission volume has been increasing steadily — the quality and quantity of your submissions has been fabulous. We only accept story submissions via our website. They are no longer accepted via mail or fax.

To contact us regarding other matters, please send us an e-mail through webmaster@chickensoupforthesoul.com, or fax or write us at:

Chicken Soup for the Soul
P.O. Box 700
Cos Cob, CT 06807-0700
Fax: 203-861-7194

One more note from your friends at Chicken Soup for the Soul: Occasionally, we receive an unsolicited book manuscript from one of our readers, and we would like to respectfully inform you that we do not accept unsolicited manuscripts and we must discard the ones that appear.

Every cloud has a silver lining. Readers will be inspired by these 101 real-life stories from people just like them, taking a positive attitude to the ups and downs of life, and remembering to be grateful and count their blessings. This book continues Chicken Soup for the Soul's focus on inspiration and hope, and its stories of optimism and faith will encourage readers to stay positive during challenging times and in their everyday lives.

978-1-935096-56-6

Inspirational Classics

Tough times won't last, but tough people will. Many people have lost money, jobs and/or homes, or made cutbacks. Others have faced life-changing natural disasters, or health and family difficulties. These encouraging and inspirational stories are all about overcoming adversity, pulling together, and finding joy in a simpler life. Stories address downsizing, resolving debt, managing chronic illness, having faith, finding new perspectives, and blessings in disguise.

978-1-935096-35-1

Inspirational Classics

Chicken Soup for the Soul.
for the Soul.
Count Your Blessings

101 Stories of Gratitude, Fortitude, and Silver Linings

Jack Canfield,
Mark Victor Hansen, Amy Newmark,
Laura Robinson & Elizabeth Bryan

This uplifting book reminds readers of the blessings in their lives, despite financial stress, natural disasters, health scares and illnesses, housing challenges and family worries. This feel-good book is a great gift for New Year's or Easter, for someone going through a difficult time, or for Christmas. These stories of optimism, faith, and strength remind us of the simple pleasures of family, home, health, and inexpensive good times.

978-1-935096-42-9

Inspirational Classics

Others share how they found their passion, purpose, and joy in life in these 101 personal and exciting stories that are sure to encourage readers to find their own happiness. Stories in this collection will inspire readers to pursue their dreams, find their passion and seek joy in their life. This book continues Chicken Soup for the Soul's focus on inspiration and hope, reminding readers that they can find their own happiness.

978-1-935096-77-1

Inspirational Classics

Chicken Soup for the Soul®

www.chickensoup.com